Jesus and the
Language of the Kingdom

NORMAN PERRIN

Jesus and the Language of the Kingdom

Symbol and Metaphor in New Testament Interpretation

FORTRESS PRESS

Philadelphia

Library of Congress Catalog Card Number 75–13045

ISBN 0–8006–0412–1

5110G75   Printed in U.S.A.   1–412

To Amos Wilder and Paul Ricoeur
who taught me to look at the problem
of hermeneutics in new ways

Table of Contents

Preface

This volume began as an attempt to revise for book publication a number of essays that I have published over the years on the Kingdom of God, on the parables of Jesus, and on the problems of New Testament hermeneutics. As I began to revise them, however, it became evident that my own thinking on the various topics had developed rapidly, especially in the years since about 1970, as Amos Wilder began to influence me very strongly and I was in constant dialogue with Paul Ricoeur. So it seemed better to rewrite than to revise, and the result is this volume, the manuscript of which was written in a concentrated period of time in December, 1974, and January, 1975.

A problem to be overcome in the writing of the manuscript was the fact that the interpretation of Kingdom of God in the message of Jesus and the interpretation of the parables are different but closely related topics. So the scholar who writes about the Kingdom of God in the message of Jesus must necessarily write about the parables, and vice versa. Moreover, the scholar who reviews the discussion of the one will also suddenly find himself reviewing the discussion of the other. I could find no solution to this problem except to accept the necessity for a certain amount of repetition. So the parables are discussed briefly in the study devoted to the Kingdom, while C. H. Dodd and Joachim Jeremias, who are equally important in the discussion of both the Kingdom of God and the parables of Jesus, simply turn up in both contexts. I have attempted to keep the element of repetition to a minimum.

A further problem was presented by the omnipresence of Rudolf Bultmann in any discussion of Kingdom of God, of the parables, or of the problem of hermeneutics. His own contributions to the related discussions have been epoch-making, and his influence on other scholars has been enormous. I was presented with the choice of either writing a special study of Bultmann and his work and influence, or of returning to him at several different places in the manuscript. In the end I chose the latter course, since it enabled me to discuss separately his hermeneutics in general (pages 10–12 below) and his particular interpretation of Kingdom of God in the message of Jesus (pages 71–80 below), and his influence on and response to the work of Ernst Fuchs (pages 108–110 below), and, more briefly, his influence on the work of Dan Via (pages 144–145 below). In each instance I am dealing with Bultmann in the context of a particular aspect of the discussion and at the same time gradually developing an overall view of his work and influence. The reader whose concern is an overall view of Bultmann and his work will be able to put together the separately presented discussions.

A further special problem was that of nomenclature for the parables. No two scholars use the same set of terms, and so I was faced with the choice of either imposing my own terms on everyone else, or of allowing variety, e.g., Laborers in the Vineyard, Workers in the Vineyard, or Vineyard Workers. In the end I chose the latter course, and I have given the cross references in the Index of Parables at the end of the book.

It is my privilege now to offer my grateful thanks to all those who have contributed to the work represented in these pages. I would mention especially the two scholars to whom I have dedicated the volume, Amos Wilder and Paul Ricoeur, whose insights have been a constant source of challenge and stimulation to me. Then, as always, the community of scholars which is the Divinity School of the University of Chicago has provided the essential context for the work I have tried to do. In this instance I am particularly conscious of my debt to David Tracy, who with Paul Ricoeur and myself conducted a seminar on the hermeneutics of religious language in which much of the material developed here was first presented. Finally, and again as always, the students at the University of Chicago have been very important to me as I pursued the themes of these studies in constant discussion with them in classroom, coffee shop, and office. In particular my graduate assistant, Mary Ann Tolbert, herself a gifted and challenging student of the problem of hermeneutics, has contributed a great deal to this volume and the work it represents.

University of Chicago   NORMAN PERRIN
Chicago, Illinois
Spring 1975

CHAPTER I

Introduction

Two subjects have concerned me particularly throughout my work as a New Testament scholar: the Kingdom of God and the parables of Jesus. The two are closely related, because the Kingdom of God is the ultimate referent of the parables of Jesus, and because the whole message of Jesus focuses upon the Kingdom of God, while the parables are today the major source for our knowledge of that message. They are therefore related at the level of life of Jesus research, and this is the level at which I began to pursue them.

In *The Kingdom of God in the Teaching of Jesus*, I was concerned with a historical understanding of Jesus' use of "Kingdom of God," and in *Rediscovering the Teaching of Jesus*, I used the parables as the major source for knowledge of that teaching. But both the Kingdom of God and the parables of Jesus are of interest to students of the New Testament at levels other than that of life of Jesus research. The former is a major biblical symbol, and the latter are a most distinctive literary form; they both offer particular challenges at the level of interpreta- *here.* tion, or, to put the matter in other words, they present fascinating problems at the level of hermeneutics. It is at this level that I am concerned with them in this current study.

I am distinguishing between "a historical understanding" on the one hand and "interpretation" or "hermeneutics" on the other. This distinction is part of a particular understanding of the hermeneutical process which I have reached, and which it is the purpose of these studies to

1

explore. I will begin therefore by setting out this understanding in general terms.

Hermeneutics is, to paraphrase Bultmann's quotation of Dilthey, the methodology for reaching an understanding of written texts held to be meaningful.[1] Among students of the New Testament it is in particular the methodology for reaching an understanding of the texts which make up the New Testament, or which can be reconstructed from the New Testament, as in the case of the teaching of Jesus. But the principles involved in the hermeneutical process are the same for any texts, sacred or secular, ancient or modern, literary or popular. There will be changes of emphasis or detail according to the nature of the text being interpreted, but the methodological principles are constant. Whether it be a biblical symbol, a parable of Jesus, a letter of Paul, Lincoln's Gettysburg address, or the transcript of a Watergate tape, the hermeneutical theory is the same despite the differences demanded by the particular nature of the text being interpreted. Bultmann quite properly gave up the claim for a special hermeneutics for scripture: "The interpretation of biblical texts is not governed by theoretical principles different from those applying to any other literature."[2] We can make the claim in reverse: hermeneutical principles arrived at by a consideration of biblical texts will be applicable also to non-biblical texts. So although what follows is related specifically to biblical texts, and in particular to the use of the biblical symbol Kingdom of God and to the parables of Jesus, it is *mutatis mutandis* applicable to any text.

The first step in the hermeneutical process is that of *textual criticism*: we begin by establishing the text to be interpreted. In the case of most modern texts this is not a matter of any great moment, but in the case of texts which have a considerable history of transmission, and of interpretation in the process of transmission, or in the case of texts from the ancient world of which we have several manuscripts, this can be a particular problem. The interpreter of the plays of Sophocles, for example, or of a dialogue of Plato, must either be a textual critic, or be building on the work of textual critics in establishing the text to be interpreted. In the case of the use of the biblical symbol Kingdom of God, and in the case of the parables of Jesus, there are particular problems at this level.

Biblical symbols, like literary symbols altogether, do not occur in a vacuum; they are always found in the context of some kind of verbali-

zation. So we find Kingdom of God, or its linguistic equivalent, in confessions, in songs of praise, in prayers, in prophetic exhortations, and so on. We are always dealing with a specific text which uses this symbol. At the same time, however, the symbol itself is not created anew each time it is used; it carries associations of meaning with itself from one context of verbalization to another. The interpreter is therefore faced with the double task of doing justice to the individualities of the various texts in which the symbol is verbalized, while, at the same time, exploring the nature of the associations which the symbol carries with itself from verbalization to verbalization, from specific text to specific text. So the interpreter of the biblical symbol must always be concerned both with the particularities of the specific text he is considering, and also with the power which the symbol has[2] to generate meaning in any text in which it is verbalized. It is not enough, therefore, to establish the text to be interpreted; the interpreter must also be concerned with the power of the symbol to transcend, and even to transform, the particular text itself.

In the case of the parables of Jesus, the interpreter faces the specific problem of reconstructing the text to be interpreted. The parables of Jesus were delivered orally; so far as we know, Jesus himself *wrote* no single word of them. We are therefore dependent upon texts which were written later, and which may or may not represent an accurate reminiscence of the parables as Jesus taught them. The texts we have represent the parables as they stood at the end of a considerable process of oral and written transmission and reinterpretation, both among the followers of Jesus during his lifetime, and among the early Christian communities after his death. No single text we possess represents less than forty years of transmission and reinterpretation, both oral and written, of the parables which Jesus taught, and one of them, the Gospel of Thomas, represents something like three hundred years of that same process! However, the difficulty is more apparent than real. The parables of Jesus were so distinctive that in broad structural outline they survived the subsequent process of transmission very well, while, at the same time, the process of reinterpretation was so obvious, and so much at variance with the original thrust of the parables themselves, that the original form and thrust of the parables have not proven difficult to reconstruct. We will discuss this in more detail below;[3] for the moment it is sufficient to point out that although mod-

ern interpreters of the parables of Jesus must reconstruct the texts they propose to interpret, this has not proven to be difficult in practice. There is broad measure of general agreement as to the text of the parables as parables *of Jesus.*

The case is similar with Jesus' use of the symbol Kingdom of God, except that in this instance it is a matter of determining the authenticity of sayings attributed to Jesus in the gospels, rather than of reconstructing sayings from later interpreted versions of them. However, appropriate criteria of authenticity have been worked out and there is a broad measure of agreement among the competent scholars, so that establishing the text to be interpreted is again not a matter to delay the interpreter; we merely note that it needs to be done.

Once we have established the text to be interpreted the next step is to reach a historical understanding of the text; we move from textual criticism to *historical criticism.* In the case of texts from another time and another culture this can be an extremely complex and difficult task, involving many different considerations, but the theoretical principles involved are both firmly established and well understood. We need to be able to understand the language in which the text is written, the nature of the text itself as a historical and literary artifact, the circumstances in which and for which it was written. We need, further, to understand as far as we can the intent of the author in writing the text, and the meaning understood by those for whom the text was written. For all of this we need a number of different critical skills, and ultimately a measure of historical imagination, as we seek to understand the text as the author intended it to be understood, or as it was understood by those who first read it. But the point is that the art of historical criticism is in fact very highly developed, the skills needed are both available and attainable, so that in most cases a firm historical understanding of a text can be reached. Moreover, it is reached by critical methods which are, so to speak, public property, methods which lie "in the public domain," so that where there is disagreement there is also the possibility of informed discussion and the hope of resolving the disagreement. There is nothing esoteric or private about historical criticism; its conclusions are openly arrived at by methods common to historical scholarship as such, so that a consensus as to the historical understanding of a given text should be possible among competent historical scholars. Moreover, if such an understanding is challenged, it

is necessarily challenged by means of evidence or arguments proper to historical scholarship, so that, again, discussion is possible and an eventual reevaluation of the evidence or arguments is to be expected.

Biblical scholars tend to be primarily historical scholars, so much so that "biblical criticism" almost always means "historical critcism of biblical texts," and the task of reaching a historical understanding of the biblical texts has been pursued both vigorously and, for the most part, successfully. There are still areas which have so far proven intractable—in the New Testament the Gospel of John is perhaps the most important example—but such areas diminish steadily as each generation of scholars succeeds in establishing a historical understanding of texts which had resisted a previous generation. The most obvious recent gain has been the new understanding of the synoptic gospels made possible by the rise of redaction criticism.[4] Both the biblical symbol Kingdom of God and the parables of Jesus have presented particular problems at the level of historical understanding, but these problems either have been, or can now be resolved, and the studies which follow will attempt—among other things!—to present a historical understanding of biblical texts using Kingdom of God and of the parables of Jesus.

The interjection "among other things" is due to the fact that historical criticism is only one stage of the hermeneutical process; hence in what follows my concern will go beyond that of reaching a historical understanding of the "Kingdom" texts and of the parables. In the hermeneutical process itself, I would claim, we need to go beyond historical criticism to a *literary criticism*; we need to concern ourselves with the nature and natural force of both the literary form and language of a text. If we are dealing with symbolic language then we must consider what a literary symbol is, how it works, what it does. If we are seeking to interpret a parable then we must ask what kind of literary entity a parable is, and what such an entity is designed to do; we must reflect on the kind of language which the parable uses and consider how that particular kind of language works. It is, for example, important to recognize that Kingdom of God is a *symbol*, and that, further, its natural function is *to evoke a myth.* It will be argued below that the extensive discussion of Kingdom of God in the teaching of Jesus has been bedeviled by the fact that scholars have thought of Kingdom of God as a conception rather than as a symbol. Conceptions are very different things from symbols, and one asks very different questions about them. For almost a hundred years scholars have been asking questions about Kingdom of God in the teaching of Jesus that have proven unanswerable; I shall argue below that they are unanswerable precisely because they are questions which are only proper if Kingdom of God is a conception, which it is not.

Similar considerations arise in connection with the parables of Jesus. The modern interpretation of these parables begins with the recognition of a literary point: they are parables and not allegories. An allegory is a narrative in which the various elements presented represent something other than themselves; essential to its interpretation is the key to the identification of the various elements, and once this key has been supplied the message of the allegory can be presented in non-allegorical language. A parable on the other hand is essentially a comparison whereby one thing is illuminated by being compared to another, and the parable makes its point as a totality. In Luke 10, the parable of the Good Samaritan is given as an answer to the question, "Who is my neighbor?" The story as a whole is directed to this question, and the further question with which the story concludes, "Which of these three, do you think, proved neighbor to the man who fell among the robbers?" demands an interpretation of the story as a whole, not an identification of the references hidden in the figures of the traveler, priest, Levite, or Samaritan. The lesser known, a definition of "neighbor," is illuminated by that which the parable makes known, a definition of neighbor in the case of the traveler on the Jericho road.[5] Parables function in this way, and in this they are very different from allegories, which function in a quite different way. In our later study of the interpretation of the parables of Jesus we shall be concerned in much greater detail with the nature and function of parable as a literary form. At the moment we wish only to make the point that an appreciation of this nature and function is an essential element in the process of interpreting the parable.

We have deliberately drawn our illustrations from the material that will concern us in detail in the studies which follow, but the point is an obvious one which could be made in many different ways. A personal letter is different from a legal decree; the realistic narrative of a popular story is different from the heavily symbolic narratives of an apocalyptic visionary or the Oglala Sioux, Black Elk.[6] Written texts can

differ radically from one another, and these differences demand different critical approaches, just as, to take an obvious example, the rock
musical *Hair* demands one kind of critical appreciation, and a performance of Richard Wagner's *Götterdämmerung* another. We need
not labor this point; the interpreter must need take seriously the nature
and natural function of the literary form and language of the text he or
she is concerned to interpret. But in this connection we must note that
the literary concern can overlap with the historical concern.

In the case of the parables of Jesus a literary concern has played a
major role in their historical interpretation, for it became essential to
recognize that they were parables and not allegories—a consideration
of literary form—in order to interpret them historically as *parables*,
and as parables *of Jesus*. Similar considerations enter into the historical
interpretation of other texts in the New Testament. It becomes important, for example, to recognize that Paul's letter to the Galatians is a
genuine letter, or that the "letter" of James is a homily; no adequate
historical understanding of them as texts is possible without a consideration of such literary features. Nor are such considerations limited to
New Testament or biblical texts; an adequate historical understanding
of any text will depend in no small part upon an adequate appreciation
of the literary form and language of the text.

I have stressed the role of literary criticism in reaching a historical
understanding of a text, because it is important to recognize that it
does help us to look backward from a text to its meaning in its original
historical context. But a text does not remain anchored in its original
historical context. Once it achieves a fixed form, normally written, in
which it can be circulated in new and different contexts, then it can be
given new and different contexts. Once a text is "published" and begins
to circulate at large, then the meaning intended by the author, or the
meaning natural to it in its original historical context, is no longer the
meaning necessarily given to that text. Again, the parables of Jesus
provide an excellent example of this point.

These parables were originally *oral* texts, comparisons made or stories told by Jesus to small groups of his contemporaries. They were
immediate texts, by which I mean that they were created for the context in which they were delivered; for example, they constantly allude
to matters of knowledge or experience or expectation common to both
Jesus and his immediate contemporaries. Moreover, they were *highly*

personal texts, deliberately designed by their author Jesus to express his personal message and to challenge his contemporaries to accept or reject it.[7] So they had a particular meaning in their original historical context. But the parables did not remain oral, immediate, and highly personal texts. They were remembered, retold, and finally written down and circulated among the followers of Jesus, and among the early Christian communities as they came into existence after the death of Jesus himself. But now their original oral, immediate, and highly personal meaning was necessarily lost. They were still held to be texts with meaning, but now that meaning had to be found anew in them as written texts circulating in the early Christian communities in the Hellenistic world.

In general this was done in three different ways. First, the parables were put in the context of a Jewish wisdom teacher using parables in a manner characteristic of the wisdom movement. The Good Samaritan, understood as a story illuminating the principle of neighborliness, referred to above, is a good example of this. Then, secondly, they were understood as teaching morality. The Unjust Steward in Luke 16:1–9 is a good example of this, because we can see in verses 8 and 9 a series of not very successful attempts to draw a moral lesson from a story about a wholly reprehensible character. But for the most part a third way was taken: the parables were interpreted as allegories, either by adding an allegorizing interpretation as a separate entity, or by adding allegorizing touches within the parable itself. An example of the former is the addition of Mark 4:14–20 to The Sower in Mark 4:3–9. This explanation makes the parable an allegory of the situation and experience of early Christians. An example of the latter is the addition of the "beloved" son motif, the quotation from Psalm 118 and allusions to Isa. 5:1–7 to The Wicked Tenants in Mark 12:1–11.[8] These additions transform the parable into an allegory of the fate of Jesus.

Such a process of reinterpretation, with its loss of original meaning and finding of new and quite different meanings, was inevitable as the parables were "published" and circulated. Moreover, the parables of Jesus are only a particularly drastic example of the potential fate of any text that is "published" and circulated in new and different historical and cultural contexts. All such texts can be given new and different meanings as they are interpreted in new and different situations.

This obvious fact raises the problem of validity in interpretation,[9] a particularly pressing problem for biblical scholars since biblical texts are notoriously subject to many and different interpretations. Biblical scholars have normally met this problem by appealing to historical criticism and arguing that the meaning of a text in its original historical context should be determinative of future possibilities for meaning in that text. But literary criticism can also be a factor in such a discussion, because it can be argued that meaning found in a text must be arrived at by a process of interpretation which does justice to the force and function of the literary form and language of that text. I have argued that point at some length elsewhere, and I intend to return to it below.[10] For the moment I am simply noting this possible significance of literary criticism in the hermeneutical process.

But literary criticism has a further and very important potential significance in the hermeneutical process: it can offer new potentialities for understanding and interpreting a text. In my study of the biblical symbol Kingdom of God below I shall be deliberately using literary-critical insights about the nature and function of literary symbols in an attempt to understand and interpret uses of the symbol Kingdom of God. Further, in the study of the modern interpretation of the parables of Jesus I shall be deliberately reviewing that discussion from the standpoint of its use of literary-critical factors and insights. Implicit in both studies is the claim that such literary-critical considerations offer *new* and *valid* possibilities for interpreting the texts concerned. The possibilities are new because they could not be discerned apart from the literary-critical considerations; they are valid because they arise out of the nature and natural force of the literary form and language of the texts.

Literary criticism is therefore a most important element in the hermeneutical process. It is important because it is an important element in moving toward a historical understanding of the text, and also because it opens up new possibilities for a valid understanding of the text in a context different from its original historical context.

This brings me to the final element in the hermeneutical process: *the act of interpretation itself*. It is proper to call the act of interpretation itself *hermeneutics*, because the other elements in the hermeneutical process, textual criticism, historical criticism, and literary criticism, are subordinate to it and designed only to serve it.

New Testament scholars tend to be particularly aware of hermeneutics as a dynamic process of interaction between text and interpreter. They tend to think of it on the model of a dialogue between text and interpreter, and they tend to think of it also as a process in the course of which not only does the interpreter interpret the text, but also the text interprets the interpreter. The reason for this is the enormous influence of Rudolf Bultmann, whose understanding of hermeneutics is necessarily the starting point for any discussion of the matter among New Testament scholars.

Bultmann begins by quoting Wilhelm Dilthey.[11] He understands hermeneutics as the methodology for understanding the expressions of human life fixed in writing, as we noted above.[12] In order to understand and appreciate this, we should perhaps consider for a moment the general circumstances in which Bultmann hammered out his understanding of hermeneutics. To begin with, Bultmann himself is a pupil of the *religionsgeschichtliche Schule*, associated with such names as Reitzenstein, Bousset, and Bultmann's own teacher Johannes Weiss.[13] He is heir therefore to the movement which, at the end of the nineteenth century and the beginning of the twentieth, established the strange and foreign nature of the New Testament to the modern world. After several generations of thinking in terms of moral principles and ethical teaching which united the New Testament with the modern world, Jesus was suddenly seen as an apocalyptic visionary, and the New Testament in general was seen as saturated by mythical thinking and by the expectation of the miraculous. A great gulf opened up between the New Testament and modern man. Bultmann himself was enormously aware of this gulf—we may call it a "hermeneutical gulf"—and his hermeneutics are ultimately an attempt to bridge it.

In his attempt to bridge the hermeneutical gulf Bultmann had recourse, first, to the understanding of written texts developed by Wilhelm Dilthey as "expressions of human life fixed in writing." But if texts are to be so understood then they can be questioned with regard to the understanding of human life which they express; they can be interrogated by the interpreter with regard to their understanding of the nature of human existence in the world. This is the "pre-understanding" (*Vorverständnis*) with which an interpreter approaches a text; it is the "direction of enquiry" (*das Woraufhin*) which determines the questions to be asked of the text. Suddenly Bultmann had bridged the hermeneutical gulf between, for example, the apocalyptic mythology Johannes Weiss had attributed to Jesus and the world of twentieth-century technological man.[14] It remained only for Bultmann to develop his understanding of human existence in the world in accordance with the philosophical analysis of that existence by Martin Heidegger, whom Bultmann knew in Marburg from 1924 to 1928, and his hermeneutics was complete.

Bultmann's particular interpretation of the apocalyptic mythology of Jesus, i.e., of Jesus' proclamation of the Kingdom of God, will concern us later.[15] For the moment we are concerned with the dynamics of the hermeneutical process as Bultmann understands it, and as he has taught two generations of New Testament scholars to understand it. He takes for granted the whole process of historical criticism, the whole procedure for arriving at a historical understanding of the text as we discussed it above.[16] He tends not to be interested in literary form and language of a text as such, but wishes to move directly to the understanding of human existence in the world which is being expressed in the text, whatever the nature of its literary form and language. His concern is with the dynamic interaction of text and interpreter as the interpreter questions the text concerning its understanding of human existence in the world, and as the interpreter in turn is questioned by the claims of the text regarding the possibilities of human existence in the world. Bultmann frequently speaks of a genuine understanding of a text as disclosing basically "the possibilities of human existence," which possibilities "are shared by the interpreter," so that "the very act of understanding" the text brings "these possibilities to full consciousness" for the interpreter. "The presupposition for any genuine interpretation" of a text, claims Bultmann characteristically, is "the living relationship between the interpreter" and the understanding of existence "being expressed directly or indirectly by the text." By this living relationship "text and interpreter are bound together"; without it, "inquiry and understanding are not possible." The interpreter interrogates the text, but "in the interrogation of a text the interpreter must allow himself to be interrogated by the text, he must listen to its claims."[17]

Aspects of Bultmann's understanding of hermeneutics will concern us at several points in the following studies: in connection with the interpretation of Jesus' use of Kingdom of God,[18] and in connection with the interpretation of the parables of Jesus by Ernst Fuchs and

Dan Via.[19] At those points we will discuss his hermeneutics further; at the moment we note his emphasis upon the dynamic interaction between text and interpreter, which we would claim is the climax of the hermeneutical process. In due course we shall develop our understanding of the matter further, and at that point we shall attempt to do more justice than Bultmann has done to literary factors and their influence on the act of interpretation itself. But Bultmann is necessarily the starting point for any discussion of hermeneutics by a New Testament scholar.

NOTES

1. "*Hermeneutik . . . (ist) die 'Kunstlehre des Verstehens schriftlich fixierter Lebensaüsserungen!*" Bultmann, "*Das Problem der Hermeneutik*" in his collected essays *Glauben und Verstehen* II (1961), pp. 211–235 (the quote is from p. 211). The English translation in Bultmann, *Essays Philosophical and Theological* (New York: Macmillan, and London: SCM Press, 1955), p. 234 reads: "Hermeneutics . . . (is) the 'technique of understanding expressions of life set in written form . . . .'" Bultmann's understanding of hermeneutics is very important indeed and will concern us in detail below, pp. 10–12, 71–80, 108–110, 144–145.

2. *Glauben und Verstehen* II, p. 231. The translation is my own, as will always be the case when the quotation is in English and the title of the work quoted in German.

3. See below, pp. 101–103, 120–121, 166.

4. See the historical understanding of these texts offered in N. Perrin, *The New Testament: An Introduction* (New York: Harcourt Brace Jovanovich, 1974). The reader will note my hesitancy in speaking of the Gospel of John in that *Introduction*.

5. This is not necessarily the purpose of the parable on the lips of Jesus. Historically speaking, Jesus used the literary form of the parable in a most distinctive manner but this does not change the point about the nature of parable as a literary form. On the meaning of The Good Samaritan on the lips of Jesus see below, pp. 106–107, 114–115, 119–120, 138–140, 162–165.

6. On apocalyptic visionaries and Black Elk, see Perrin, *The New Testament: An Introduction*, pp. 83–85.

7. In making these statements, I am assuming the results of modern research on the parables of Jesus. This research will be discussed in detail below.

8. A version of the parable without these allegorizing additions has been found in the Gospel of Thomas. On the whole matter see J. D. Crossan, *In Parables* (New York: Harper & Row, 1973), pp. 91–96.

9. An intentional allusion to the book by E. D. Hirsch, *Validity in Interpretation* (New Haven: Yale University Press, 1967). Hirsch discusses the

problem in relationship to the critical interpretation of literary texts and is reacting against a literary criticism which deliberately ignored the intent of the author in determining the possibilities for meaning of a text. "When critics deliberately banished the original author, they themselves usurped his place. . . . Where before there had been but one author, there now arose a multiplicity of authors, each carrying as much authority as the next. To banish the author as the determiner of meaning was to reject the only compelling normative principle that could lend validity to an interpretation" (Hirsch, p. 5). For Hirsch the author is the determiner of meaning in a text. New Testament scholars in general would welcome this viewpoint, and we shall see that most New Testament scholarship is concerned to restore to the parables the meaning intended by their author, Jesus. But we shall see that this view is being challenged by Dan Via, on not inconsiderable grounds. See below, pp. 142–144.

10. Perrin, "Historical Criticism, Literary Criticism, and Hermeneutics: The Interpretation of the Parables of Jesus and the Gospel of Mark Today," *JR* 52 (1972), pp. 361–375. See further below.

11. Bultmann's more important publications on the subject are as follows:

"The Problem of Hermeneutics," in Bultmann, *Essays*. German original in Bultmann, *Glauben und Verstehen* II (1952), pp. 211–235, and *ZTK* 47 (1950), pp. 47–69. This is a systematic statement of his hermeneutics, particularly important in showing the relationship of his hermeneutics to those of Schleiermacher and Dilthey.

"New Testament and Mythology," now in *Keryma and Myth* (London: SPCK, 1953, and Harper Torchbook no. 80; New York: Harper & Row, 1961). Originally published in 1941, this is Bultmann's initial statement of "demythologizing."

Jesus Christ and Mythology (New York: Scribner's, 1958, and London: SCM Press, 1960). Originally written in English, this is a more developed statement of "demythologizing."

History and Eschatology: The Presence of Eternity (Harper Torchbook no. 91; New York: Harper & Row, 1962), also available as *History and Eschatology* (Edinburgh: Edinburgh University Press, 1957). Originally written in English, as the Gifford Lectures for 1955, this is an important statement of Bultmann's views in general and of his hermeneutics in particular, especially interesting in that it relates his views to those of R. H. Collingwood.

"The Primitive Christian Kerygma and the Historical Jesus," in *The Historical Jesus and the Kerygmatic Christ*, ed. C. E. Braaten and R. A. Harrisville (New York and Nashville: Abingdon Press, 1964). This is Bultmann's definitive statement of his views on the relationship between the historical Jesus and the Christian proclamation, a matter extremely important in the interpretation of texts which ultimately reflect the message of Jesus.

12. See above, p. 2 and n. 1.

13. There is a convenient presentation of this movement in W. G. Kümmel, *The New Testament: The History of the Investigation of Its Problems* (New York and Nashville: Abingdon Press, 1972, and London: SCM Press, 1973), pp. 206–280.

14. On this see below, pp. 71–76.

15. See below, pp. 71–80.
16. Bultmann, *Essays*, pp. 235–240.
17. Bultmann, *Glauben und Verstehen* II, pp. 226, 227, 228.
18. See below, pp. 71–80.
19. See below, pp. 108–110 and 144–145.

CHAPTER II

The Interpretation of Kingdom of God in the Message of Jesus

In the whole realm of New Testament hermeneutics there is no more intractable problem than that of the interpretation of the symbol "Kingdom of God" in the message of Jesus. This is a problem at every stage of the hermeneutical process. As long ago as 1892 Johannes Weiss raised the *historical question* of the meaning of the symbol in the message of Jesus, and the purport of Jesus' teaching concerning it. Today the questions he raised are still unresolved. So far as the *literary-critical question* of the nature and force of the symbol, and of the linguistic context in which it is found, is concerned, there is general agreement that the background of Jesus' use is the language and symbolism of ancient Jewish apocalyptic. But to say that is to raise a whole set of further questions, questions with regard to the nature and force of apocalyptic symbols, and questions with regard to the possibility of a non-apocalyptic use of the symbol by Jesus. With regard to the *hermeneutical interaction* between the text of Jesus' message concerning the Kingdom of God and the interpreter, one can find every possible variety of opinion: that the message should be taken literally as apocalyptic and the world view it represents either accepted or rejected by the interpreter; that the message need not be taken literally as apocalyptic and hence that it may be interpreted in a variety of ways.

The problems involved in understanding and interpreting "Kingdom of God" in the message of Jesus have concerned me ever since I wrote my doctoral dissertation on "The Kingdom of God in the Teaching of

Jesus" at Göttingen in 1957–59 and published a revised version of it in 1963 (London: SCM Press, and Philadelphia: Westminster Press). In light of developments in my own understanding of the problems and possibilities of interpreting the New Testament, I have returned to the matter again and again: *Rediscovering the Teaching of Jesus* (New York: Harper & Row, and London: SCM Press, 1967); *The New Testament: An Introduction* (New York: Harcourt Brace Jovanovich, 1974), "Wisdom and Apocalyptic in the Message of Jesus" (*The Society of Biblical Literature One Hundred Eighth Annual Meeting Proceedings*, ed. Lane C. McGaughy [Missoula, Montana: SBL, 1972], II, pp. 543–70); "Eschatology and Hermeneutics," *JBL* 93 (1974), pp. 1–14; "The Interpretation of a Biblical Symbol" (to be published in 1975 in the *Journal of Religion*). It is my purpose to return to the matter now in light of the interpretation theory developed in the studies which make up this volume. In the course of this new, extended study, I shall be using material presented and insights developed in the course of my previous work, especially in the three articles mentioned immediately above, but this study is itself new, and the attentive reader will discover some development from, and revisions of, my previously expressed opinions.

In the course of this study I shall attempt both to use and to develop further the insights concerning the interpretation of the New Testament indicated in the Introduction, and it is my hope to contribute both to the continuing discussion of "Kingdom of God" in the message of Jesus, and also to the rapidly developing discussion of method in the interpretation of the New Testament.

I will begin this study by considering the origin and use of Kingdom of God in the ancient Jewish literature, including under that rubric Jewish literature representing the period down to the destruction of the Jerusalem temple by the Romans in 70 A.D.

A. KINGDOM OF GOD IN THE ANCIENT
JEWISH LITERATURE

The roots of the symbol Kingdom of God lie in the ancient Near Eastern myth of the kingship of God. This "was taken over by the Israelites from the Canaanites, who had received it from the great kingdoms on the Euphrates and Tigris and Nile, where it had been developed as early as ancient Sumerian times."[1] In this myth the god had acted as king in creating the world, in the course of which he had overcome and slain the primeval monster. Further, the god continued to act as king by annually renewing the fertility of the earth, and he showed himself to be king of a particular people by sustaining them in their place in the world. This myth is common to all the peoples of the ancient Near East, and elements from one version of the myth were freely used in others. Essentially it is only the name of the god which changes as we move from people to people. In Babylonia Marduk is king; in Assyria, Asshur; in Ammon, Milhom; in Tyre, Melkart; in Israel, Yahweh.

A feature of this myth of the kingship of God was that it was celebrated annually in cultic ritual. In the ancient world life was seen as a constant struggle between good and evil powers, and the world as the arena of this struggle. So each winter threatened to become a permanent blight on the fertility of the earth; and each spring was a renewal of the primeval victory of the god over the monster, as each spring the god renews the fertility of the earth against the threat of his enemies and man's. It was this that was celebrated cultically in an annual New Year festival. In the cultic ritual of this festival the god became king as he reenacted the primeval victory of creation; he acted as king as he renewed the fertility of the earth; his people experienced him as king as he entered once more into their lives.

That ancient Israel learned to think of their god in this way, and to celebrate his kingship in this way, can be seen from the so-called enthronement psalms, Psalms 47, 93, 96, 97, 98, 99, with their constant refrain, "Yahweh has become king!" a cultic avowal often mistranslated, "The Lord reigns."[2]

Yahweh has become king; he is robed in majesty;
   Yahweh is robed, he is girded with strength.
Yea, the world is established; it shall not be moved;
   thy throne is established from of old;
   thou art from everlasting.

Ps. 93:1–2

Yahweh has become king: let the earth rejoice;
   let the many coastlands be glad!
Clouds and the thick darkness are round about him;
   righteousness and justice are the foundation of his throne.

Ps. 97:1–2

> Say among the nations, "Yahweh has become king!
> Yea, the world is established, it shall never be moved;
> he will judge the peoples with equity."

Ps. 96:10

Already in those latter two quotations we can see a characteristic Israelite emphasis being introduced into the myth; "righteousness and justice are the foundation of his throne" and "he will judge the peoples with equity" are reminiscent of the language of covenant traditions, and this is a reminder that major elements of Israelite theology were established among the Israelite tribes *before* they adopted the myth of the kingship of God from their Canaanite neighbors. The adoption of the myth has to date from the period of the monarchy,[3] but already in the days of tribal confederacy (amphictyony) the (future) Israelite was confessing the *Salvation History*.

My father was a wandering Aramaean. He went down into Egypt to find refuge there, few in numbers; but there he became a nation, great, mighty, and strong. The Egyptians ill-treated us, they gave us no peace and inflicted harsh slavery on us. But we called on Yahweh the God of our fathers. Yahweh heard our voice and saw our misery, our toil and our oppression; and Yahweh brought us out of Egypt with mighty hand and outstretched arm, with great terror, and with signs and wonders. He brought us here and gave us this land, a land where milk and honey flow. Here then I bring the first fruits of the produce of the soil that you, Yahweh, have given me.

Deut. 26:5b–10 (Jer. Bible)

The conception of the Salvation History (*Heilsgeschichte*) is one introduced into the discussion of the theology of the Old Testament by Gerhard von Rad, who points out that in Deut. 26:5b–9 we have what he calls a Credo, a confessional summary of the activity of God on behalf of his people.[4] Such Credos are found elsewhere, for example, Deut. 6:20–24, Josh. 24:2b–13, and characteristically they dwell on the activity of God on behalf of his people in a sequence of events: the migrations of the Patriarchs and the Promise of the Land (Canaan) to them; the Descent into Egypt and prosperity and oppression there; the Deliverance from Egypt at the Exodus; the Red Sea miracle; the Wilderness Wandering; the Giving of the Land (Canaan, the land promised to the Patriarchs). This constitutes the Salvation History, the history of God's acts of salvation on behalf of his people, and it plays a major role in the development of ancient Israelite theology, as also in the development of ancient Israelite literature, since it provides the basic structure for the pentateuchal sources J, E, and P, and hence ultimately for the Pentateuch itself.

The conception of a Salvation History, and the practice of its confessional recitation at a festival at one or more of the amphictyonic sanctuaries antedates, therefore, the myth of God as king and its celebration in the temple at Jerusalem, but the question of comparative dating is not important. What is important is that Israel inherited two traditions which concerned themselves in a very special way with the activity of God. One, the ancient Near Eastern myth, celebrated the activity of God in the act of creation, and in the annual renewal of the world; the other, the amphictyonic *Heilsgeschichte*, celebrated the activity of God at crucial moments in the history of his people. It was natural and inevitable that these two should be brought together.

The two traditions are brought together in various ways. In the first place, the enthronement psalms extend the act of the creation of the world by God to the act of God creating and choosing his own people, i.e., to include the fundamental thrust of the Salvation History.

> Moses, Aaron one of his priests, and Samuel
> his votary, all invoked Yahweh:[5]
>   and he answered them.
> He talked with them in the pillar of cloud;
> they obeyed his decrees, the Law he gave them.
>   Ps. 99:6–7 (Jer. Bible)

Then, secondly, elements from the Salvation History were interpreted in terms of characteristics of the creation myth. "The sea where the Egyptians perished becomes the primeval sea (cf. Exod. 15:5, 8), Egypt is turned into 'Rahab,' the primeval dragon (cf. Isa. 30:7; 41:9; Ps. 87:4; 89:11)."[6] Finally, the two are brought together in literary units, as in Psalm 136.

> O give thanks to Yahweh, for he is good;
> O give thanks to the God of gods;
> O give thanks to the Lord of lords;
> To him who alone does great wonders,
> To him who by understanding made the heavens,
> To him who spread out the earth upon the waters,
> To him who made the great lights,
> The sun to rule over the day,

The moon and the stars to rule over the night;
To him who smote the first-born of Egypt,
And brought Israel out from among them,
With a strong hand and an outstretched arm;
To him who divided the Red Sea in sunder,
And made Israel pass through the midst of it,
But overthrew Pharaoh and his host in the Red Sea;
To him who led his people through the wilderness,
To him who smote great kings,
And slew famous kings,
Sihon, king of the Amorites,
And Og, king of Bashan,
And gave their land as a heritage,
A heritage to Israel his servant;
It is he who remembered us in our low estate,
And rescued us from our foes,
He who gives food to all flesh;
O give thanks to the God of heaven.[7]

But the most obvious example of this process is the Pentateuch itself. At the time of the Solomonic enlightenment the J document was written in Jerusalem: the J document is virtually a narrative account of Creation and *Salvation History*. At the Exile the P document followed this pattern, and it remained the pattern of the Pentateuch as we know it, with the necessary changes introduced when the Deuteronomic history was united with the Creation plus Salvation History narrative.[8] That the Pentateuch itself represents an amalgam of two originally separate traditions can be seen rather dramatically in the fact that the E source does not include Creation but begins directly with the Patriarchs, i.e., it covers only the Salvation History.

With the bringing together of the two originally separate entities— the myth of God as king with its emphasis on creation and renewal, and the myth of the Salvation History with its emphasis on the activity of God on behalf of his people at key moments in their history—the stage was set for the emergence of the symbol Kingdom of God. At the level of language the symbol is derived from the myth of the kingship of God, for *malkuth*, "reign" or "kingdom," is an abstract noun formed from the root *m-l-k* "reign, be king." At the level of immediate reference, however, the symbol evokes the features of the Salvation History. What happened was that the two myths came together to form one, the myth of God who created the world and is active on behalf of his people in the history of that world, and the symbol evolved to evoke that myth. We will quote two characteristic passages to illustrate the meaning and use of Kingdom (of God)[9] in the Old Testament.

> All thy creatures praise thee, Lord,
>   and thy servants bless thee.
> They talk of the glory of the kingdom
>   and tell of thy might,
> they proclaim to their fellows how mighty
>   are thy deeds
>   how glorious the majesty of thy kingdom.
> Thy kingdom is an everlasting kingdom,
>   and thy dominion stands for all generations.
>   Ps. 145:10–14 (NEB)

From this we can see that to speak of the "glory of [God's] kingdom" is to speak of "his might," of his "mighty deeds." Moreover to say that the Kingdom of God is "an everlasting kingdom" is to say that God's "dominion stands for all generations." As a further definition of this the psalm continues

> In all his promises the Lord keeps faith,
>   he is unchanging in all his works;
> the Lord holds up those who stumble
>   and straightens backs which are bent.

In other words, to speak of the Kingdom of God is to speak of the mighty power of God, of his kingly activity, of the things which he does in which it becomes manifest that he is indeed king.

Moving from the meaning of the symbol to that which it evokes, we turn to the song of Moses in Exodus 15 (quoting NEB). This concludes with the cry of exaltation, "The Lord shall reign for ever and ever," and consists essentially of a recital of what are understood to be the mighty acts of God on behalf of his people, i.e., the Salvation History. God has delivered his people from their captivity in Egypt and destroyed those who pursued them:

> The chariots of Pharaoh and his army
>   he has cast into the sea;
> the flower of his officers
>   are engulfed in the Red Sea.

He has guided them through the wilderness and brought them to the Promised Land:

In thy constant love thou hast led the people
whom thou didst ransom:
thou hast guided them by thy strength
to the holy dwelling-place.

Moreover God has brought his people not only to the Promised Land
but also to Mount Zion, to Jerusalem and the temple that can now be
established there:

Thou broughtest them in and didst plant them
in the mount that is thy possession,
the dwelling-place, O Lord, of thy own making,
the sanctuary, O Lord, which thy own hands prepared.

In all this God was acting as king, and it is to be expected that he will
continue to act as king on behalf of his people: "The Lord shall reign
for ever and ever."

In these early uses of the symbol we have a consistent myth, the
myth of a God who created the world and was continually active in
that world on behalf of his people, with the emphasis upon the continuing activity of God. The symbol functions by evoking the myth, and
in turn the myth is effective because it interprets the historical experience of the Jewish people in the world. They knew themselves as the
people who had successfully escaped from Egypt, who had settled in
Canaan, who had built a temple to their God on Mount Zion. In their
myth it was God who had done these things on their behalf, and by
using the symbol in their songs of praise they evoke the myth and so
celebrate their history as the people of God.

It is obvious that at this point I have begun to use the word myth in
a particular way. Myth is a word that is notoriously difficult to define,
but in the case of the myth of God acting as king I like Alan Watts's
statement, as quoted by Philip Wheelwright: "Myth is to be defined as
a complex of stories—some no doubt fact, and some fantasy—which,
for various reasons, human beings regard as demonstrations of the
inner meaning of the universe and of human life."[10] "A complex of
stories—some no doubt fact, and some fantasy," that statement describes exactly the ancient Israelite people's understanding of their
deliverance from Egypt, their conquest of Canaan, the bringing of the
Ark to Mount Zion by David and the building of a temple there by

Solomon. "A complex of stories . . . which, for various reasons, human beings regard as demonstrations of the inner meaning of the universe and of human life," that too describes exactly the Israelite understanding of life in the world as being under the direct control of the God who had acted as king on their behalf *and who would continue to do so.* The ancient Israelite people believed that their myth of the kingly activity of God demonstrated "the inner meaning of the universe" and gave them a true understanding of the nature of human life in the world. It is because they believed this that the symbol was so effective: it was effective precisely because it evoked the myth by means of which they had come to understand themselves as the people of God, the beneficiaries of his kingly activity in the world. The symbol is dependent upon the myth, and it is effective because of its power to evoke the myth. The myth in turn derives its power from its ability to make sense of the life of the Jewish people in the world.

With this understanding of things the historical destiny of the Jewish people in the world becomes an important factor in the functioning of the symbol and the effectiveness of the myth. So long as the people could celebrate their freedom as the people of God in the land God had given them they could celebrate his reign or kingdom in their temple, but in fact the freedom of the people of God in the land God had given them was a precarious historical phenomenon. Ancient Palestine was a buffer state between the two world powers centered on the fertile crescent of Mesopotamia to the north and on the river Nile to the south. Historically speaking the ancient Israelite people were able to enter Palestine from the desert about 1100 B.C. because at that time both the power to the north and the power to the south were comparatively ineffective. In Mesopotamia Assyria was only just coming to power, and in Egypt the so-called New Empire was in decline. This international situation continued, and so David was able to establish an independent Jewish state about 1000 B.C. But the situation did not continue indefinitely. In the north Assyria came to power, and in the south Egypt revived, and so Palestine became again a buffer state between two world empires, its little independent kingdoms subject again to the control of the world powers. The Israelite kingdom had split into two at the death of Solomon in 922 B.C., and the northern kingdom eventually fell to an aggressive Assyrian king in 721 B.C., while the southern kingdom, comparatively small and out of the way, managed to survive until 587 B.C., when it fell to a new power from the north, the Babylonians.

The details of all of this are of course unimportant in a discussion of the interpretation of the biblical symbol, but what is important is the impact of these historical events upon the use of the symbol Kingdom of God with its evocation of the myth of God active as king on behalf of his people in the world. To put the matter in a very summary form, what happened was that prophets arose who interpreted these events in such a way that the myth maintained its force. The catastrophes were the judgment of God upon his people and their kings for not remaining true to him; the temporary reprieves were signs that God was still active on behalf of his people. Above all the prophets used the ancient symbolism to express the hope for a new act of God as king on behalf of his people, an act whereby he would deliver them from their new captivity to Assyria or Babylon as once he had delivered them from Egypt.

> For the Lord our judge, the Lord our law-giver,
> the Lord our king—he himself will save us.
>   Isa. 33:22 (NEB)

> How lovely on the mountains are the feet of the herald
> who comes to proclaim prosperity and bring good news,
>   the news of deliverance,
> calling to Zion, "Your God is king."
> . . . .
> The Lord has bared his holy arm in the sight of
>   all the nations,
>   and the whole world from end to end
>   shall see the deliverance of our God.
>   Away from Babylon; come out, come out. . . .
>   Isa. 52:7–11 (NEB)

The most important element in the intricate historical process is perhaps that this particular hope was in fact fulfilled. The Babylonians conquered Jerusalem and exiled many of its people to Babylon in 587 B.C. Within fifty years, in 529 B.C., Cyrus, king of the Medes and Persians, conquered Babylon and took control of all the former Babylonian territories, including Syria and Palestine. Cyrus' policy was to allow people conquered and transported by the Babylonians to return home and rebuild their temples and sanctuaries, and within a year the

Jews had permission to return to Jerusalem and to rebuild their temple. Under these circumstances the Jewish prophets were able to assert their myth and claim that Cyrus was in fact the servant of their God.

> Thus says the Lord to Cyrus his anointed,
>   Cyrus whom he has taken by the hand
> . . . .
> I will give you treasures from dark vaults,
>   hoarded in secret places,
> that you may know that I am the Lord,
>   Israel's God who calls you by name.
>   Isa. 45:1–3 (NEB)

Not only did the Jewish prophets reassert the myth, they also returned to a use of the symbolism of the Kingdom of God.

> Zion, cry out for joy;
>   raise the shout of triumph, Israel;
> be glad, rejoice with all your heart,
>   daughter of Jerusalem.
> The Lord has rid you of your adversaries,
>   he has swept away your foes;
> the Lord is among you as king, O Israel;
>   never again shall you fear disaster.
>   Zeph. 3:14–15 (NEB)

"The Lord is among you as king, O Israel; never again shall you fear disaster," thus exulted the prophet Zephania as the exiled Jews returned to Jerusalem and began the tasks of rebuilding their temple and reconstructing the forms and expressions of their faith. Once again, however, the events of history called into question the validity of the myth. For two hundred years or so the Jewish people lived quietly in Jerusalem and its environs as a theocracy ruled in the name of God by the High Priest. But in 333 B.C. the Persian Empire was conquered by Alexander the Great, and after his death and the establishment by his generals of their independent kingdoms, Palestine resumed its age-old status of an embattled buffer state between empires to the north and to the south. To the north was Syria, ruled by the Seleucids; to the south was, as always, Egypt, now ruled by the Ptolemies. The days of virtual independence for a small Jewish state centered on Jerusalem were over. Events resumed their ancient pattern: the Jews were first under the control of the Ptolemies and then of the Seleucids. Then there came a period of decline of both the Syrian and Egyptian powers, and the

Jews achieved independence again in 164 B.C., under Judas Maccabee and his brothers. More than that, the successors of the Maccabees were able to rebuild the Jewish state to something like the size it had attained under David and Solomon. But this was due, as always, to the comparative decline of the world powers. Syria and Egypt were comparatively impotent, and Rome had not yet begun to exercise power in the eastern Mediterranean. But in 63 B.C. this situation changed, and the Roman general Pompey appeared in Palestine to regulate the affairs of the eastern Mediterranean on behalf of Rome. Roman power was irresistible, and the Jewish people again lost their independence as a result of a change in the international political situation.

After 63 B.C. the situation of the Jews in Palestine was a particularly bitter one. They had returned from their captivity in Babylon exulting in God as king who had again delivered them. They had then known almost two centuries of virtual independence only to fall prey again to Egyptians and Syrians. Under Judas Maccabee and his successors they had known another century of independence, and even a restoration of their state to something of its ancient glory. But now their situation was worse than ever. The Romans ruled in the land, and Jewish High Priests, the representatives of God to the people and of the people before God, were appointed by Roman fiat. After 6 A.D. the situation worsened, for at that time the Romans began to rule Jerusalem directly by means of a Roman procurator.

Under these circumstances the Jewish people continued to evoke the ancient myth, but now the formulations have a note of intensity about them, a note almost of despairing hope. In the Assumption of Moses, an apocalyptic work written shortly before the time of Jesus, we find the symbolic language of the Kingdom of God used as follows:

> And then his [God's] kingdom shall appear
>   throughout his creation,
> And then Satan shall be no more,
> And sorrow shall depart with him.
> . . . .
> For the Heavenly One will arise from his
>   royal throne,
> And he will go forth from his holy habitation
> With indignation and wrath on account of his sons.
> . . . .

For the Most High will arise, the Eternal God
    alone,
And he will appear to punish the Gentiles
Then thou, O Israel, shalt be happy.
. . . .
And God will exalt thee,
And he will cause thee to approach the heaven
    of the stars.

Assumption of Moses 10

Here we have the symbolic language of the Kingdom of God being used again to express the hopes of the people. The myth remains the same—that of God as king active on behalf of his people—and the symbol remains the same—it is God's Kingdom that will appear—but the formulation has changed. On the one hand, the language has grown more metaphorical: ". . . Satan shall be no more, and sorrow shall depart with him. . . ." ". . . the Heavenly One will arise from his royal throne . . . with indignation and wrath on account of his sons. . . ." On the other hand, the hope itself is coming to take a form in which the expectation is for a dramatic change in the circumstances of the Jews over against the hated Gentiles. ". . . the Most High will arise . . . he will appear to punish the Gentiles . . . Then thou, O Israel, shalt be happy . . . God will exalt thee . . . he will cause thee to approach the heaven of the stars. . . ."

This is the language of apocalyptic, as this is the apocalyptic hope, and there is some question as to what the apocalyptic writers actually expected. It has been pointed out, above all perhaps by Amos Wilder,[11] that apocalyptic imagery is a natural form of expression when one is in extreme circumstances, and Wilder himself has turned to it in poetry arising out of his combat experiences in the First World War. What one can say perhaps is that the extremity of the situation of the Jews under the Romans in Palestine after 63 B.C. escalated their use of language in the expression of the characteristic hope for the activity of God on their behalf, as it also created circumstances under which they were no longer sure what they hoped for—except that it was for a deliverance like those from Egypt and Babylon in the past, but this time a permanent deliverance from all the evils of history.

One particularly prominent form of this apocalyptic hope for a deliverance from history itself is that of the hope to begin a war against Rome in which God would intervene, and which God would bring to an end by destroying the Gentiles and their Jewish collaborators or sympathizers, and by creating a world transformed, a world in which "Satan and sin will be no more." Just how widespread and realistic this particular form of the apocalyptic hope was can be seen from the fact that the Jewish people rose in revolt against Rome in 66 A.D., and again in 132; both times they began a war against Rome in which they expected God to intervene and which they expected God to bring to an end in victory for them as his people.

The people we have come to know through the Dead Sea Scrolls shared this hope. Indeed one of the Dead Sea Scrolls is a battle plan for this war against Rome, and all evil, the war in which God would intervene and which he would bring to victory on their behalf. This is the so-called War Scroll (IQM) and in it we find a use of the symbolic language of the Kingdom of God. We read, "And to the God of Israel shall be the Kingdom, and among his people will he display might," and, "Thou, O God, resplendent in the glory of thy Kingdom . . . [art] in our midst as a perpetual help," (IQM 6:6 and 12:7). In both instances the symbol Kingdom of God is being used to express the hope, indeed the expectation, that God would act on behalf of his people by intervening in a war against Rome and the Roman legions. In this hope and expectation they began the war, but the war itself, contrary to their expectation, went the way of Rome and of the Roman legions.

One last use of the symbol in ancient Judaism remains to be mentioned, the use in the Kaddish prayer, a prayer in regular use in the Jewish synagogues immediately before the time of Jesus, and for that matter still in use today. In an English translation of the ancient form, the prayer is as follows:

> Magnified and sanctified be his
>   great name in the world that he
>   has created according to his will.
> May he establish his kingdom in your
>   lifetime and in your days and in
>   the lifetime of all the house of
>   Israel, even speedily and at a
>   near time.

This is so close to a central petition of the prayer that Jesus taught his disciples,

Hallowed be thy name
Thy kingdom come

that the two must be related, and the most reasonable supposition is that the prayer of Jesus is a deliberate modification of the Kaddish prayer, a point to which I shall return below. But for the moment I wish to make the point that this is a use of the symbol in a prayer used regularly by the synagogue community *as a community*. The very fact that the symbol is being used in prayer by a whole group of people means that while it will always have evoked the myth of God active as king on behalf of his people, the form of the expectation expressed by the petition, "May he establish his kingdom," will have varied from individual to individual, and no doubt that for many Jews living in the period between Pompey's "settlement" of the East in 63 B.C. and the beginning of the Jewish revolt against Rome in 66 A.D. the prayer will have expressed the hope for the kind of dramatic irruption of God into human history that is the central theme of ancient Jewish (and Christian) apocalyptic. But it can never have been *limited* to the expression of that hope, for it is of the very nature of religious symbols that they are plurisignificant, that they can never be exhausted in any one apprehension of meaning, and this is, of course, true of most symbols.

Before we can make any final statement of the use of the symbol "Kingdom of God" in ancient Jewish apocalyptic, therefore, we need to digress somewhat and discuss the nature and function of symbols altogether. We will do this in relationship to two modern discussions of symbols: Philip Wheelwright, *Metaphor and Reality* (1962), and Paul Ricoeur, *The Symbolism of Evil* (1969). This is a valid approach to the use of a particular symbol in ancient Jewish apocalyptic, and in the message of Jesus, for the nature and function of symbol are of the very stuff of language itself and do not change in essentials from language to language, or from age to age.

I will begin this digression on the nature and function of symbol with Philip Wheelwright's definition of a symbol: "A symbol, in general, is a relatively stable and repeatable element of perceptual experience, standing for some larger meaning or set of meanings which cannot be given, or not fully given, in perceptual experience itself."[12] A symbol therefore represents something else, and Wheelwright makes a most important distinction within symbols in terms of their relationship with that which they represent. A symbol can have a one-to-one relationship to that which it represents, such as the mathematical symbol *pi*, in which case it is, in Wheelwright's terms, a "steno-symbol," or it can have a set of meanings that can neither be exhausted nor adequately expressed by any one referent, in which case it is a "tensive symbol."

Paul Ricoeur makes a similar distinction. For Ricoeur a symbol is a sign, something which points beyond itself to something else. Not all signs are symbols, however, for sometimes a sign is transparent of meaning and is exhausted by its "first or literal intentionality." But in the case of a symbol the meaning is opaque and we have to erect a second intentionality upon the first, an intentionality which proceeds by analogy to ever deeper meanings. Concerned with the symbolism of evil, Ricoeur discusses "defilement." This is a sign in that it has a first, literal intentionality; it points beyond itself to "stain" or "unclean." But "defilement" is also a symbol because we can, by analogy, go further to a "certain situation of man in the sacred which is precisely that of being defiled, impure."[13] What for Wheelwright is a distinction between a "steno-symbol" and a "tensive symbol" is for Ricoeur a distinction between a "sign" and a "symbol."

We now return to the symbol "Kingdom of God" in ancient Jewish apocalyptic, and I want to take up this aspect of the discussion by quoting a paragraph from my SBL Presidential Address, delivered in 1973.

Let me begin this aspect of my discussion by pointing out that in ancient Jewish apocalyptic in general—and for that matter in early Christian apocalyptic in general—the symbols used are, in Wheelwright's terms, "steno-symbols"; in Ricoeur's, "signs" rather than "symbols." Typically, the apocalyptic seer told the story of the history of his people in symbols where each symbol bore a one-to-one relationship with that which it depicted. This thing was Antiochus IV Epiphanes, that thing was Judas Maccabee, the other thing was the coming of the Romans, and so on. But if this was the case, and it certainly was, then when the seer left the known facts of the past and present to express his expectation of the future his symbols remained "steno-symbols," and his expectation concerned singular concrete historical events. To take an actual example, if in chapters 11 and 12 of the Book of Daniel the "abomination that makes desolate" is a historical artifact—and it is—and if those who "make many understand" and the "little help" are historically identifiable individuals—and they are—then the "Michael" of Dan. 12:1 is also someone who will be historically identifiable, and the general resurrection of Dan. 12:2 is an event of the same historical order as the setting up of the altar to Zeus in the Jerusalem temple. The series of events described in Daniel 11 and 12 are events within history; insofar as they are described in symbols, those symbols are "steno-symbols" (Wheelwright), or they are "signs" rather than "symbols" (Ricoeur).[14]

In the year since I made that statement a number of my friends and colleagues have challenged it, and in the light of their challenges I have rethought the matter as carefully as I could. It now seems to me that I have pressed too hard the distinction between a "steno-" and a "tensive" symbol in the case of apocalyptic symbols. It is still a most important distinction, and it is still true that most apocalyptic symbols are steno-symbols. But it is also true that the distinction is not hard and fast, and that in the case of such major symbols as the coming of Michael and the resurrection of the dead, or the establishment by God of his Kingdom—or the coming of Jesus as Son of Man—then no hard and fast line could be drawn, and some seers no doubt saw the symbols as steno-symbols while others saw them as tensive.

What this means is that, for example, in the case of the symbols used to represent God's irruption into history, it was always possible to see the symbols as steno-symbols, and for Jews to identify the Messiah and seek signs of the coming of the one historical moment of God's final intervention on behalf of his people. Similarly for Christians it was always possible to see the symbol of Jesus coming "on the clouds of heaven" as Son of Man as a steno-symbol, and to seek to calculate the time and place of that coming. There is ample evidence that large numbers of both Jews and Christians did in fact do exactly those things, that, to use the words we are now using, large numbers of both Jews and Christians used and understood the symbols of God's eschatological activity on behalf of his people as steno-symbols. But the point I now concede—indeed the point I am now eager to embrace!—is that this was not necessarily the case in any one instance. We have to investigate each case on its merits, recognizing that symbols of the order of those representing the eschatological activity of God can be either steno- or tensive symbols.

If we view the symbol Kingdom of God in ancient Judaism in this light, then we can see that fundamentally it is a tensive symbol and that its meaning could never be exhausted, nor adequately expressed, by any one referent. However, in view of the identification of historical individuals as the Messiah, and in view of the undoubted expectation that God would intervene in the course of the war against Syria at the time of the Maccabees and that this would be the active beginning of the End—as well as in view of similar expectations in the case of the Jewish War and the Bar Cochba revolt—we would have to conclude that in ancient Jewish apocalyptic Kingdom of God was predominantly understood as a steno-symbol. But then there is the Kaddish prayer to remind us that even during the heyday of ancient Jewish apocalyptic such an understanding was neither necessary nor universal.

As we approach the message of Jesus, then, there are three things to bear in mind. In the first place, "Kingdom of God" is a symbol with deep roots in the Jewish consciousness of themselves as the people of God. Then, secondly, it functions within the context of the myth of God active in history on behalf of his people; indeed by the time of Jesus it had come to represent particularly the expectation of a final, eschatological act of God on behalf of his people. Thirdly, it could be understood and used either as a steno- or as a tensive symbol, to use a modern but nonetheless appropriate distinction. It is against this background that we must view the message of Jesus.

B. KINGDOM OF GOD IN THE MESSAGE OF JESUS

In this section of our study we attempt to arrive at a historical understanding of the meaning and use of Kingdom of God in the message of Jesus. At this time we are not considering the possible significance of the message of Jesus concerning the Kingdom for a subsequent generation of hearers, with the possible meaning of that message in a context other than that in which it was first delivered. These latter aspects of the matter will concern us at a later stage in this study.

The message of Jesus concerning the Kingdom of God has been the subject of an intensive scholarly investigation ever since Johannes Weiss published the first edition of his *Die Predigt Jesu vom Reiche Gottes* in 1892.[15] In general this discussion has not differentiated between the historical and the hermeneutical aspects of the problem. The participants in the discussion have generally assumed that there was an immediate and direct correlation between a historical understanding of the message of Jesus and a hermeneutical appreciation of its possible significance for the present (i.e., for the present of the scholar or interpreter). Indeed, much of the historical aspect of the discussion has been strongly influenced by what these scholars held to be the hermeneutical possibilities of their findings. Weiss himself, however, did keep the two aspects separate, and we shall attempt to do so. To repeat: our present focus is with the historical aspect of the discussion only.

It is my intention to make brief reference to the discussion and to isolate some of the issues upon which it has turned. Before I do this, however, there is a further point to be made with regard to the discussion itself, a point that is of some importance. Weiss constantly spoke of "the *concept* Kingdom of God," of Jesus' "*conception* of the Kingdom of God,"[16] and this kind of language is common parlance in the discussion. It may indeed be said to be a discussion of Jesus' "conception," "understanding," "idea," "*Vorstellung*," or "*Idee*" of the Kingdom. All of us who have participated have spoken in these terms. In a book published as lately as spring, 1974, I find that I have done so myself![17] But I now want to argue that such language is imprecise. "Kingdom of God" is not an *idea* or a *conception*, it is a *symbol*. As a symbol it can *represent* or *evoke* a whole range or series of conceptions or ideas, but it only becomes a conception or idea if it constantly represents or evokes that one conception or idea, and we then take the step of creating a kind of verbal shorthand in speaking of the "conception of the Kingdom." If we speak of "Jesus' conception of the Kingdom of God," then we are prejudging a whole range of really important issues, for we are assuming that there is one constant conception in the message of Jesus represented by the symbol "Kingdom of God": we make Kingdom of God a steno-symbol on the lips of Jesus.

It would be my claim today that this is the reason for the fact that the discussion begun by Johannes Weiss in 1892 has reached no satisfactory conclusion. It can reach no satisfactory conclusion because it is bedeviled by a concern for Jesus' *conception* of the Kingdom, and to put the matter in that way is to prejudge issues upon which the discussion should focus attention. The first part of this study claimed that Kingdom of God is a symbol which evokes the myth of the activity of God as king on behalf of his people. Further, it was argued that this activity of God could be understood in different ways. Even in ancient Jewish apocalyptic the hope evoked by the use of the symbolic language could vary enormously; it could take many varied forms. Moreover, it was pointed out that even in the time of maximum apocalyptic influence the Kaddish prayer was in regular use, which means that the symbolic language could evoke other and different forms of the hope for the kingly activity of God on behalf of his people. To speak of Jesus' *conception* of the Kingdom is to imply that for Jesus Kingdom of God evoked a consistent well-defined understanding of the nature and form of the activity of God represented by that symbolic language. This is to set limits to the discussion within the confines of which it could never be settled, limits, moreover, which it constantly strove to break.

It is my claim that to speak of Kingdom of God as a symbol, and then to ask questions with regard to its nature as a symbol—and with regard to what it evoked or represented in the message of Jesus—is to adopt a procedure which will bring the whole matter into clearer and more satisfactory focus. We turn now to a brief review of some aspects of the scholarly discussion.[18]

1. The Scholarly Discussion of Kingdom of God in the Message of Jesus

We begin where the discussion begins, with Johannes Weiss. Weiss developed his views in conscious opposition to those of Albrecht Ritschl, who saw the Kingdom of God as the moral organization of humanity through action inspired by love.[19] Weiss had a conscious concern to build upon a historical exegesis of the New Testament texts and to take into account the Jewish apocalyptic literature. He reached the conclusion that, in the message of Jesus, Kingdom of God was essentially an apocalyptic concept, "the breaking out of an overpowering divine storm which erupts into history to destroy and to renew, and which a man can neither further nor influence."[20] "The disciples were to pray for the coming of the Kingdom, but men could do nothing to establish it." This Kingdom was imminent, indeed Jesus "even had moments of prophetic vision when he perceived the opposing kingdom of Satan as already overcome and broken [at which moments] he declared with daring faith that the Kingdom of God had already dawned." But this was proleptic vision, "in general . . . the actualization of the Kingdom of God has yet to take place."[21] It is in the context of this imminent expectation of the eruption of the overwhelming divine storm of the Kingdom that Jesus proclaimed his ethical teaching. He demanded "the righteousness of the Kingdom of God [which] does not signify the ethical perfection which members of the Kingdom possess or achieve *in the Kingdom of God*, but rather the *dikaiosynē* which is the *condition for entrance into* the Kingdom of God."[22] The translator-editors of Weiss's book speak of this understanding of the ethical teaching of Jesus as "The Ethics of Preparation," in the heading they supply for this section. Schweitzer was to develop it as "interim ethics," ethical teaching valid only for the short period of time which remained between Jesus' proclamation of the coming of the Kingdom and the actual coming of that Kingdom.[23]

With the publication of Weiss's views, and their subsequent popularization by Albert Schweitzer in *The Quest of the Historical Jesus*,[24] the scholarly discussion got under way, and it followed the lines laid down by Weiss and Schweitzer, dealing with the issues in the terms in which they had raised them. As we pointed out above, the discussion has concerned itself with Jesus' *conception* of the Kingdom, and the first question examined was whether Weiss and Schweitzer were right in claiming that Kingdom of God was an *apocalyptic* conception in the message of Jesus. In general this came to be accepted, but in the very act of accepting this contention scholars sought to blunt its force by arguing that Jesus had transformed the conception as he used it. William Sanday spoke of Jesus "starting from" the apocalyptic idea but "transcending" it; F. C. Burkitt claimed that Jesus' use of the term Kingdom of God was "almost as much a criticism of the popular ideals as a preaching of them."[25] For a time this was the dominant note in the discussion,[26] while there were still voices raised claiming that Jesus was not dependent upon apocalyptic,[27] but in 1927 a conference of English and German theologians agreed that Kingdom of God was an apocalyptic concept in the message of Jesus,[28] and from that moment forward this was accepted as a basic tenet in the discussion. Scholars still developed variations on the theme of Jesus' transformation of apocalyptic, but now this was done on the basis of a detailed exegesis of aspects of the teaching of Jesus rather than on more general considerations.

The two most important contributions at this stage were those by R. Bultmann in his book *Jesus* (1926), and C. H. Dodd (a participant in the Cambridge conference) in his *Parables of the Kingdom* (1935). We will discuss each of these briefly.

In his book *Jesus* Bultmann makes an extended statement about

Kingdom of God (he actually uses the phrase Reign of God rather than Kingdom of God, *Gottesherrschaft* rather than *Gottesreich,* but in our present context that is unimportant) in the message of Jesus, a statement worth quoting at some length.

[In the message of Jesus] Reign of God is a power which wholly determines the present although in itself it is entirely future. It determines the present in that it forces man to decision. . . . Because Jesus so sees man as standing in the crisis of decision before the activity of God, it is understandable that in him the Jewish expectation becomes the absolute certainty that now the hour of the breaking-in of the Reign of God has come. If man stands in the crisis of decision then . . . it is understandable that for Jesus the whole contemporary mythology should be pressed into the service of this conception of human existence. . . .[29]

Bultmann reached this understanding of Kingdom of God in the message of Jesus on the basis of a very sophisticated process of interpretation.[30] He begins by accepting the Schleiermacher-Dilthey contention that a text is an "expression of life" (*Lebensäusserung*), so that the proclamation of Jesus is an expression of Jesus' understanding of the nature of human existence in the world. But in reaching an understanding of a statement of the nature of human existence in the world one may use categories such as those developed by a modern philosophy, in this instance Heideggerian existentialism, insofar as they can be shown to be appropriate.[31] In the case of the message of Jesus I would regard them as appropriate; so in my view Bultmann may speak of man "standing in the crisis of decision" and of Jesus' "conception of human existence." Although he is using these modern categories, he is still making a historical statement.

Bultmann's understanding of Kingdom of God in the message of Jesus has been enormously influential. In many respects it anticipates by almost fifty years the views I shall be developing below. But I would regard my restatement of the case as not unimportant because I am not starting from Jesus' *conception* of the Kingdom. Bultmann can do what he does because for him Jesus' conception of the Kingdom is ultimately a "conception of human existence" in the world. That is a brilliant insight, but it is somewhat forced, and I think it is better not to start with Jesus' "conception" of the Kingdom.

Although Bultmann is making a historical statement about the message of Jesus, he is also and at the same time creating a possibility at the level of hermeneutics. What he has done is to create the possibility of bridging the gap between the ancient Jewish apocalyptic preacher and the modern interpreter. As he understands it both are concerned to come to an understanding of the nature and possibilities of human existence in the world; hence meaningful dialogue can take place between them. This aspect of Bultmann's contribution to the discussion will concern us later;[32] we mention it now only for the sake of completeness.

C. H. Dodd's *Parables of the Kingdom*, published in 1935, also made a major contribution to the discussion. He raised the question of the time element in the proclamation of Jesus. Weiss and Schweitzer had claimed that Jesus proclaimed the Kingdom as imminent, and in some sense even perhaps proleptically present, but nonetheless as future. The Kingdom is "at hand," but its actualization is still to be expected in the future. Against this view Dodd argued that Jesus claimed that the Kingdom had actually come in his ministry, that the eschatology of Jesus was a "realized eschatology." He argued that both the Greek *ēggiken* of Mark 1:15 and the *ephthasen* of Matt. 12:28 = Luke 11:20 go back to a Semitic original which should be translated "has come," giving us, "The Kingdom of God has come." Other sayings either claim or imply the same thing: Luke 10:9–11, the Kingdom has come whether men repent or not; the sayings about the blessedness of the disciples and the greater than Solomon or Jonah, Luke 10:23–26; 11:31–32, both imply the actual presence of the Kingdom as does the reply to the Baptist's question, Matt. 11:4–6. Matt. 11:12 implies a contrast between the past of the law and the prophets and the present of the Kingdom of God. Dodd summarized his discussion of the Kingdom sayings as follows:

Whatever we may make of them, the sayings which declare the Kingdom of God to have come are explicit and unequivocal. They are moreover the most characteristic and distinctive of the Gospel sayings on the subject. They have no parallel in Jewish teaching or prayers of the period. If therefore we are seeking the differentia of the teaching of Jesus upon the Kingdom of God, it is here that it must be found.[33]

There are, of course, Kingdom sayings which seem unequivocally to point to a future coming of the Kingdom, e.g., Mark 9:1, which Dodd regarded as authentic. In his discussion of these sayings Dodd has to resort to a series of stratagems to maintain his "realized eschatology."

Some he explains away. Mark 9:1, for example, refers to the hearers of Jesus coming to realize that the Kingdom had indeed come in the ministry of Jesus. Others he interpreted as referring to "a world beyond this," to the "transcendent order beyond time and space."[34] This aspect of Dodd's work has never been found convincing.[35]

A further aspect of Dodd's work, and a most important one, was the fact that he introduced the parables of Jesus into the discussion of the Kingdom of God in the message of Jesus. This had most important consequences, both for the interpretation of the parables, and for the understanding of Jesus' use of Kingdom of God. We shall discuss the consequence for the interpretation of the parables in our second study;[36] here our concern is with the consequence for the understanding of Jesus' use of Kingdom of God. We will begin this aspect of our review of Dodd's work by summarizing his interpretation of the parables.

In general, Dodd argues, the burden of the message of the parables is that the great crisis, the coming of the Kingdom, is something present in the ministry of Jesus. In The Hid Treasure and The Costly Pearl (Matt. 13:44–46) the possession of the highest good, the Kingdom of God, is a present opportunity. The Tower-builder and The King Going to War (Luke 14:28–33) challenge men to take great risks with open eyes, in view of the presence of the crisis. The Children in the Marketplace calls attention to the egregious folly of childish behavior in the presence of the supreme crisis of history. Mark 2:18–19, in which Jesus is the Bridegroom, equates the present time with the time of blessing which is the object of Jewish expectation. The Patched Garment and The Old Wine-skins implies that the ministry of Jesus cannot be accommodated to traditional Judaism. In the ministry of Jesus the Kingdom has come, and one of the features of its coming was an unprecedented concern for the lost. This is the theme of The Lost Sheep and The Lost Coin, and the background to such sayings as Mark 2:17. The Prodigal Son has reference to the same situation, the calling of the outcasts in the ministry of Jesus, a situation which finds more elaborate expression in the parable of the Great Feast. The generosity and compassion of the employer/in The Laborers in the Vineyard has a similar reference.

The parables of crisis (The Faithful and Unfaithful Servants, The Waiting Servants, The Thief at Night and The Ten Virgins), as we have them, are intended to be referred directly to the expected second advent of Christ. In their original context in the ministry of Jesus, however, they were to enforce the appeal to men to recognize that the Kingdom of God was present, and that by their conduct in the presence of this crisis they would "judge themselves as faithful or unfaithful, wise or foolish."[37]

The parables of growth (The Sower, Tares, Seed Growing Secretly and Mustard Seed) are considered together with the parables of the Leaven and the Dragnet and are now interpreted as having reference to the harvest which is being reaped in the ministry of Jesus, the sowing having taken place before the beginning of that ministry.[38]

This interpretation of the parables, particularly as developed by Jeremias, has been very influential. Its importance is that it does introduce the parables into the discussion of the Kingdom, and this is absolutely justifiable. Indeed, it is essential. Not only do many of the parables begin with an express, or implied comparison, "The Kingdom of God is like . . .", all of them clearly have as their ultimate referent the Kingdom of God. An understanding of their message is therefore essential to an understanding of the message of Jesus concerning the Kingdom of God. More than that, Dodd is clearly justified in claiming that the challenge of the parables implies the presence of the Kingdom. If we agree to discuss the Kingdom in terms of "present" and "future" then Dodd was correct: the parables of Jesus imply the presence of the Kingdom. Whatever may be the weaknesses of other aspects of Dodd's "realized eschatology," in his reliance on the parables he was on firm ground. The development of the discussion after Dodd's contribution supported him in this: it became generally accepted that there was a "present" emphasis in the message of Jesus concerning the Kingdom, but not that this was the only emphasis.

Following the publication of Dodd's *Parables of the Kingdom* it became generally accepted that there was both a present and a future aspect to the message of Jesus concerning the Kingdom of God. Dodd carried the discussion with regard to a present aspect, but he did not carry it with regard to a present aspect *only*, and most scholars opted for some variation on the theme of an eschatology "in the process of realization" (Jeremias: *sich realisierenden Eschatologie*).[39] In my own previous discussions of the subject I have argued for "the Kingdom of God as both present and future in the teaching of Jesus";[40] as late as the spring of 1974 I was saying that "in the message of Jesus there is a very real tension between the Kingdom as present and the Kingdom as future, between the power of God as known in the present and the power of God to be known in the future."[41] In this I was not only representing my own views, I was also expressing the consensus of the discussion.[42] The question to be raised, however, is not whether this consensus is correct, but rather whether it is legitimate to think of Jesus' use of Kingdom of God in terms of "present" and "future" at all.

There is no need for us to review the discussion any further. With Bultmann's existentialist interpretation of Kingdom of God in the message of Jesus, with Dodd's "realized eschatology" and its subsequent modification to "eschatology in the process of realization," we have covered the essentials. The more recent discussion has really offered only variations on the positions reached by Weiss and Schweitzer, or by Bultmann, or by Dodd and by Jeremias modifying Dodd. As one who has both chronicled the discussion and participated in it, I can report that reading subsequent contributions—including my own—gives one a strong feeling of *déjà vu!*

The purpose of this present study is to offer what I hope will prove to be a new perspective on the discussion by approaching Kingdom of God as a *symbol*, and by approaching the message of Jesus concerning the Kingdom of God in terms of Jesus' use of the symbol. I therefore now restate the conclusion of the first section of this study. Kingdom of God is a symbol with deep roots in the Jews' consciousness of themselves as the people of God. It functions within the context of the myth of God active in history on behalf of his people; indeed by the time of Jesus it had come to represent particularly the expectation of a final eschatological act of God on behalf of his people. Moreover, it can be used either as a steno- or as a tensive symbol. It is against this background that we turn now to the teaching of Jesus.

2. The Use of Kingdom of God in the Message of Jesus

In turning to the message of Jesus we must turn to specific sayings and parables in the gospels, including the Gospel of Thomas. But this raises immediately the question of establishing the text to be interpreted, because the material attributed to Jesus in the gospels stems in large part from the early Christian communities, and even that which has claims to authenticity will have been edited and reinterpreted through many years of oral and written transmission in the early Christian communities. Moreover it may have been edited and reinterpreted further by the evangelists themselves. New Testament scholars have recognized this problem and have developed critical methods for reconstructing the earliest form of a saying or parable, and then criteria for determining the claims to authenticity of that earliest form. The details of this process in the case of the parables will concern us throughout the study of the interpretation of the parables below, and I have discussed the details of the process in the case of other material elsewhere.[43] I do not propose to repeat that discussion here but simply to claim that competent scholarly opinion would recognize as authentic *at least* the following material.

(a) The *Kingdom sayings*, Luke 11:20; 17:20–21; Matt. 11:12.
(b) The *Lord's Prayer* in a version close to Luke 11:2–4.
(c) The *proverbial sayings*, Mark 3:27; 3:24–26; 8:35; Luke 9:62; Mark 10:23b, 25; Luke 9:60a; Matt. 7:13–14; Mark 10:31; 7:15; 10:15; Luke 14:11 (cf. 16:15); Matt. 5:39b–41; 5:44–48.
(d) The *major parables*:
The Hid Treasure and The Pearl, Matt. 13:44–40.
The Lost Sheep, Lost Coin, Lost (Prodigal) Son, Luke 15:3–32.
The Great Supper, Matt. 22:1–14; Luke 14:16–24; Gos. Thom. 92:10–35.
The Unjust Steward, Luke 16:1–9.
The Workers in the Vineyard, Matt. 20:1–16.
The Two Sons, Matt. 21:28–32.
The Children in the Marketplace, Matt. 11:16–19.
The Pharisee and the Tax-Collector, Luke 18:9–14.
The Good Samaritan, Luke 10:29–37.
The Unmerciful Servant, Matt. 18:23–35.
The Tower Builder and King Going to War, Luke 14:28–32.
The Friend at Midnight, Luke 11:5–8.
The Unjust Judge, Luke 18:1–8.
The Leaven, Luke 13:20–21; Gos. Thom. 97:2–6.
The Mustard Seed, Mark 4:30–32; Gos. Thom. 84:26–33.
The Seed Growing by Itself, Mark 4:26–29; Gos. Thom. 85:15–19.
The Sower, Mark 4:3–8; Gos. Thom. 82:3–13.
The Wicked Tenants, Mark 12:1–12; Gos. Thom. 93:1–18.

This list of the parables is meant to be illustrative rather than exhaustive; in general scholars will accept any parable that can be reconstructed as a parable as distinct from an allegory. To avoid multiple references I have given only the Markan or Lukan references even when there are parallels for Mark in Matthew and Luke, or for Luke in Matthew. Gospel of Thomas references are added only when they are particularly interesting, usually because that gospel offers an unallegorized form of the parable.

I now offer a discussion of some items from each of these categories, beginning with the *Kingdom sayings*. Where appropriate I make reference to my previous exegesis of these sayings in *The Kingdom of God in the Teaching of Jesus* (=*Kingdom*) and *Rediscovering the Teaching of Jesus* (=*Rediscovering*), an exegesis I am usually supplementing and sometimes correcting. I also include references to *The New Testament: An Introduction* (=*Introduction*) where appropriate.

(a) The Kingdom Sayings

In the case of these sayings in particular I am revising my previous exegesis, even that offered as recently as 1974 in my *Introduction*. The reason for this is the fact that only now am I in a position to appreciate the difference made by recognizing Kingdom of God as a symbol. Even at the time of writing the *Introduction* I had not grasped the matter as fully as I now have.

(i) Luke 11:20 "But if it is by the finger of God that I cast out demons then the kingdom of God has come (*ephthasen*) upon you."

Previous exegesis: *Rediscovering*, pp. 63–67 and the reference there to *Kingdom*. See also *Introduction*, pp. 288–291.

It may be taken as established that in this saying Jesus is interpreting his exorcisms. Historically speaking Jesus had a reputation as a successful exorcist; ancient Jewish sources speak of him as one who "practiced sorcery," and the gospel accounts of the exorcisms have a core of historical reality.[44] This saying shows that Jesus claimed that his exorcisms were a manifestation of the power of God as king. If we discuss the Kingdom in terms of "present" or "future," then this saying is strong evidence for the Kingdom as present in the ministry of Jesus, for the exorcisms were a historical reality and there can be no doubt but that *ephthasen*, and any reasonable Semitic language original, really means "has come." But these are not the right terms in which to discuss it. Rather, we should recognize that Jesus is deliberately evoking the myth of the activity of God on behalf of his people, and claiming that the exorcisms are a manifestation of that activity in the experience of his hearers. Kingdom of God is here a symbol, and it is used in this saying because of its evocative power. The saying is a challenge to the hearers to take the ancient myth with renewed seriousness, and to begin to anticipate the manifestation of the reality of which it speaks in the concrete actuality of their experience.

A second and unmistakable aspect of this saying is its link with the Kaddish prayer, "May he establish his Kingdom in your lifetime . . ." or, in the form in which Jesus taught it to his disciples, "Thy Kingdom come." As we pointed out earlier, constant use of this prayer—and it was a prayer for constant use—would inevitably lead to a wide variety of forms of anticipation of the kingly activity of God on behalf of the petitioner. It would inevitably come to be anticipated, not only in terms of the kind of cosmic activity anticipated by the apocalyptic writers, but also in terms of the immediate and personal needs of the people at prayer. The use of the symbol in connection with so immediate and personal a need as the healing of an individual must be understood as a reinforcement of the trend from the cosmic to the personally experienced reality.

A last consequence of this saying is that it establishes the fact that Kingdom of God is not a steno- but a tensive symbol on the lips of Jesus. Clearly the exorcisms do not exhaust the possibilities with regard to the activity of God on behalf of his people; the meaning of the symbol is not exhausted by any one apprehension of the reality it represents.

(ii) Luke 17:20–21 "The kingdom of God is not coming with signs to be observed; nor will they say, 'Lo here it is!' or 'There!' for behold, the kingdom of God *entos hymōn estin.*"

Previous exegesis: *Rediscovering,* pp. 68–74 and the reference there to *Kingdom.* See also *Introduction,* pp. 288–291.

An interpretation of this saying must take very seriously the fact that it is a negative saying; its concern is not to proclaim, but to guard against the misunderstanding of a proclamation. What it affirms it affirms in deliberate and self-conscious contrast to what it denies.

When I first attempted an exegesis of this saying,[45] I thought that
what was being denied was the apocalyptic view of history (i.e., one
concerned with the totality of history) and what was being affirmed
was the prophetic view of history (i.e., one concerned with specific
events within history). Later I argued that Jesus was modifying the
prophetic view of history that he was affirming to the extent that the
specific events in terms of which the Kingdom might be known were
the events of "the experience of the individual."[46] Today I want to
look at the matter in terms of symbol and myth.

The apocalyptic practice of "sign seeking" was dependent upon a
view of myth as allegory,[47] and upon the treatment of symbols as
steno-symbols. Typically the apocalyptic seer told the story of the history of his people in symbols where, as we pointed out earlier in this
study, for the most part each symbol bore a one-to-one relationship to
that which it depicted. This thing was Antiochus Epiphanes, that thing
was Judas Maccabee, the other thing was the coming of the Romans,
and so on. The story is myth because it is a narrative account of the
history of the people of God, climaxing in an account of God's eschatological redemption of his people which still uses symbols. But the
symbols are steno-symbols and this makes the myth an allegory. In
the case of an allegory, once the symbols have been correctly identified
the allegory itself can be abandoned and the story retold in steno-
language. Insofar as he can correctly identify the symbols—and insofar as the seer got his facts straight!—the historian can retell the story
of these apocalyptic visions in the language of critical historiography,
as the commentaries upon Daniel, Revelation, and the other Jewish
or Christian apocalypses testify.

The important point in the present context however is that if the
symbols in these allegorical myths are steno-symbols down to the account of the actual redemption of the people of God, then the symbols
in the account of that redemption can also be steno-symbols. If, as I
put the matter above, in Daniel 11–12, "the abomination that makes
desolate" is a historical artifact—and it is—and if those who "make
many understand" and the "little help" are historically identifiable
individuals—and they are—then "Michael" can also be someone who
will be historically identifiable and the general resurrection can be an
event of the same historical order as the setting up of "the abomination
that makes desolate." It is precisely the acceptance of this way of

thinking that makes possible a seeking after "signs to be observed." What was sought was a steno-symbol which could be identified as an event in the apocalyptic drama, and which would identify the person concerned as one of the *dramatis personae*. But all this is dependent upon the treatment of the myth of the activity of God on behalf of his people as allegory and its symbols as steno-symbols.

Jesus categorically rejected the seeking after "signs to be observed" and in so doing necessarily equally categorically rejected the treatment of the myth as allegory and its symbols as steno-symbols. In the message of Jesus the myth is true myth and the symbols of God's redemptive activity are tensive symbols. This is the meaning I would now give to the enigmatic "the kingdom of God *entos hymōn estin*." It means that the symbol of the kingly activity of God on behalf of his people confronts the hearers of Jesus as a true tensive symbol with its evocation of a whole set of meanings, and that the myth is, in the message of Jesus, true myth with its power to mediate the experience of existential reality.

At this point I want to digress from the discussion of the Kingdom sayings for a moment to turn to the refusal of Jesus to give a sign. There are four passages from the synoptic gospels which relate Jesus' refusal to give a sign: Matt. 12:39 and 16:4; Luke 11:29–32; and Mark 8:11–13. These have been examined by my pupil Richard A. Edwards[18] who shows that there is a fundamental pericope at the basis of the gospel traditions, a pericope now best represented by Mark 8:11–12.

The Pharisees came and began to argue with him, seeking from him a sign from heaven, to test him. And he sighed deeply in his spirit, and said, "Why does this generation seek a sign? Truly, I say to you, no sign shall be given to this generation."

In some such version as this, although probably without specific reference to Pharisees, the pericope has claims to authenticity. It is early in the tradition, underlying both Mark and Q, and it represents an attitude to "signs" dissimilar to both ancient Judaism and primitive Christianity—Jewish and Christian apocalyptic regularly looked for and identified "signs." Of course it is possible that "sign" in this pericope refers to something that Jesus might do to validate his personal authority, and that the pericope, therefore, should be interpreted as part of the evidence that Jesus specifically refused to make personal claims, that he put all his emphasis upon the proclamation of the Kingdom rather than upon the person of the proclaimer. But in light of Luke 17:20–21 it is also possible that the refusal is a refusal to enter into the common apocalyptic practice of identifying "signs" which indicated the imminence of the eschatological act of God.[49]

(iii) Matt. 11:12 From the days of John the Baptist until now, the Kingdom of Heaven has suffered violence, and men of violence plunder it.

Previous exegesis, and defense of the translation: *Rediscovering*, pp. 74–77 and *Kingdom*, pp. 171–176. See also *Introduction*, pp. 288–291.

This has proven a most difficult saying to interpret. It is obvious that it envisages the Kingdom as a present reality, but the idea of the Kingdom suffering violence and being plundered was difficult to understand. However, when we think in terms of the Kingdom as a symbol evoking a myth then the matter becomes clear. The myth evoked here is a variation of the myth of God active as king; it is the myth of God engaged in eschatological conflict with the power of evil. The reality of this myth to the hearers of Jesus is obvious from the apocalyptic literature in general and the Qumran scroll, "The War of the Sons of Light against the Sons of Darkness," (IQM) in particular. What is unique, and indeed breathtaking about this saying, is that it relates the myth to the fate of John the Baptist, and to the potential fate of Jesus and his disciples. In my earlier exegesis I followed Käsemann in seeing the import of the logion as "the Kingdom of God suffers violence from the days of the Baptist until now and is hindered by men of violence,"[50] and I have become convinced that the saying refers to the death of the Baptist and the prospective suffering of Jesus and his disciples.[51] The point I wish to emphasize now is that this reflection is carried on in the context of an evocation of the myth of the eschatological war. In Luke 11:20–21 the use of Kingdom of God evokes the myth of the eschatological activity of God and interprets the exorcism of Jesus as a manifestation of that activity. In Matt. 11:12 the use of Kingdom of Heaven (=God) evokes the myth of the eschatological war between God and the powers of evil and interprets the fate of John the Baptist, and the potential fate of Jesus and his disciples, as a manifestation of that conflict.

(b) The Lord's Prayer

As we noted earlier, most scholars are prepared to accept as authentic the prayer in a version close to Luke 11:2–4 which reads (RSV):

> "Father,
> Hallowed be thy name,
> Thy kingdom come.
> Give us each day our daily bread;
> And forgive us our sins, for we ourselves forgive
>   every one who is indebted to us;
> And lead us not into temptation."

Previous exegesis: *Rediscovering*, pp. 160–161, *Kingdom*, pp. 191–198. See also *Introduction*, p. 299.

In our present context the most important element in the prayer is that to which we have already called attention, the parallelism between the Kingdom petition and the Kaddish prayer of the ancient Jewish synagogue.[52] The parallelism is too close to be accidental, and the differences—the brevity of the petition in the Lord's Prayer and the change from the formal third person to the intimate second person singular—are characteristic of the language style of Jesus himself, as compared to that of the ancient Jewish synagogue.[53] The petition is to be considered a deliberate echo of the Kaddish prayer, revised in expression in accordance with the language style of Jesus himself.

We have already noted that the Kaddish prayer represents a tensive use of the symbol Kingdom of God in ancient Judaism, that the expectation it evoked must have varied from individual to individual, and even for the same individual from time to time. The parallel use in the Lord's Prayer is, therefore, further evidence for Jesus' use of Kingdom of God as a tensive symbol. Once it is recognized that Kingdom of God is being used as a tensive symbol in the opening petition of the prayer, then the remaining petitions become particularly interesting; they represent realistic possibilities for the personal or communal experience of God as king. God is to be experienced as king in the provision of "daily bread,"[54] in the experienced reality of the forgiveness of sins, and in support in the face of "temptation."[55] It is very evident that the symbol Kingdom of God evokes the expectation of the activity of God on behalf of the petitioner, and that the symbol is by no means exhausted in any one manifestation of that which it evokes. The petitions which follow are, as it were, explorations of fundamental possibilities for the experience of God as king in human life; they are neither mutually exclusive nor exhaustive.

In view of what we shall find to be the case in the proverbial sayings and the parables, to be explored immediately below, it is particularly interesting that one of the petitions envisages a positive role for the response of the petitioner to the experience of God as king: "Forgive us our sins, for we ourselves forgive every one who is indebted to us." I still regard it as most probable that this should be understood as, "Forgive us . . . as we herewith forgive . . .",[56] and in any case the intent to link the experience of God to the response of man is quite clear. We shall find a similar element in both the proverbial sayings and the parables, so this is a point to which we shall be returning.

(c) The Proverbial Sayings

See Perrin, *Introduction*, pp. 296–299, of which the following is an expansion with only minor revisions.

As I indicated above, I am accepting as authentic a specific group of sayings.[57] This group was first isolated and established as authentic by R. Bultmann in a brilliant discussion of "Jesus as a teacher of wisdom," in his justly famous *History of Synoptic Tradition*. Bultmann divided the sayings into four categories: sayings arising from the exaltation of an eschatological mood: Mark 3:27; 3:24–26; sayings which are the product of an energetic summons to repentance: Mark 8:35; Luke 9:62; Mark 10:23b, 25; Luke 9:60a; Matt. 7:13–14; sayings concerning reversal: Mark 10:31; Matt. 22:14; sayings which demand a new disposition of mind: Mark 7:15; 10:15; Luke 14:11; Matt. 5:39b–41.

After discussing the sayings, Bultmann reached a conclusion on them as a group which is worth quoting in full:

All these sayings, which admittedly are in part no longer specific examples of logia, contain something characteristic, new, reaching out beyond popular wisdom and piety and yet are in no sense scribal or rabbinic nor yet Jewish apocalyptic. So here if anywhere we can find what is characteristic of the preaching of Jesus.[58]

After Bultmann, the discussion of the proverbial sayings of Jesus was not pursued vigorously until they were taken up in America by William A. Beardslee.[59] Beardslee is very important because he was the first scholar to approach these sayings from the standpoint of *literary criticism*. He is concerned with the nature and natural function of the proverb as a literary form. A proverb is "a statement about a particular kind of occurrence or situation, an orderly tract of experience which can be repeated."[60] But while the proverb may be a kind of generalization, it really is a prediscursive form of thought and represents a flash of insight: "What a collection of proverbs confronts one with is not a systematic general analysis of existence, but a cluster of insights."[61] But the proverb not only represents a flash of insight, it also compels insight. The proverb's function is not simply declarative; its compressed form commands insight. There is "an implied imperative in the declarative in the sense that there is an implied challenge to see it this way."[62]

In the Jewish wisdom tradition the "secular" form, the proverb, came to be used in the context of a faith in God and so its imperative effect was heightened. As the natural point of contact with the moralistic side of the (Jewish) wisdom tradition, the proverb is not just an empirical statement; it is a statement related to some kind of human happening. As such, it implies a summons to action, even though the secular proverbs base that action simply on the observed consequences of what men do. By tremendously heightening the "imperative" implication of the proverb and by bringing it into relation with God's will, the Jewish wisdom tradition came to use this form for affirmations that were not merely empirical, but were "affirmations of faith in God's just and orderly rule of the world."[63] So in Jewish wisdom the proverb has the double motif of "observing bits of life and of expressing faith in God's moral order."[64]

But in the synoptic gospels and Q the context is often not that of "faith in God's just and orderly rule of the world" but rather that of a strongly eschatological setting. The beatitudes are not just intimations of the future; they see the present in light of the future. They represent a viewpoint in which "the present is secretly transformed by the power of the future."[65] A further characteristic of some of these proverbs is that they represent an *intensification of proverbial insight*. In Q the saying "No servant can serve two masters," which could well express a typical proverbial flash of insight, declares "the total claim of God."[66] "In the most characteristic Synoptic sayings . . . (general folk) wisdom is immensely concentrated and intensified."[67]

This recognition of the intensification of the normal proverbial insight in some of the most characteristic proverbial sayings in the synoptic gospels and Q is very important indeed. Beardslee points to the antithesis of the reversal situation ("The first will be last," etc.) which is sharpened to paradox in Luke 17:33 (cf. Mark 8:35) "Whoever loses his life will preserve it."[68] Further, while hyperbole is widespread in proverbial literature it reaches a "distinctive intensification" in "Love your enemies, do good to those who hate you." So distinctive is this intensification of the hyperbole that the Christian literature shows a marked tendency to shrink back from it. Didache 1:3 illustrates the tendency of Christian wisdom to draw such a hyperbolic saying back into the continuity of the project of life: "Love your enemies and you will have no enemy."[69]

"Common sense" reasserts itself in the textual expansion of the Sermon on the Mount. "Whoever is angry with his brother *without a cause* shall be liable to judgment"; "your father who sees in secret will reward you *openly*." In these cases we see how readers familiar with the "tit for tat" or retributive theme of moral religious wisdom assume that this must be intended by the sayings of Q.[70]

But much the most important thing about this intensification of the normal proverbial insight is the way it functions:

The characteristic thrust of the synoptic proverbs, however, is not the cautious and balanced judgment so typical of much proverbial literature. Such middle-of-the-road style has as its presupposition the project of making a continuous whole out of one's existence. The intensification of the proverb as paradox and hyperbole *functions precisely to call this project into question, to jolt the hearer out of this effort, and into a new judgment about his own existence.*[71]

Beardslee does not concern himself directly with the question of whether this intensification of proverbial insight, and the setting of such intensified proverbial sayings in a strongly eschatological context, is to be attributed to Jesus himself, although he "presumes" that it is.[72] Characteristically, he does not address himself to the question of Jesus as a teacher of Wisdom but to the use of the wisdom form, the proverb, in the gospels and Q. But there can be no doubt of the fact that his observations are applicable to Jesus as a teacher of Wisdom. The most characteristic of the sayings which concern him are on Bultmann's list; and better examples of sayings that would meet the criterion of dissimilarity it would be hard to imagine. I will take the liberty, therefore, of applying Beardslee's insights to these sayings as sayings of Jesus.

The work of Bultmann on "Jesus as a Teacher of Wisdom" and that of Beardslee on "The Proverb in the Synoptic Gospels and Q," and my own further work on the various sayings have convinced me that there are three things that have to be considered as carefully as possible with regard to the proverbial sayings of Jesus: their intensely eschatological context; their intensification of the normal proverbial insight; and their function in jolting the hearer out of the project of making a continuous whole out of his or her existence and into the passing of a judgment about, and indeed, upon, that existence. In light of these considerations, I now offer a brief analysis of the proverbial sayings of Jesus.

(i) The most radical sayings: Luke 9:60a; Matt. 5:39b–41

Luke 9:60a "Leave the dead to bury their own dead."

Matt. 5:39b–41 "If anyone strikes you on the right cheek, turn to him the other also; and if any one would use you and take your coat, let him have your cloak as well; and if any one forces you to go one mile, go with him two miles."

These are the most radical of the proverbial sayings of Jesus. Indeed, they are so radical that they shatter the form of proverbial saying altogether and become something quite different. Where proverbial sayings normally reflect upon life in the world and are concerned, as Beardslee puts it, "to make a continuous whole out of one's existence," these sayings shatter the whole idea of orderly existence in the world. To "leave the dead to bury their own dead" is to act so irresponsibly as to deny the very fabric which makes possible communal existence in the world; it is a fundamental denial of the kind of personal and communal sense of responsibility which makes possible the act of living in community. The giving of the "cloak as well" and the going of the "second mile" are commandments, and it is impossible to take them literally as moral imperatives. In the first one, the results would be "indecent exposure," and in the second, a lifetime of impressed service.

The history of the interpretation of these sayings is a history of mellowing them down to the point where they become barely possible of fulfillment and hence extraordinarily radical challenges. In connection with the first we may quote the evangelist Luke, who adds, "but as for you, go and proclaim the kingdom of God" (Luke 9:60b), and so makes the saying a dramatic and radical challenge to Christian discipleship. In connection with the second we may quote T. W. Manson, who says of the second mile: "The first mile renders to Caesar the things that are Caesar's; the second mile, by meeting opposition with kindness, renders to God the things that are God's."[73] I was sufficiently impressed by these ancient and modern interpretations to write earlier that the challenge to leave the dead to bury their dead meant that "the challenge of the Kingdom is all-demanding,"[74] and that the cloak and second mile "are intended to be vivid examples of a radical demand."[75] But all of this interpretation, ancient or modern, is irrelevant to a historical understanding of the message of Jesus.

In the context of the message of Jesus these are not radical demands but themselves part of the proclamation of the Kingdom of God. They challenge the hearer, not to radical obedience, but to radical questioning. To use Beardslee's extraordinarily apposite phrase, they jolt the hearer out of the effort to make a continuous whole out of his or her existence and into a judgment about that existence.

(ii) The Eschatological Reversal Sayings:
Mark 8:35; 10:23b, 25; 10:31; Luke 14:11

Mark 8:35 "For whoever would save his life will lose it; and whoever loses his life for my sake and the gospel's will save it." [The original probably ran something like ". . . for the sake of the kingdom of God."]

Mark 10:23b, 25 "How hard it will be for those who have riches to enter the kingdom of God. . . . It is easier for a camel to go through the eye of a needle than for a rich man to enter the kingdom of God."

Mark 10:31 "But many that are first will be last and the last first."

Luke 14:11 "Every one who exalts himself will be humbled, and he who humbles himself will be exalted."

These sayings need not delay us. The theme of eschatological reversal is one of the best attested themes of the message of Jesus. It proclaims the Kingdom as eschatological reversal of the present and so invites, indeed demands, judgment upon that present.

(iii) The Conflict Sayings: Mark 3:27; 3:24–26

Mark 3:27 "No one can enter a strong man's house and plunder his goods, unless he first binds the strong man; then indeed he may plunder his house."

Mark 3:24–26 "If a kingdom is divided against itself, that kingdom cannot stand. And if a house is divided against itself, that house will not be able to stand. And if Satan has risen up against himself and is divided, he cannot stand, but is coming to an end."

Here we have the same myth of the eschatological war that we find in the Kingdom saying, Matt. 11:12. The interpretation by Jesus of his and his disciples' experience in terms of that myth clearly has multiple attestation in the tradition. This again is a form of proclamation of the Kingdom of God.

> (iv) *The Parenetical Sayings: Luke 9:62; Matt. 7:13–14; Mark 7:15; 10:15; Matt. 5:44–48*

Luke 9:62 "No one who puts his hand to the plough and looks back is fit for the kingdom of God."

Matt. 7:13–14 "Enter by the narrow gate; for the gate is wide and the way is easy that leads to destruction, and those who enter it are many. For the gate is narrow and the way is hard, that leads to life, and those who find it are few."

Mark 7:15 "There is nothing outside a man which by going into him can defile him; but the things which come out of a man are what defile him."

Mark 10:15 "Whoever does not receive the kingdom of God like a child shall not enter it."

Matt. 5:44–48 "Love your enemies and pray for those who persecute you, so that you may be sons of your Father. . . . for he makes his sun rise on the evil and on the good, and sends rain on the just and on the unjust. For if you love those who love you, what reward have you? Do not even the tax collectors do the same? And if you salute only your brethren, what more are you doing than others? Do not even the Gentiles do the same? You, therefore, must be perfect, as your heavenly Father is perfect."

The proverbial sayings we have discussed thus far, the most radical sayings, the eschatological reversal sayings, and the conflict sayings, all are forms of proclamation: they are designed to jolt the hearer out of an effort to make a continuous whole out of existence in the world and into a judgment upon that existence; they are forms of Jesus' proclamation of the Kingdom of God. Indeed, the conflict sayings have obvious links with one of the Kingdom sayings, Matt. 11:12. When seen in connection with the Kingdom sayings, these proverbial sayings seem to serve the function of preparing the hearer for an experience of God in terms of radical questioning, of reversal, of a conflict both personal and eschatological. To use a phrase I owe to Dominic Crossan, it is as if Jesus proclaims the coming of the Kingdom, not in terms of the end of the world, but in terms of the end of world itself. But if these sayings link up with the Kingdom sayings, as they appear to do, then the parenetical sayings we are now discussing appear to link up most naturally with the "as we herewith forgive . . ." of the Lord's Prayer. They seem to be part of a consistent attempt on the part of Jesus to link the experience of God which the Kingdom language symbolizes most definitely with a response on the part of the hearer.

In this connection it is particularly interesting that two of the parenetical sayings use the symbol: Luke 9:62 speaks of "being fit for the kingdom of God"; Mark 10:15 of "receiving" and "entering" the Kingdom. Kingdom being the symbol it is, the verbs used are certainly to be understood metaphorically. One cannot "be fit for" or "receive" or "enter" a symbol; one can only respond in various ways to that which the symbol evokes, in this instance the experience of God as king. They and the other three sayings, Matt. 7:13–14; Mark 7:15; Matt. 5:44–48, are to be understood as metaphors of response. They take up themes well known from Jewish parenetical traditions and transform them. In the context of the message of Jesus as we can now understand it historically they are not concerned with "gates" and "ways," or with "defilement," or with being perfect in imitation of God, in the way that these themes are approached in the contemporary Jewish literature—or in the subsequent Christian literature (see Mark 7:17–19) which brings the saying back into the normal categories of religious exhortation. Rather, they are concerned with these things as metaphors of response to that which the symbol evoked.

As we seek to understand historically the Kingdom sayings, the Lord's Prayer, and the proverbial sayings as integral and integrated elements of the message of Jesus, it becomes evident that a pattern begins to emerge. It is a pattern which has as its center the claim to mediate an experience of God as king, an experience of such an order that it brings world to an end. On the one side there is the symbolic language of the Kingdom with its enormous evocative power, and on the other the various metaphors of response. As we turn to the parables, we shall find that they exhibit the same pattern.

(d) The Parables

Since the parables of Jesus will be the subject of our second study, we will not discuss them in any detail here. In anticipation of that discussion, however, we may say that the parables are directly related to the Kingdom of God. Many of the parables begin with the formal introduction. "The Kingdom of God is like . . ." or its equivalent, especially the so-called parables of the Kingdom in Mark 4 and Matthew 13. This setting could have been provided in the tradition in which the parables were transmitted before reaching the hands of the evangelists, and one has to raise the question as to whether it is the setting originally given by Jesus himself. We shall see that such settings have often been provided in the tradition, or by the evangelists. But in this instance the setting is wholly appropriate to the historical message of Jesus. The Kingdom of God is the ultimate referent of all the parables of Jesus, and many of them must have been delivered in a form which began with "The Kingdom of God is like . . ." or "It is the case with the Kingdom of God as with. . . ." Such forms have multiple attestation in the gospel tradition[76] and they would have been wholly appropriate to the historical message of Jesus. I need not labor this point; today no scholar doubts it.

In the context of Jewish wisdom teaching at the time of Jesus, and the parable is a literary form developed in the wisdom movement, the natural expectation is that the parable is a means of instruction, or a way of making a point in a debate or controversy. So in the case of a parable beginning "The Kingdom of God is like . . ." the natural expectation is that the parable would explain some aspect of the speaker's understanding of the Kingdom of God, much as The Good Samaritan in Luke 10 explains something of the understanding of "neighbor" being developed by the Jesus of that narrative in response to the lawyer's question.[77] Or, alternatively, the parable of the Prodigal Son could have been used very naturally in the context of use of parables in ancient Jewish wisdom as a weapon of controversy, as it is so presented in Jesus' use of this parable in Luke 15 to defend his conduct in eating with "sinners."[78]

Modern research on the parables of Jesus, however, particularly the more recent work carried on in America,[79] has shown that the parables of Jesus were much more than illustrations explaining a difficult point, or than telling weapons in a controversy; they were bearers of the

parable = bearer
of the reality.

reality with which they were concerned. It is the claim of this research
that the parables of Jesus mediated to the hearer an experience of the
Kingdom of God. In this respect the parables are like the use by Jesus
of the symbol Kingdom of God in other forms of his proclamation. A
parable is an extended metaphor, and "a true metaphor or symbol is
more than a sign, it is a bearer of the reality to which it refers."[80] As I
shall put the matter in the course of the discussion of the interpretation
of the parables,[81] these words are the essential clue to understanding
both the symbolic language of the Kingdom sayings and the metaphorical language of the parables on the lips of Jesus. Precisely because of
the function of symbol and metaphor they mediated the reality evoked
by the symbol of God to the hearer.

I must leave the justification of this claim concerning the parables to
the discussion to follow below, but there is one point to be added now,
and that is that the pattern we observed in the case of the proverbial
sayings also functions in the case of the parables. A major function of
the parables of Jesus was proclamation, and proclamation with the
implicit claim to mediate experience of the reality being proclaimed.
But at the same time there were parables which functioned as parenesis, parables concerned to develop the theme of response, just as there
were parenetical proverbial sayings.[82]

An extended summary of Jesus' use of Kingdom of God would be
out of place. Jesus characteristically used proclamatory sayings, proverbial sayings, and parables, and he taught his disciples a prayer. All
our knowledge of his use of the symbol Kingdom of God has to be
derived from these sayings and parables, and from the prayer, as we
have attempted to derive such knowledge above. But it is of the very
nature of such forms of language that they resist translation into another mode of discourse; we will not, therefore, attempt to summarize
Jesus' use of Kingdom of God in the form of propositional statements.
We will simply repeat our basic contentions, that Jesus used Kingdom
of God as a tensive symbol, and that the literary forms and language
he used were such as to mediate the reality evoked by that symbol.

C. KINGDOM OF GOD IN CHRISTIAN LITERATURE

Kingdom of God has been widely used in Christian literature from
the composition of the synoptic gospel source Q to the present day;

even a minimal survey of the available material would require at least a substantial volume. Moreover the expression has been used in such a variety of ways, with such varying degrees of dependence upon Jesus' use—and with varying degrees of understanding of that use!—that a thematic summary is virtually impossible. But my concern is with the interpretation of the biblical symbol and so I may select a few examples that I find particularly interesting from that perspective. I will therefore discuss an interpretation of a Kingdom saying of Jesus in the *synoptic gospel* passage Luke 17:20–37; the use of Kingdom of God by *Augustine*; the interpretation of Jesus' use of the symbol by *Johannes Weiss* which began the modern discussion, and include a brief statement about *Albrecht Ritschl* from whom Weiss was consciously departing. I shall then take up the return to an equivalent of the biblical use by *Walter Rauschenbusch* and *Bultmann's* demythologizing of Jesus' proclamation of the Kingdom.

1. An Interpretation of Kingdom of God in Luke 17:20–37

It would be very interesting to reinvestigate the use of Kingdom of God in the New Testament as a whole in light of the thesis of the use by Jesus that I have presented above, but that is a task for another occasion. For the moment I will discuss only one example of the reinterpretation of Jesus' use in the New Testament literature, that in Luke 17:20–37.

In the Revised Standard Version Luke 17:20–21 reads as follows:

Being asked by the Pharisees when the kingdom of God was coming, he answered them, "The kingdom of God is not coming with signs to be observed; nor will they say, 'Lo, here it is!' or 'There!' for behold, the kingdom of God is in the midst of you."

We have already discussed the core of this, the saying, as an authentic saying of Jesus. At this point I would simply add that the saying is being transmitted in the narrative context of a question by "the Pharisees." This narrative context will have been provided within the tradition itself, and the Pharisees' question will have been formed within the tradition, most probably by inference from the saying itself. Our interest at the moment is in the following passage, Luke 17:22–37, which begins:

And he said to the disciples, "The days are coming when you will desire
to see one of the days of the Son of man, and you will not see it. And they
will say to you, 'Lo, there!' or 'Lo, here!' Do not go, do not follow them."

Luke 17:22–23

This passage is deliberately linked to the previous one in two ways.
In the first place, it is represented as private teaching to the disciples
after a more public form of teaching. This is a favorite literary device
for adding interpretations to teaching previously presented in the
synoptic gospels. Then, secondly, the " 'Lo, there!' or 'Lo, here!' " obviously picks up the previous " 'Lo, here it is' or 'There!' " We are therefore justified in reading 17:22–23 as an interpretation of 17:20–21,
which means that Jesus' reference to the coming of the Kingdom of
God *is being interpreted as a reference to the coming of the Son of
Man.*

The remainder of the passage, verses 24–37, develops the theme of
the coming of the Son of Man. That coming will be as lightning flash-
ing and lighting up the sky; it will be analogous to the judgmental
catastrophes of the days of Noah and of Lot; it must be preceded by
the suffering and rejection of the Son of Man, a Lukan passion prediction; and so on. The details are unimportant; what is important is
that this passage interprets Jesus' proclamation of the coming of the
Kingdom of God as a proclamation of the coming of Jesus himself as
Son of Man. Equally unimportant is the question whether this act of
interpretation was actually carried out by the scribes who produced the
synoptic gospel source Q, by some other early Christian scribes, or by
the evangelist Luke himself, although this last is most unlikely. What
matters is the clear case of an interpretation of Jesus' use of Kingdom
of God in terms of a use of Son of Man in the New Testament traditions.

This is one of the more dramatic of the Christian interpretations of
Jesus' proclamation of the Kingdom of God. Earliest Christianity did
not go on proclaiming the coming of the Kingdom of God as Jesus had
proclaimed it; rather, earliest Christianity proclaimed the coming of
Jesus as Son of Man. As Bultmann likes to put it: the Proclaimer
became the Proclaimed. If we wished to use theological language then
we could say that as Jesus proclaimed the Kingdom as eschatological
event, so earliest Christianity proclaimed him as eschatological event.
But I will stay with the language I have been using and say, rather,

that earliest Christianity used the symbol Son of Man to evoke the myth of apocalyptic redemption where Jesus had used the symbol Kingdom of God to evoke the myth of the activity of God.

The development of the imagery of the coming of the Son of Man as apocalyptic judge and redeemer was a rather complex process in earliest Christianity,[83] but in our present context those details are not important. The imagery of the coming of the Son of Man as apocalyptic judge and redeemer is one possible variation of the theme of the apocalyptic redemption which was the central hope of Jewish apocalyptic at the time of Jesus and of earliest Christianity. We discussed this in some detail earlier[84] and it is obvious that the symbolism could vary enormously—one could speak of the coming of the Kingdom, of the archangel Michael, of the Man from the Sea (4 Ezra), of Enoch as Son of Man or Elect One, of the Shoot of David, and so on, almost indefinitely. But behind the variety of symbols there is a consistency of myth: apocalyptic is always concerned with the myth of the final and decisive redemptive act of God on behalf of his people.

In moving from the symbol Kingdom of God to a symbol of apocalyptic redemption such as that of the coming of the Son of Man, earliest Christianity may be said to have stayed within the same mythological framework but to have considerably changed the focus. In comparing Jesus with Jewish apocalyptic one is necessarily struck by the fact that the symbol he chooses to use is one that is necessarily a tensive symbol; only with the greatest of difficulty, if at all, could Kingdom of God be reduced to a steno-symbol. But Son of Man is a very different matter. Like the parallel symbols Shoot of David, Man from the Sea, archangel Michael, etc., it invites treatment as a steno-symbol, and it invites the kind of sign-seeking that Jesus had always rejected. The Son of Man is perhaps not necessarily a steno-symbol, but the Christian identification of Jesus as Son of Man makes it difficult to make it anything more. Jesus-as-Son-of-Man-to-come-as-apocalyptic-redeemer invites calculation of the time and seeking for signs. In this respect it is interesting that Luke 17:22–37 is virtually an apocalyptic discourse, like Mark 13; Matthew 24; Luke 21; Assumption of Moses 10; 1 Enoch 1:3–9; 1 Enoch 46:1–8; 4 Ezra 6:13–18.[85] In the context of an apocalyptic discourse, Luke 17:23 contrasts very sharply with 17:21. In the genuine saying of Jesus, the kind of thing that is represented by "Lo, here it is!" or "There!" is flatly rejected. In the reinterpretation "Lo, there!" or "Lo, here!" is negated only to the extent that it is difficult to locate a lightning flash. The context of an apocalyptic discourse rules out the kind of flat rejection of signs characteristic of Luke 17:21, and of the genuine teaching of Jesus. In Mark 13, for example, the apocalyptic discourse *par excellence* in the New Testament; "Look, here is the Christ!" or "Look, there he is!" is similarly only partially negated—in effect Mark 13:21–22 negates the "Look, here!" or "Look, there!" only to the extent that these are false Christs, not that the Christ could never be found in that way—while in verses 24–25 a series of signs are given by which it may be known that the Son of Man is about to appear.

The first major interpretation of Jesus' use of Kingdom of God in the Christian traditions is the interpretation of the coming of the Kingdom of God in terms of the coming of Jesus as Son of Man. This remains within the general framework of the myth of God as active on behalf of his people, but the change is unmistakable. The tensive symbolism has given way to the steno-symbolism more usual in Jewish and Christian apocalyptic. Under certain circumstances the Son of Man symbolism of Christian apocalyptic could become tensive symbolism, but this does not appear to be the case in the apocalyptic discourses which are its natural context in the New Testament. In any case the shift *toward* steno-symbolism is unmistakable in the move from Jesus to earliest Christianity.

2. The Use of Kingdom of God by Augustine

In the long centuries which separate the first century from the twentieth, there are many uses of the symbol but we will discuss only two, the first of these being the use by Augustine, 354–430, a major Christian theological figure. Augustine blended together what had become characteristically Christian ways of thinking with the rich heritage of Greek and Roman philosophy, and he did this at a time when the Roman world was falling apart under barbarian onslaughts—Rome itself fell to Alaric the Hun in 410. Augustine is the first major theologian to use the symbol, and he uses it speculatively or reflectively. In this he is characteristic of theologians to come after him, for such a use by theologians continues into the present.

In order to discuss Augustine effectively we must turn again to Paul Ricoeur and his book *The Symbolism of Evil*, for Ricoeur turns to

Augustine at a key point in his discussion.[86] Ricoeur is concerned with primordial symbols that are used almost universally by man as man, with the "fundamental symbols elaborated in the living experience of defilement, sin and guilt."[87] Having identified these symbols he goes on to observe that they are antecedent to the myths which explain and interpret them, a myth such as that of the fall of mankind in the person of the primordial ancestor, the Adamic myth. The myth is "an interpretation, a hermeneutics, of the primordial symbols in which the prior consciousness of sin gave itself form."[88] The leit-motif of Ricoeur's interpretation of symbols is that "the symbol gives rise to thought." So, in this instance, the primordial symbols give rise to the Adamic myth. But the matter does not end there for there is a third level, a level reached as the symbols and their mythic interpretation give rise to speculation. We have a "second-degree rehandling" of the symbols and the myth in "the more intellectualized symbols of original sin."[89] Stated in summary form, Ricoeur's insight is that we must "distinguish three levels: first that of the primordial symbols of sin, then that of the Adamic myth, and finally the speculative cipher of original sin; and we shall understand the second as first-degree hermeneutics, the third as second-degree hermeneutics."[90] But we may distinguish three levels only if we start with the symbols themselves. Actually there is something prior to the symbols: there is "the living experience of defilement, sin and guilt" in which "the fundamental symbols [are] elaborated"; there is "the prior consciousness of sin" which "gave itself form" in the primordial symbols.[91]

In the discussion of primordial or archetypal symbols we may, therefore, distinguish four levels. First, the level of the consciousness or experience of man as man which gives rise to or is expressed in the symbols. Then, secondly, the symbols themselves. Thirdly, we have the myths by means of which the symbols are interpreted. Fourthly, we may find the speculative reflection on the symbols and myths which further interprets them.

Assuming the first level, Ricoeur distinguishes the three further levels in connection with the symbolism of evil as follows: "first that of the primordial symbols of sin, then that of the Adamic myth, and finally the speculative cipher of original sin."[92] So we have the myth of the fall of primordial man, Adam, which interprets those symbols; then, further, we have speculation concerning original sin, which is secondary to the myth and tertiary to the symbols. In the context of our discussion it is important to note that Ricoeur recognizes that this speculative or reflective use of the symbols in Western thought is largely due to Augustine. This speculative use of the symbol is only, as he describes it, "a relationship of the second degree," and he deplores "the harm that has been done to souls, during the centuries of Christianity, first by the literal interpretation of the story of Adam, and then by the confusion of this myth, treated as history, with later speculations, *principally Augustinian*, about original sin. . . ."[93]

It is evident that we will have to make distinctions in the possibilities of the relationship between symbol and myth. Ricoeur, concerned with primordial symbols, sees myth as a hermeneutics of the symbol. If we are dealing with primordial or archetypal symbols then this is the case; the symbol is prior to the myth which interprets it. But in the case of other classes of symbols this is not necessarily the case. The biblical symbol Kingdom of God is not a primordial or archetypal symbol. If we use the categories established by Wheelwright, summarized in note 91 above, then it is rather a "symbol of cultural range," a symbol having "a significant life for members of a community, of a cult, or of a larger secular or religious body." Kingdom of God is a symbol having a significant life for the members of the community using the ancient Jewish literature, and for the ongoing Christian community.

In the case of such symbols, and the major biblical symbols would belong in this class, the symbol does not arise from the primordial experience of man as man, but rather from the historical experience of the community for which the symbol has meaning, and from the myths by means of which that community comes to understand itself as a community and to make sense of its historical experience. Such is the case with the symbol Kingdom of God. As we have seen, the symbol came into being in the context of the historical experience of the ancient Israelites, and in the context of the amalgam of the two myths by means of which the Israelite community interpreted that experience and understood itself as a community. It then came to function in the cultural continuity of that community through the centuries. In this instance the myth does not interpret the symbol, but rather the symbol evokes the myth; and I suspect that an investigation of other major biblical symbols would reveal a similar state of affairs.

But if the relationship between symbol and myth is different in the case of "symbols of cultural range" than it is in the case of "primordial" or "archetypal" symbols, then that difference is at the first two levels of Ricoeur's concern. These are the levels at which we have symbols and their mythic interpretation, or myths and their symbolic representation. Once we reach the third level we find that both can give rise to speculation, and both in fact do so in the writings of Augustine. At the hands of Augustine the primordial symbols of sin, which had produced the myth of the fall of Adam, came to produce the speculative idea of original sin. Also at the hands of Augustine the myth of God active as king in the world on behalf of his people, which had produced the symbol of the Reign or Kingdom of God, came to produce the speculative idea of the church as the Kingdom of God, and the Kingdom of God as the totality of redeemed humanity. Except that Augustine called this entity the city of God, the city of the saints.

For the city of the saints is up above, although it produces citizens here below, and in their persons the City is on pilgrimage until the time of its kingdom comes. At that time it will assemble all those citizens as they rise again in their bodies; and then they will be given the promised kingdom, where with their Prince, they will reign, world without end.

Augustine, *City of God*, XV 1

This Kingdom of God, this City of God, is, for Augustine, the church, not necessarily the church as it now is but as it will be at the end of time (e.g., *City of God*, XX 9). It was, of course, easy enough for the church of the Middle Ages to take the next step and to equate the Kingdom of God with the hierarchical church in the world, and the omnipotent church became the Kingdom of God.

I do not have time to pursue these matters in any detail but I would like to point out that in the use of the symbol Kingdom of God to represent the church by Augustine and in the Middle Ages two very important factors are at work, one linguistic, and one sociological. The linguistic factor has to do with the use of the symbolic language involved. In ancient Judaism, down to and including the proclamation of Jesus, the symbolic language is used *directly* in songs of praise, in exhortation, in the interpretation of events, or it is the referent of similes and parables. The myth lies only one stage removed from the symbolic language and the purpose of the language is directly to evoke the myth. But by the time of Augustine we have reached a culture dominated by allegory, in which the symbol is not directly used but in

which it is always represented by something else. If we take a characteristic passage from Augustine's *City of God* we find him puzzling
over the allegorical representation of the Kingdom of God in the texts
of the New Testament.

We must certainly rule out any reference to that Kingdom [i.e., the ultimate
Kingdom of God] which he is to speak of at the end of the world, in the
words, "Come you that have my Father's blessing, take possession of the
kingdom prepared for you" [a reference to Matt. 25:34]; and so, even now,
although in some other and far inferior way, his saints must be reigning with
him, the saints to whom he says, "See, I am always with you, right up to the
end of the world" [a reference to Matt. 28:20]; for otherwise the Church
could surely not be called his kingdom, or the kingdom of heaven.

Augustine, *City of God*, XX 9

Here we can see that the symbolic language of the Kingdom of God
is not being used directly but rather it is being found represented in
texts taken from the gospels. The direct reference to the symbol, and
the evocation of the myth by the symbol is lost. Instead of evocation of
the myth of the activity of God on behalf of his people we have
reflection on the symbol indirectly represented in the text: we have
room for speculation, in this instance speculation about the relationship
between the church and the kingdom. The evocative power of the
symbol is lost in the speculative reflection upon what are held to be
indirect references to it in the text of the gospels.

The second factor is the sociological factor of the change in the
status of the community using the symbol. Israel was never an important state in the ancient Near East, and we have seen how difficult it
was to maintain the use of the symbol Kingdom of God when the
Jewish state was, historically speaking, usually under the control of
more important powers, her destiny shaped by events over which she
had no control. Moreover, the group of Jesus and his followers was an
insignificant group in Roman-controlled Palestine, and for the first
three centuries of her existence the Christian church was a small embattled sect in the Roman Empire. But by the time of Augustine
Christianity was the official religion of the Empire, and after the fall of
Rome in 410 the church was the hope for civilization in the ruins of the
Empire. It is extremely interesting that precisely at this point the identification between the church and the Kingdom of God begins to be
made. The dramatic change in the sociological status of the community

using the symbol has made possible an equally dramatic shift in the use of the symbol.

This all too brief discussion of Augustine, and Ricoeur, will have shown that Reign or Kingdom of God is a symbol of a different order or class than the symbols of guilt or sin, which are primordial or archetypal symbols. If we adopt Wheelwright's classification, then Reign or Kingdom of God is a "symbol of cultural range." But more important for our purpose is to notice the different function of myth in the case of the different symbols. In the case of the primordial symbols, the myth interprets the symbols, and the consciousness or experience of man which the symbols evoke or elaborate. But in the case of the symbol Reign or Kingdom of God, the myth is prior to the symbol, and the symbol is dependent upon it. The symbol evokes the myth, and when the myth becomes questionable or unacceptable then the use of the symbol changes, or the effectiveness of the symbol is lost. The symbol is effective only where the myth is held to be valid.

The relationship between the validity of the myth and the effectiveness of the symbol becomes evident in the use of Kingdom of God in twentieth-century Christian tradition, but before turning to twentieth-century uses we will pause for a moment in the nineteenth century and consider further the work of Johannes Weiss.

3. Johannes Weiss: The Thoroughgoing Historical Understanding of Jesus' Proclamation of the Kingdom of God

Augustine introduced into the Christian tradition the use of Kingdom of God as a speculative theological conception, and from that moment until the present day we have a continuing use of Kingdom of God in this way in Christian theology. We will not consider this long tradition of the speculative theological use of the symbol. To do so would involve us in a study of inordinate length,[94] as it would also take me into areas in which I can claim no particular competence. We will therefore limit our present discussion to the self-conscious attempt to interpret Jesus' use of the symbol, or to the return to the direct use of the symbol in the case of Rauschenbusch.

The self-conscious attempt to interpret Jesus' use of the symbol necessarily had to wait for the rise of the historical sciences. Once the kind of understanding of the New Testament texts we saw in Augustine became established, then nothing that we would recognize as historical knowledge of the message of Jesus, and hence of his use of Kingdom of God, was possible. Only with the coming of modern historical criticism could *Jesus'* use of the symbol become the object of further interpretation. It is therefore not surprising that our discussion resumes with Johannes Weiss,[95] for he was a leader of the German *religionsgeschichtliche Schule* at the end of the nineteenth century. I have mentioned this movement already;[96] at this point I may simply add that it brought the science of the historical investigation of the New Testament to the peak of its development. The scholars of this school pioneered in the thoroughgoing historical approach to the New Testament; at that level contemporary scholars are still following the trails they blazed, although passage of time has, of course, brought a certain refinement of method.[97]

Johannes Weiss was the pupil and son-in-law of Albrecht Ritschl, a leading nineteenth-century German liberal theologian. Ritschl himself used Kingdom of God as a fundamental concept in the development of his own theological system; indeed Weiss wrote, "The concept of the Kingdom of God has been brought to the centre of current theological interest through Albrecht Ritschl."[98] But Ritschl's concept was in the speculative theological tradition begun by Augustine. Ritschl understood Kingdom of God as the goal of the redemptive activity of God in Christ, and of the human ethical activity which that divine redemptive activity made possible. It is the teleological aspect of Christianity, the common end of God and of Christians as a community: it is the moral organization of humanity through action inspired by love.[99] Weiss says that as a student with Ritschl he began to be troubled by the feeling that Ritschl's conception of the Kingdom and the concept in the teaching of Jesus were two very different things.[100] In this comment we see the mind set of the historically oriented scholar: if one is going to make major use of a key concept from the teaching of Jesus then one should begin by reaching a historical understanding of that concept in the teaching.

Weiss reached a historical understanding of Jesus' proclamation of the Kingdom of God, and published his findings in 1892, *Die Predigt Jesu vom Reiche Gottes*, a book only sixty-five pages long. Few books of that size can have made such an impact. In retrospect one can see that the whole modern interpretation of Jesus and his teaching stems from those sixty-five pages;[101] and the book is also a major contribution to the recognition of the problem of hermeneutics among New Testament scholars.[102] In its own day in the eighteen nineties the book presented an understanding of Jesus' proclamation so radically different from anything conceivable to the dominant liberal German theology that a veritable storm broke around the author's head. In self-defense he reworked his thesis, and the historical evidence and arguments for it, publishing in 1900 a second edition of his book which had grown to 214 pages. He also wrote a critical review of the use of the concept Kingdom of God in theology, *Die Idee des Reiche Gottes in der Theologie*, publishing that also in 1900.

Weiss begins by investigating the historical background to the use of Kingdom of God by Jesus.[103] He determines that there were two uses of the concept[104] in ancient Judaism, depending upon whether the emphasis was put upon God as ruler or upon man as subject of that rule. The latter emphasis reaches its high point in the rabbinic concept of an act of obedience whereby a man or a people take upon themselves the yoke of the Kingdom of God. Involved in this conception is the idea of the rule of God as eternal, a continuous and lasting ordering of things that a man may accept or reject. To the man who accepts the yoke in an act of obedience, the Kingdom of God becomes manifest in his experience.[105] In the message of Jesus, however, the emphasis is put upon God as ruler, and the Kingdom of God is conceived of as "the breaking out of an overpowering divine storm which erupts into history to destroy and to renew . . . and which man can neither further nor influence."[106] Weiss was adamant on the point that the Kingdom of God is solely and only the activity of God: "The disciples were to pray for the coming of the Kingdom, but man could do nothing to establish it . . . *Not even Jesus* can bring, establish, or found the Kingdom of God; only God can do so."[107]

In this way Weiss broke with the scholarship of his day, insisting that a historical understanding of Kingdom of God in the message of Jesus must recognize that it was essentially an apocalyptic concept. Moreover, he claimed that it must be understood as being in opposition to the Kingdom of Satan. Jesus was "conscious of carrying on a struggle against the Satanic kingdom . . . [as] is to be seen most clearly in the exorcisms. . . . He knew that he was doing decisive damage to the well-organized kingdom of Satan."[108] But although Jesus saw this, it was only a proleptic vision. For Jesus the coming of the Kingdom of

God was an object of imminent expectation, but that coming still lay in the future. "Jesus' activity is governed by the strong and unwavering feeling that the messianic time is imminent. Indeed he even had moments of prophetic vision when he perceived the opposing Kingdom of Satan as already overcome and broken. . . . In general, however, the actualization of the Kingdom of God has yet to take place."[109]

The importance of Weiss, from the perspective of our discussion, is that he established the necessity for a historical understanding of Kingdom of God in the message of Jesus, an understanding to be arrived at by setting the message of Jesus firmly in the context of ancient Judaism. The details of his findings are comparatively unimportant today; the discussion Weiss inaugurated has long since overtaken his particular historical understanding of Jesus' use of Kingdom of God. But it has not overtaken his particular historical method, as can be seen from the structure of the study I am pursuing here. From the perspective of this study, however, there is a further point about Weiss, and a most important one. I am particularly concerned with the relationship between historical criticism and hermeneutics, between a historical understanding of Jesus' use of Kingdom of God and the possibility of finding significance in that understanding for the present. Here Weiss made a remarkable contribution: he flatly denied that Jesus' use of Kingdom of God had any significance for the later generation for which he, Weiss, was writing. In the preface to the second edition of *Die Predigt Jesu* he writes: "I am still of the opinion that his [Ritschl's] theological system, and especially this central concept [of the Kingdom of God], presents that form of teaching concerning the Christian faith which is most effectively designed to bring our generation nearer to the Christian religion, and, properly understood and rightly used, to awaken and further a sound and strong religious life such as we need today."[110] Weiss is fully prepared to leave the historical Jesus and his teaching in the past. "It is self-evident that Jesus did not intend . . . to promulgate for Christianity in all ages a continuing ethical law, an 'ordinance for the Kingdom of God.' "[111] Weiss has not only seen the "hermeneutical gulf"; he has no intention of trying to bridge it!

All in all Weiss is as interesting as he was important. He established the method for arriving at a historical understanding of Jesus' use of Kingdom of God, but then he simply decided that Jesus' use, however historically interesting, was irrelevant to Europe at the end of the nineteenth century. He wanted to keep his colleagues honest. If they were going to talk about the Kingdom of God in the message of Jesus, then let it be *Jesus'* concept they were talking about. But if they wished to use a quite different understanding of the concept, one they held to be more suitable for the world for which they wrote, then that was perfectly permissible. Weiss himself was fully prepared to define Kingdom of God for himself and his contemporaries as "the *Rule* of God [which] is the highest Good and the supreme ethical ideal," while admitting that "this conception of ours . . . parts company with Jesus' at the most decisive point," because Jesus himself "did not use the term 'Kingdom of God' to refer to the 'supreme ethical ideal.' "[112] In his thinking Weiss remained a man of the late nineteenth century, and in his theology he remained a Ritschlian. At the level of a historical understanding of Jesus there could be a conflict—"the eschatological Kingdom vs. the Ritschlian"[113]—but at the level of contemporary use of the concept it was strictly *no contest*; Weiss remained a Ritschlian, despite his historical findings.

Fundamentally Weiss saw Kingdom of God as a concept in the message of Jesus, and as a concept which he could not accept. But I have argued at length that Kingdom of God is not a concept but a symbol, and a symbol evoking a myth. To think in terms of a concept is to start off on the wrong foot so far as interpretation is concerned. Fundamentally, the act of interpretation turns on the acceptability or meaningfulness of the myth of God acting as king. If the myth is acceptable or meaningful then the symbol evoking that myth is powerful, and the use of Kingdom of God language becomes natural. If the myth is not acceptable or meaningful, however, then the symbol becomes ineffective and the language becomes archaic. Weiss thought in terms of a concept and found the concept unacceptable so he sought to replace it with another, acceptable one. But this is only an acceptable procedure if we agree to ignore the nature and function of the language involved, and to ignore the nature and function of the language of a text is a very dubious hermeneutical procedure. Kingdom of God is a symbol, and a symbol which functions by evoking a myth; a valid hermeneutical procedure must take these considerations very seriously into account. In practice everything turns upon the status of the myth: if the myth is held to be acceptable or meaningful then we have one hermeneutical possibility; if it is not so held then we have a second and very different one. We turn, therefore, to a consideration of Walter Rauschenbusch, as a representative of the first possibility, and to Rudolf Bultmann, as the self-conscious pioneer of the second.

4. Walter Rauschenbusch: A Modern Acceptance of the Ancient Myth

We have seen that the symbolic language of the Kingdom of God evokes the ancient Jewish myth of God acting as king, and that a vital use of the language is dependent therefore upon the full acceptance of the myth as meaningful. This remains a possibility in the twentieth century, every bit as much as it was a possibility in the first. The most obvious name to quote here is that of Walter Rauschenbusch (1861–1918) who, in the period immediately before the First World War, deservedly came to be known as "the American prophet," and who was a leading force in the movement in American Christianity known as "the social gospel." Rauschenbusch deliberately made the symbol, the Kingdom of God, the central theme of his preaching and teaching.

He was able to do this because he believed passionately in the ancient myth of a God active in the world on behalf of his people. The Kingdom of God, proclaimed Rauschenbusch, is "the energy of God realizing itself in human life."[114] For him the ancient myth was a living reality, and it was for this reason that his use of the symbolic language of the Kingdom of God carried conviction. At the same time a sociological conditioning factor was also at work. Rauschenbusch began his career by working as a Baptist minister in the notorious "Hell's Kitchen" area of New York City and for eleven years he labored among people who, in the shadow of the world's greatest wealth, were "out of work, out of clothes, out of shoes, and out of hope." He was never to forget the endless procession of needy men and women who, as he put it, "wore down our threshold and wore away our hearts,"[115] and he came to see God as active precisely in the struggle to right their wrongs. He composed a litany for use in the church which in part reads as follows:

> From the corruption of the franchise, and of
> civil government, from greed and from the
> arbitrary love of power:
> Good Lord, deliver us.
> From the fear of unemployment and the evils

of overwork, from the curse of child-labor
and the ill-paid toil of women:
Good Lord, deliver us.[116]

Rauschenbusch saw God active in history precisely in the social
struggle; he believed deeply and passionately in the Kingdom of God
as "the energy of God realizing itself in human life"; and it was this
which enabled him to speak of the Kingdom of God so effectively and
so naturally. "The Kingdom of God is divine in its origin, progress and
consummation. It was initiated by Jesus Christ, in whom the prophetic
spirit came to its consummation, and it will be brought to its fulfillment
by the power of God in his own time. . . . [It] is the continuous
revelation of the power, the righteousness and the love of God."[117]
Statements like this are possible and natural for someone for whom the
ancient myth is a living reality, for whom the Kingdom of God is "the
energy of God realizing itself in human life."

I have quoted Rauschenbusch only as one example of the way in
which the acceptance of the ancient myth makes the use of Kingdom
of God language natural and powerful. Another example would be the
Christian "freedom riders" of the nineteen sixties, who had a slogan:
"Go out in the world and find out what in the world God is doing,"
who believed that "the energy of God" was being realized in a voter
registration drive, and who could use Kingdom of God language naturally. The reader will be able to provide other examples, for with the
acceptance of the myth the symbol becomes effective and the language
natural.

5. Rudolf Bultmann: The Existentialist Interpretation of Kingdom of God in the Message of Jesus

It is Bultmann, above all others, who has recognized that ancient
myths can die, and their language, therefore, can become archaic. He
has recognized this possibility and faced it squarely. If the myth is
dead, he claims in effect, then we can either enshrine it in our museums
as an interesting and once-meaningful entity, or we can seek to interpret it in such a way that the meaning once expressed in the language
of the myth can now once again be expressed in meaningful language.
This is the hermeneutics of "demythologizing," and it is built upon the
claim that there is something prior even to the myth. The symbol

may evoke the myth, but the myth itself is secondary to, and is an expression of, an understanding of human existence in the world. The interpreter must seek therefore to reach the myth's "understanding of existence" and to interpret that understanding of existence to modern man.

We can best approach Bultmann here by considering his actual interpretation of Jesus' use of Kingdom of God, expanding on our earlier discussion of this,[118] and bringing together the key passage from his book *Jesus* (1926) and some passages from *Jesus Christ and Mythology* (1958). We begin with the key passage from *Jesus*, already quoted in part above.

The Reign of God is a power which wholly determines the present although in itself it is entirely future. It determines the present in that it forces man to decision; he becomes one thing or the other, chosen or rejected, his entire present existence wholly determined by it. . . . The coming of the Kingdom of God is not therefore actually an event in the course of time, which will come within time and to which a man will be able to take up a position, or even hold himself neutral. Rather, before he takes up a position he is already revealed for what he is, and he must therefore realize that the necessity for decision is the essential quality of his being. Because Jesus so sees man as standing in this crisis of decision before the activity of God, it is understandable that in him the Jewish expectation becomes the absolute certainty that now the hour of the breaking-in of the Reign of God has come. If man stands in the crisis of decision, and if this is the essential characteristic of his being as a man, then indeed every hour is the last hour and it is understandable that for Jesus the whole contemporary mythology should be pressed into the service of this conception of human existence, and that in light of this he should understand and proclaim his hour as the last hour.[119]

This is a very tightly packed statement, but if I may be allowed to use the terms I have been using, then we can see that Bultmann is thinking, at the deepest level, of Jesus' "conception of human existence." This, in turn, is expressed in terms of "the whole contemporary mythology" which is "pressed into the service" of this conception. Then, finally, the whole is caught up into the use of the symbol Reign or Kingdom of God. Except that Bultmann does not think of Kingdom of God as a symbol but as a conception. In his book *Jesus* Bultmann does not tell us how he reached these views, but years later he did so in his *Jesus Christ and Mythology*.[120] In this book Bultmann begins, as we have done, with Johannes Weiss.

The year 1892 saw the publication of *The Preaching of Jesus about the Kingdom of God* by Johannes Weiss. This epoch-making book refuted the interpretation which was hitherto generally accepted. Weiss showed that the Kingdom of God is not immanent in the world and does not grow as part of the world's history, but is rather eschatological, i.e., the Kingdom of God transcends the historical order. It will come into being not through the moral endeavour of man, but solely through the supernatural action of God. God will suddenly put an end to the world and to history, and He will bring in a new world, the world of eternal blessedness.[121]

Having presented Weiss' historical understanding of the meaning of Kingdom of God at the time of Jesus, Bultmann turns to Jesus himself.

This conception of the Kingdom of God was not an invention of Jesus. It was a conception familiar in certain circles of Jews who were waiting for the end of the world. This picture of the eschatological drama was drawn in Jewish apocalyptic literature. . . . The preaching of Jesus is distinguished from the typical apocalyptic pictures of the eschatological drama and of the blessedness of the coming new age insofar as Jesus refrained from drawing detailed pictures. He confined himself to the statement that the Kingdom of God will come and that men must be prepared to face the coming judgment. Otherwise he shared the eschatological expectation of his contemporaries. . . .

Jesus envisaged the inauguration of the Kingdom of God as a tremendous cosmic drama. The Son of Man will come with the clouds of heaven, the dead will be raised and the day of judgment will arrive; for the righteous the time of bliss will begin, whereas the damned will be delivered to the torments of hell.[122]

In this passage we see the importance of viewing Kingdom of God as a *conception* in the message of Jesus. It is a conception of human existence expressed in mythological terms. In this case the conception can be correct but the mythological expression incorrect, and this was in fact the case with Jesus and the early Christian community. Both understood Kingdom of God in those mythological terms, and so far as the mythology was concerned both were mistaken. "This hope of Jesus and of the early Christian community was not fulfilled. The same world still exists and history continues. The course of history has refuted mythology."[123]

When Bultmann calls the expectation of the coming of the Kingdom "mythological," he uses that word in a very special way: *for Bultmann "mythological" means prescientific.*

The conception "Kingdom of God" is mythological, as is the conception of the eschatological drama. . . . The whole conception of the world which is presupposed in the preaching of Jesus as in the New Testament generally is mythological, i.e., the conception of the world as being structured in three stories, heaven, earth and hell; the conception of the intervention of super-natural powers in the course of events, and the conception of miracles, especially the conception of the intervention of supernatural powers in the inner life of the soul, the conception that men can be tempted and corrupted by the devil and possessed by evil spirits. This conception of the world we call mythological because it is different from the conception of the world which has been formed and developed by science since its inception in ancient Greece. . . .[124]

So Bultmann is making a series of distinctions, in the course of which he is using a number of words in a very special way. He thinks of Jesus as having a particular understanding of existence, as understanding man as standing in the crisis of decision before God. Then he thinks of Jesus pressing the whole contemporary mythology into the service of this understanding of existence, meaning by mythology a prescientific cosmology. So we reach Jesus' *conception* of the Kingdom of God, a conception which Jesus shared with his contemporaries, and which was refuted by the actual course of historical events.

Bultmann therefore finds himself faced with a discredited mytholog-ical proclamation of Jesus, but he does not then imitate his teacher Johannes Weiss, shrug his shoulders, and abandon the proclamation of Jesus to the antiquarian. Instead of this he begins to examine the proclamation with regard to its central *conception*, the Kingdom of God, and to analyze this conception with regard to its outer mythologi-cal form, the trappings of a prescientific cosmology, and its inner core of meaning, its understanding of human existence. He then takes the decisive step of seeing the mythology as dispensable and the meaning as translatable. He can dispense with mythology, and he can translate the understanding of existence into a modern existentialist language. At this point he is helped by his understanding of texts to be interpreted as being Diltheyan "expressions of life," as the expression of an under-standing of human existence in the world. Although expressed in terms of a discredited mythology the proclamation of Jesus is an "expression of life" and so it can be translated into terms developed by Bultmann in dialogue with Martin Heidegger in the nineteen twenties, in terms, that is, of man being confronted by the necessity for decision and

realizing his potentiality for existence in the making of that decision.[125] So Bultmann can write of Jesus seeing "man as standing in the
crisis of decision before the activity of God," of Jesus understanding
the Reign or Kingdom of God as the power which "determines the
present in that it forces man to decision."

In all of this Bultmann is concerned to achieve a historical description of the message of Jesus, and he is concerned that that description
should be intelligible to the modern reader, and that it should be able
to challenge the modern reader at the level of that reader's understanding of his or her human existence in the world. All texts that are
"expressions of life" do this, or can do this when properly interpreted,
including the texts of Jesus' proclamation of the Kingdom of God. But
Bultmann sharply distinguishes between texts which challenge the
reader at the level of the understanding of existence, and texts which
do this and then *in addition* mediate to the reader the possibility of
achieving authentic existence in the world. These latter texts, those that
mediate the possibility of achieving authentic existence in the world,
are the texts of the proclamation of the church, not the texts of the
proclamation of Jesus. The texts of the proclamation of Jesus can challenge an understanding of existence but they cannot mediate the possibility of authentic existence; only the texts of the proclamation of the
church can do this. The texts of the proclamation of Jesus could do this
only insofar as they became texts of the proclamation of the church,
but then we would no longer be understanding them historically in
connection with Jesus.

So far as Bultmann is concerned, the words of Jesus may be en
countered *historically*, and when they are so encountered "*they* meet *us*
with the question of how we are to interpret our existence."[126] But in
this respect the words of Jesus are not different from the words of other
significant figures from the past. All words which reflect the understanding of existence of a significant individual from the past challenge
us at the level of our understanding of our existence, those of Jesus no
less, and no more, than those of Plato, Shakespeare, or Goethe. The
words of Jesus are not part of the kerygma of the church which alone
can mediate the possibility of authentic existence.[127] One obvious
question is whether, historically speaking, the words of Jesus may be
held to have mediated the possibility of authentic existence to his
hearers, and a further question is whether there is any way in which

one can hold to the general framework of the Bultmannian understanding of things and nonetheless give more authority to the words of Jesus than Bultmann is prepared to do. Both of these questions were raised by Bultmann's own pupils, and the second of them specifically gave rise to the so-called Question or New Quest of the historical Jesus. One of the leaders in raising these questions among Bultmann's pupils was Ernst Fuchs, but his work was done fundamentally in connection with the parables. We shall therefore be discussing it in the course of our second study, and at that time we will offer a further discussion of this particular aspect of Bultmann's hermeneutics. We now turn to a critical discussion of Bultmann's interpretation of Jesus' proclamation of the Kingdom of God, deliberately excluding, however, a discussion of the "Question," or "New Quest" of the historical Jesus. Such a discussion would require a major study devoted to it alone, and that is clearly impossible in this present volume.[128]

Concerning Bultmann's understanding and interpretation of Jesus' proclamation of the Kingdom of God, the first thing that needs to be said is that it is much the most important contribution to the discussion of Jesus' use of Kingdom of God, and that it is the necessary starting point for any further discussion of the issues involved. What Bultmann has done, in effect, is to offer a solution to the problem of the relationship between historical criticism and hermeneutics. By means of historical criticism he establishes that Jesus made use of ancient Jewish apocalyptic mythology in his proclamation. At that point his understanding of hermeneutics takes over, and he views the oral text of this proclamation as an expression of Jesus' understanding of human existence in the world. Now it no longer matters that Jesus was mistaken about the coming end of the world. What matters is not the accuracy of Jesus' expectation concerning the future of the world but the validity of his understanding of human existence in the world. At the same time Bultmann has succeeded in bridging the hermeneutical gulf, opened up by his teacher Johannes Weiss, between the ancient Jewish apocalyptic preacher and the modern interpreter. Both are concerned with the understanding of human existence in the world and hence meaningful dialogue can take place between them.[129]

At this point I have two critical comments to offer, one at the level of historical criticism, and one at the level of literary criticism.[130] At the level of historical criticism I would challenge Bultmann's understanding of the message of Jesus. As we saw above, Bultmann claims that "Jesus envisaged the inauguration of the Kingdom of God as a tremendous cosmic drama," a drama which includes the coming of the Son of Man "with the clouds of heaven," the resurrection of the dead, and the arrival of the day of judgment. The difference between Jesus and other first-century Jewish apocalypticists in this connection was only that Jesus "refrained from drawing detailed pictures." Now that, in my view, is simply not the case. Historical investigation of the message of Jesus shows that he did not proclaim the coming of the Son of Man, and that, further, the references to the raising of the dead and a day of judgment that would arrive on a calendar day are to be ascribed to early Christianity, not to Jesus.[131] In point of fact the difference between Jesus and ancient Jewish apocalyptic is much greater than Bultmann will allow, a difference I have tried to express in the literary-critical terms of a distinction between tensive symbols and steno-symbols. It is at the level of literary criticism that the most important challenge to Bultmann can be made and this is my second criticism of his views.

At the level of literary criticism one must question Bultmann's understanding of the symbols in ancient Jewish apocalyptic and in the proclamation of Jesus, an understanding implicit in his view of Kingdom of God as a conception in the message of Jesus. But a conception of the Kingdom which features a coming of the Kingdom at a definite point in time, accompanied by an apocalyptic scenario, and which can be disproved by the failure of such events to occur at definite moments in chronological time, such a conception necessarily is using the symbols of ancient Jewish apocalyptic as steno-symbols. The symbols concerned are being understood as having single historical referents in which they are exhausted.

In my view Bultmann, like most interpreters, is wrong in speaking of the Kingdom of God as a conception, because that is an imprecise use of language and hides the possibilities for understanding and interpretation that are present when the Kingdom is recognized as a symbol. But he is wrong, further, in understanding it as the particular conception he does—a conception including the literal fulfillment of the apocalyptic scenario—because that is wrong both at the historical level, the point I made above, and also at the literary level. It is wrong at the literary level in that it understands the symbol used by Jesus as a steno-symbol which it was not, and in that it understands the symbols of Jewish apocalyptic in general as steno-symbols, which they often are but need not necessarily be.

If we turn to the question of Jesus' use of Kingdom of God as a symbol, then I would claim that it can be shown that Jesus used it as a tensive symbol. But if Kingdom of God is a tensive symbol in the proclamation of Jesus then the mythology of Jesus has not been discredited by the subsequent course of history. A steno-symbol can be interpreted as referring specifically to one concrete event to be expected at a specific date in chronological time, and as being exhausted in that one referent. Because of this the myth involved can be invalidated by the failure of the event to take place. But a tensive symbol is not like that. A tensive symbol can never be regarded as referring only to one concrete event, as being exhausted in that referent. Hence the myth involved can never be invalidated by a failure in the case of one supposed referent.

A similar problem arises in connection with Bultmann's understanding of myth. It is not only that by myth he tends to mean prescientific cosmology, as I pointed out above. It is also that, when he thinks of myth, he tends to think in terms of what I called earlier *allegorical* myth.[132] He thinks in terms of a myth in which the symbols have a one-to-one reference to something beyond themselves, and of a myth which conveys a message which can also be expressed in non-mythological language. Hence his concern to "demythologize," i.e., to express the message of the myth in non-mythological language. In the case of a myth in which the symbols are steno-symbols this hermeneutical method would be appropriate, and if Jesus were proclaiming the coming of the Son of Man as the early church proclaimed that coming— i.e., with the "coming" functioning as a steno-symbol to be exhausted by one event on a calendar date in chronological time—then Bultmann would be correct. The non-occurrence of the expected event would discredit the myth and demand an expression of its implicit understanding of existence in non-mythological language. But it is my claim that Kingdom of God is not a steno-symbol in the message of Jesus, and that the myth involved is not allegorical myth.

It is obvious that we are here moving into an area which will also concern us in our second study, because in making a distinction between allegorical myth and another kind of myth we are paralleling a distinction between allegory and parable. Indeed there is every reason to hold that as Kingdom of God is the central symbol of the message of Jesus, so is the parable the most characteristic literary form of that message. Before we can go further in discussing the interpretation of Kingdom of God in the message of Jesus, therefore, we must turn to an attempt to understand and interpret the parables. But before leaving Bultmann I would like to attempt to summarize his significance in this discussion, as I understand it.

The significance of Bultmann is to be seen at the two levels at which he must also be challenged: the levels of historical and of literary criticism. At the level of historical criticism he develops the insights and methods of his teacher Weiss, and he does so with such thoroughness and consistency that we are forced to a renewed historical study of the message of Jesus to see whether Bultmann's claims concerning that message are justified. He accepted the results of Weiss's research, and his own, fully and honestly, and he forces us to a further intensive investigation of the message of Jesus. In particular we have to investigate the Son of Man element in that message because the understanding of the apocalyptic element in the message of Jesus depends to a very great extent on whether he did or did not proclaim the coming of the Son of Man as apocalyptic redeemer.

It is at the level of literary criticism that Bultmann is most open to challenge, but it is no small part of his contribution to the discussion that he raises it to the level of literary criticism. In interpreting the mythology of the message of Jesus so consistently as a prescientific cosmology he forces us to recognize that this is an inadequate understanding of myth, but that myth is nonetheless involved in Jesus' use of Kingdom of God. After Bultmann there is no going back from the recognition that myth is a factor in our understanding of Jesus' message; it remains to recognize more adequately the nature of the myth and the function of the symbol Kingdom of God in connection with it. In particular we have to face the question as to whether the myth is dead and the Kingdom language, therefore, archaic. We shall also find a similar problem in the case of the parables, where the question is whether their fundamental metaphors are dead or only dormant. We shall therefore be returning to this matter in our next study and in our final discussion.

But Bultmann's major contribution to the discussion lies at the level of hermeneutics. He does not allow us to shrug our shoulders at the hermeneutical gulf but insists that we attempt to bridge it. One possible bridge is the one he attempts to build by understanding the proclamation of Jesus as an "expression of life" to be interpreted in terms of its challenge to an understanding of human existence in the world. One may or may not want to use this particular bridge, but after Bultmann there is no escaping the challenge of hermeneutical bridge-building. His understanding of the task to be faced becomes normative, even if the way of facing it does not. Again, this is a matter for further discussion after we have reviewed the interpretation of the parables.

NOTES

1. S. Mowinckel, *The Psalms in Israel's Worship* (New York and Nashville: Abingdon Press, and Oxford: Basil Blackwell, 1962), I, p. 114.

2. Ibid., p. 107. The English translations all have "The Lord reigns," or the equivalent. RSV: "The Lord reigns"; NEB: "The Lord is king"; Jerusalem Bible: "Yahweh is king."

3. Ibid., p. 125: ". . . the concept of Yahweh as a king would hardly be adopted by the Israelites until they themselves had got a king, and, with him, an obvious occasion to bestow on Yahweh this highest title of honor."

4. G. von Rad, *The Problem of the Hexateuch* (New York: McGraw-Hill, and Edinburgh: Oliver & Boyd, 1966; German original, 1938). The insight is developed further in von Rad's *Old Testament Theology*, I *The Theology of Israel's Historical Traditions* (New York: Harper & Row, and Edinburgh: Oliver & Boyd, 1962; German original, 1957).

5. In the monarchial period the Salvation History was extended to include the foundation of the monarchy and the united kingdom, and the establishment of the temple at Jerusalem. It also expanded to include the theophany and giving of the Law at Sinai, an element conspicuously absent from the early formulations to which von Rad called attention. The relationship between the Sinai tradition and the other elements of the Salvation History is a matter of dispute among the competent scholars. For recent discussions see F. M. Cross, *Canaanite Myth and Hebrew Epic* (Cambridge: Harvard University Press, 1973), pp. 79–90 and *passim*, and E. W. Nicholson, *Exodus and Sinai in History and Tradition* (Oxford: Basil Blackwell, 1973, and Atlanta: John Knox Press, 1974).

6. Mowinckel, *Psalms*, p. 108.

7. The translation is taken from von Rad, *Problem*, pp. 9–10. (Refrains omitted).

8. The original narrative of the Creation plus Salvation History must have included an account of the Conquest, i.e., the account must have gone from Numbers to Joshua. "The break which the Book of Deuteronomy causes

between the narratives in the Book of Numbers and those in Joshua is unnatural in the extreme." James A. Sanders, *Torah and Canon* (Philadelphia: Fortress Press, 1972), pp. 1–30, "The Shape of the Torah." The quotation is from p. 25.

9. From the point of view of linguistic usage the form "Kingdom of God" is comparatively late; it may even be specifically Christian. Ancient Judaism tended to use the noun "Kingdom" with a personal pronoun referring to God ("his," "thy"), or to use the verb "to reign, be king" with God as subject. In New Testament times the Jews were using a form "Kingdom of Heaven," where Heaven was a circumlocution for God. It should be recognized that there is no satisfactory English translation of the Hebrew or Aramaic phrases involved. We use Kingdom of God as the traditional term, developing the meaning to be given to it as we proceed.

10. Philip Wheelwright, *Metaphor and Reality* (Bloomington: Indiana University Press, 1962 [Midland Book edition, 1968]), p. 130. A problem in this particular discussion is that we are dealing with two different kinds of myth. On the one hand, we have the myth of Creation, the cosmogonic myth, mediated to Israel by its Canaanite neighbors, and forming the basis for the slightly different myth of the kingship of God. Then, on the other hand, we have the myth of the Salvation History, the myth of God active as king in the history of the Israelite people. Because of the link with history in the case of the Salvation History, some scholars tend to resist the use of the word myth in this connection. F. M. Cross, for example, prefers to speak of "epic," and the title of his book, "Canaanite Myth and Hebrew Epic," expresses his understanding of the contrast between the cosmogonic myth and the epic of the redemptive history. (Cross prefers History-of-Redemption to Salvation History to represent the German *Heilsgeschichte*, e.g., p. 83). But the element of history involved in the Salvation History does not make it any less a myth, in the sense of the Watts definition, which I accept as a valid definition of this kind of myth. The cosmogonic myth and the Salvation History myth are different kinds of myths, but they are both myths, and they both function as myths in ancient Israel, especially as they are amalgamated. Moreover, the Salvation History myth continues to function as myth right into the present, as we shall argue in the course of this study. For an introductory discussion of the element of history in biblical myths see Perrin, *The New Testament: An Introduction* (New York: Harcourt Brace Jovanovich, 1974), pp. 21–33.

11. See, for example, A. Wilder, "The Rhetoric of Ancient and Modern Apocalyptic," *Interpretation* 25 (1971), pp. 436–453.

12. Wheelwright, *Metaphor and Reality*, p. 92.

13. P. Ricoeur, *The Symbolism of Evil* (Boston: Beacon Press, 1969), p. 15.

14. Perrin, "Eschatology and Hermeneutics," *JBL* 93 (1974), p. 11.

15. Recently edited and translated into English, with an introduction, by Richard H. Hiers and David L. Holland as *Jesus' Proclamation of the Kingdom of God* (Philadelphia: Fortress Press, and London: SCM Press, 1971). For an extended discussion of Weiss and his views see N. Perrin, *The Kingdom of God in the Teaching of Jesus* (Philadelphia: Westminster Press, and London: SCM Press, 1963), pp. 16–23.

16. Weiss, *Jesus' Proclamation*, pp. 57, 61. On p. 59 we find "this central idea of Jesus."

17. Perrin, *The New Testament: An Introduction*, p. 67. "The Assumption of Moses . . . is particularly interesting because of its use of 'Kingdom of God,' a key concept in the teaching of Jesus."

18. In what follows I am drawing on my previous reviews of the discussion, especially Perrin, *Kingdom of God in the Teaching of Jesus* (=*Kingdom*).

19. We will discuss Ritschl's views in more detail below, p. 66.

20. Weiss as quoted in Perrin, *Kingdom*, p. 18. The quotation is from the second edition of Weiss's book.

21. Weiss, *Jesus' Proclamation*, p. 129.

22. Ibid., p. 105. Weiss's italics.

23. Perrin, *Kingdom*, p. 30.

24. English translation of *Vom Reimarus zu Wrede* (1906). Subsequent German editions were entitled *Die Geschichte der Leben-Jesu-Forschung*. For a presentation of Schweitzer's views in some detail see Perrin, *Kingdom*, pp. 28–36.

25. Perrin, *Kingdom*, pp. 38, 40.

26. Ibid., pp. 41–45, "The Transformation of Apocalyptic."

27. Ibid., pp. 49–52, "The Denial of Apocalyptic."

28. Ibid., pp. 56–57.

29. From the translation in ibid., p. 116.

30. What follows is my own reconstruction of the path which Bultmann has followed. He has not spoken in these terms, but I believe this is a reasonable presentation in view of his essay *Das Problem der Hermeneutik* and other works. See also Perrin, "Eschatology and Hermeneutics," pp. 7–9, and the introduction to this volume, above, pp. 10–12. We shall have occasion to return to Bultmann's hermeneutics and to his interpretation of Kingdom of God, below, pp. 71–80.

31. I would regard Bultmann's use of Heidegger's categories as legitimate in the same way that I regard my use of Wheelwright's distinction between steno- and tensive symbols as legitimate.

32. See below, pp. 71–80.

33. C. H. Dodd, *The Parables of the Kingdom* (rev. ed., New York: Scribner's, 1961), p. 34. Perrin, *Kingdom*, p. 61.

34. Dodd, *Parables*, pp. 54–56. Perrin, *Kingdom*, p. 61.

35. See Perrin, *Kingdom*, pp. 67–73, for a brief review of the discussion.

36. See below, pp. 97–100.

37. Dodd, *Parables*, p. 139.

38. Ibid., pp. 140–156.

39. Perrin, *Kingdom*, p. 73.

40. The title of chap. V of *Kingdom*.

41. Perrin, *The New Testament: An Introduction*, p. 289.

42. The only recent attempt to deny this consensus known to me is Richard H. Hiers, *The Kingdom of God in the Synoptic Tradition* (Gainesville: University of Florida Press, 1970), and Hiers and Holland in the Introduction to their translation of Weiss, *Jesus' Proclamation*. This is an attempt to reinstate the views of Weiss against the current consensus.

43. N. Perrin, *Rediscovering the Teaching of Jesus* (New York: Harper & Row, and London: SCM Press, 1967), pp. 15–53; *The New Testament: An Introduction*, pp. 280–282.

44. Perrin, *The New Testament: An Introduction*, p. 284, and *Rediscovering*, p. 65.

45. *Kingdom*, pp. 174–178.

46. N. Perrin, *Rediscovering*, pp. 73–74.

47. On this see Ricoeur, *Symbolism of Evil*, pp. 163–164.

48. *The Sign of Jonah in the Theology of the Evangelists and Q* (London: SCM Press, 1971).

49. This statement is a deliberate modification of the one in "Eschatology and Hermeneutics," where I claimed that this pericope did refer to apocalyptic sign-giving, p. 12. I now recognize that statement as being too hastily made. However, the fundamental point I was making then, and am making now, is not affected: Jesus did repudiate apocalyptic sign-giving; Luke 17:20–21 shows that.

50. *Rediscovering*, p. 77: "It may be that the saying was originally inspired by the fate of the Baptist." See Ernst Käsemann, *Essays on New Testament Themes* (London: SCM Press, 1964), p. 42.

51. Modern life of Jesus research has established that Jesus had a high view of the Baptist (*Rediscovering*, pp. 75–76) and if this is the case then he must have reflected on the fate of the Baptist and its meaning in relationship to the Kingdom of God. It is reasonable to claim that Matt. 11·12 is a result of such reflection, and that it reflects not on the fate of the Baptist only but also on the potential fate of Jesus and his disciples.

52. See above pp. 28–29.

53. On this see especially Perrin, *The New Testament: An Introduction*, p. 200.

54. This is a difficult phrase to interpret (Perrin, *Kingdom*, pp. 193–194) but whatever its exact meaning it is clearly a reference to something essential to man which is of God's providing.

55. Again difficult to interpret (Perrin, *Kingdom*, pp. 196–198) but obviously a further reference to the experienced reality of God in a critical human situation.

56. Perrin, *Kingdom*, p. 196.

57. See above, p. 41.

58. R. Bultmann, *History of the Synoptic Tradition* (New York: Harper & Row, and Oxford: Basil Blackwell, 2d ed., 1968 [the first German edition appeared in 1921]), p. 115.

59. W. A. Beardslee, "Uses of the Proverb in the Synoptic Gospels," *Interpretation* 24 (1970), pp. 61–76; "The Proverb," chap. III of his *Literary Criticism and the New Testament* (Philadelphia: Fortress Press, 1970).

60. Beardslee, "Uses of the Proverb," p. 65.

61. Ibid., p. 66.

62. Beardslee, *Literary Criticism*, p. 31.

63. Ibid., pp. 32–33.

64. Ibid., p. 33.

65. Ibid., p. 38.

66. Ibid., p. 39.

67. Beardslee, "Uses of the Proverb," p. 66.
68. Ibid., p. 67.
69. Ibid., p. 69.
70. Beardslee, *Literary Criticism*, p. 40.
71. Beardslee, "Uses of the Proverb," p. 71 (italics supplied).
72. Ibid.
73. T. W. Manson, *The Sayings of Jesus* (London: SCM Press, 1949), p. 160.
74. Perrin, *Rediscovering*, p. 144.
75. Ibid., pp. 147–148.
76. See J. Jeremias, *The Parables of Jesus* (rev. ed.; New York: Scribner's 1963 and 3rd rev. ed., London: SCM Press, 1972), pp. 101–103, for examples of the variations of this introductory formula.
77. This is in fact the understanding of the parable and its purpose reached by the community, or individual, responsible for the present form of Luke 10:25–37. We shall see below, however, that this does not represent the historical intent of Jesus in using the parable. The Jesus of the narrative in Luke 10 is not necessarily the Jesus of the original form and use of the parable.
78. In this instance modern scholars tend to see the narrative as representing the situation of the historical Jesus, and this use of the parable as characteristic of Jesus himself.
79. The reference is particularly to the work of Wilder, Via, Funk, and Crossan, to be discussed in detail below.
80. Amos Wilder, quoted below, p. 130.
81. See below, p. 130.
82. I shall develop this theme in connection with the parables. See below, pp. 195–196.
83. I have outlined the process as I understand it, and argued for that understanding, in N. Perrin, *A Modern Pilgrimage in New Testament Christology* (Philadelphia: Fortress Press, 1974).
84. See above, pp. 26–28.
85. On apocalyptic discourse as a genre, see Perrin, *The New Testament: An Introduction*, p. 79, and the further references given there.
86. For previous references to Ricoeur, see above, pp. 29, 30, 31.
87. Ricoeur, *Symbolism of Evil*, p. 237.
88. Ibid.
89. Ibid.
90. Ibid.
91. We can support Ricoeur's point about what he calls "primordial symbols" by referring to Philip Wheelwright, who has a most important discussion of symbols in his book *Metaphor and Reality*. Wheelwright defines a symbol as "a relatively stable and repeatable element of perceptual experience, standing for some larger meaning or set of meanings which cannot be given, or not fully given, in perceptual experience itself" (p. 92). Concerning himself with literary symbols Wheelwright speaks of *five classes of symbols*: (1) *the presiding image of a single poem*; (2) *the personal symbol* (one that "has continuing vitality and relevance for a poet's imaginative and perhaps actual life" [p. 102]); (3) *symbols of ancestral vitality*

(symbols "lifted by one poet, for his own creative purposes, from earlier written sources" [p. 105]); (4) *symbols of cultural range* ("those which have a significant life for members of a community, of a cult, or of a larger secular or religious body" [pp. 108–109]); (5) *archetypal symbols* ("those which carry the same or very similar meanings for a large portion, if not all, of mankind" [p. 111]). This graduation of symbols is extraordinarily suggestive; at the very least it challenges us to attempt something similar with regard to biblical symbols. For the moment, however, we simply note that in isolating "archetypal symbols" Wheelwright is calling attention to the class of symbols which Ricoeur calls "primordial symbols."

92. Ricoeur, *Symbolism of Evil*, p. 237.

93. Ibid., p. 239, italics added.

94. A reasonably comprehensive presentation of the use of Kingdom of God in Christian tradition to 1964 by Ernst Staehlen, *Die Verkündigung des Reiches Gottes in der Kirche Jesu Christi* takes up seven large volumes (Basel: Verlag Friedrich Reinhardt, 1961–65). It would be easy to compile a further volume to cover the last decade.

95. Johannes Weiss, 1863–1914. Three of his publications concern us: *Die Predigt Jesu vom Reiche Gottes* (1892); *Die Predigt Jesu vom Reiche Gottes*[2] (1900); *Die Idee des Reiches Gottes in der Theologie* (1900). I enumerate the two editions of *Predigt* separately because the second edition is a new book. Among other things it has grown from 65 to 214 pages! As I mentioned earlier, above note 15, the first edition of *Predigt* has been edited and translated into English by Richard H. Hiers and D. Larrimore Holland as *Jesus' Proclamation of the Kingdom of God*. The discussion of Weiss we now give here is an expansion of the earlier mention of him, above pp. 34–35.

96. See above, p. 10.

97. It would take us too far afield to discuss this in any detail, but if I may be permitted a passing remark, the major refinements have been an increasing concern for the use of insights of a comparative as well as a purely historical approach to religion (*Religionswissenschaft* in addition to *Religionsgeschichte*), and an increasing concern for the literary and linguistic aspects of the texts involved. But these are only refinements; we do nothing today that was not inherent in the work of a Reitzenstein, Bousset, or Weiss.

98. Weiss, *Die Idee des Reiches Gottes*, quoted in Perrin, *Kingdom*, pp. 14–15.

99. From the summary of Ritschl in Perrin, *Kingdom*, pp. 14–16.

100. "The clear perception that Ritschl's idea of the Kingdom of God and the corresponding idea in the proclamation of Jesus were two very different things disturbed me quite early." Weiss, *Predigt*[2] in the Foreword, commented on in Perrin, *Kingdom*, p. 17. See also *Jesus' Proclamation*, p. 6, for Hiers and Holland on the same point.

101. It was the first truly historical treatment of the teaching of Jesus, and it established the fact that Jesus' use of Kingdom of God had to be understood against the background of Jewish apocalyptic, as I am still attempting to understand it in this study more than 80 years later. It also began the tendency to interpret Jesus as a historical phenomenon altogether, and not simply his use of Kingdom of God, against that same background, a *Tendenz* that grew to be dominant in *Leben-Jesu-Forschung*—through its

popularization by Albert Schweitzer and *The Quest of the Historical Jesus*—and which also continues to this day. On Weiss and his impact see further Hiers and Holland in their Introduction to *Jesus' Proclamation*.

102. The book established the "hermeneutical gulf" between Jesus and the modern world by claiming that the historical understanding of Jesus' proclamation of the Kingdom was irrelevant to a modern use of the conception. See immediately below.

103. I am now repeating aspects of my earlier summary of Weiss in Perrin, *Kingdom*, pp. 16–23.

104. We are using "concept" now rather than "symbol," because Weiss thought of Kingdom of God in this way.

105. Once it became established that one should seek the meaning of Kingdom of God in the message of Jesus in the immediate historical context of ancient Judaism, there were many scholars who saw in this rabbinical concept the key to understanding that meaning. Two examples are Gustaf Dalman in Germany and T. W. Manson in England. See Perrin, *Kingdom*, pp. 18, 25–26, 92.

106. Weiss, *Predigt*[2], p. 5. Perrin, *Kingdom*, p. 18.

107. Weiss, *Jesus' Proclamation*, pp. 129–130, italics supplied.

108. Ibid., pp. 76–77.

109. Ibid., p. 129.

110. *Predigt*[2], p. v.

111. *Predigt*[2], p. 143, translated and quoted by Hiers and Holland, *Jesus' Proclamation*, p. 21. Hiers and Holland have an extended and perceptive discussion of this aspect of Weiss's thought, pp. 16–24.

112. Weiss, *Jesus' Proclamation*, pp. 134–135. See Perrin, "Eschatology and Hermeneutics," p. 6.

113. The heading of a section of the treatment of this matter by Hiers and Holland, *Jesus' Proclamation*, p. 7.

114. My quotations of Rauschenbusch are from *A Gospel for the Social Awakening: Selections from the Writings of Walter Rauschenbusch*, compiled by B. E. Mays with an introduction by C. E. Hopkins (New York: Association Press, 1950). This one is on p. 45.

115. Ibid., 14–15.

116. Ibid., 171–172.

117. Ibid., p. 44.

118. See above, pp. 35–37. See also the earlier discussion of his hermeneutical method, above pp. 10–12. We shall return to his hermeneutical method again in connection with our discussion of the interpretation of the parables by Ernst Fuchs and by Dan Via, below pp. 108–113, 144–145.

119. Bultmann, *Jesus*, pp. 46–47 (cf. the English translation, *Jesus and the Word* [New York: Scribner's, 1934; paperback, 1958, and London: Fontana Books, 1960], pp. 51–52). See Perrin, *Kingdom*, p. 116; "Eschatology and Hermeneutics," pp. 7–8.

120. R. Bultmann, *Jesus Christ and Mythology* (New York: Scribner's, 1958, and London: SCM Press, 1960). This book consists of lectures delivered by Bultmann in America in 1951.

121. Ibid., pp. 11–12.

122. Ibid., pp. 12–13.

123. Ibid., p. 14.

124. Ibid., pp. 14–15.

125. In brief, Heidegger saw human existence in the world as threatened by "care" and by the inescapability of death. Facing these twin threats to the reality of his existence in the world, man could make a resolute decision to accept them, and by the reality of that decision achieve a level of authentic existence in the world. Bultmann modified this in accordance with what he regarded as a Christian understanding of existence. He distinguished between "inauthentic" and "authentic" existence, and he accepted the contention that the transition from inauthentic to authentic existence came as the consequence of man's *decision*. But this decision, for Bultmann, was not a decision in face of "care" and the inescapability of death, but a decision made as man is confronted by the Word of God, the Word of God normally confronting man in the proclamation of the church. The essentials for Bultmann are: the distinction between "inauthentic" and "authentic" existence; the fact that the transition from one to the other comes as a consequence of decision; and the claim that the decision is made as one is confronted by the Word of God. Whether the proclamation of Jesus was the Word of God to his contemporaries in this sense is a good question, but in any case the proclamation of Jesus is not the Word of God in this transition-enabling sense to modern man. To modern man the transition-enabling Word of God is the proclamation of the church. We go into more detail on these matters in our discussion of Fuchs's interpretation of the parables, below, pp. 108–113.

126. Bultmann, *Jesus and the Word*, p. 11. See Perrin, *The Promise of Bultmann* (Philadelphia: Lippincott, 1969), p. 58.

127. Perrin, ibid. Bultmann never quite says this in so many words but it is implicit in his whole theological position.

128. I discussed the matter in chap. V of *Rediscovering the Teaching of Jesus*, pp. 207–248 and 262–266 (annotated bibliography). Today I am if anything more sympathetic to Bultmann's position than I was when I published *Rediscovering*, but the matter requires intensive further discussion, especially in light of the findings of redaction criticism with regard to the essential nature of the synoptic tradition and the synoptic gospels. No such discussion is possible here but I hope for an opportunity to turn to the matter at some future date.

129. See my earlier statement of this in "Eschatology and Hermeneutics," p. 8.

130. In my SBL Presidential Address I said of Bultmann's historical-critical understanding of the proclamation of Jesus that "by and large it is still valid" (ibid., p. 9), and then I went on to develop certain criticisms of it. In the more detailed discussion here I am expanding on the limitation implied by the "by and large" and developing the criticisms further and more explicitly.

131. The crux of the matter here is certainly the question of the Son of Man as apocalyptic redeemer. Neither Bultmann, nor any other scholar competent in life of Jesus research would build a case for such a view of the message of Jesus on the strength of the claims to authenticity of references to a general resurrection or a calendar-dated day of judgment. But if the proclamation of the coming of the Son of Man as apocalyptic redeemer is authentic,

then much of the remainder of the typical ancient Jewish apocalyptic scenario would have to be regarded as authentic also. The Son of Man question is crucial, and it is because I recognize this that I have spent so much time working on the problem. Here I can only repeat what I have argued in detail in *Rediscovering the Teaching of Jesus* and in *A Modern Pilgrimage in New Testament Christology*: Jesus did not proclaim the coming of an apocalyptic Son of Man; indeed he did not use Son of Man in any formal designatory sense at all.

132. See the discussion above, p. 44, and the reference in note 47 there to Paul Ricoeur, *Symbolism of Evil*, pp. 163–64.

CHAPTER III

The Modern Interpretation
of the Parables of Jesus

There is no better case study of the problems and possibilities of hermeneutics than that provided by the modern interpretation of the
parables of Jesus. Here, as we pointed out in the Introduction above,
every facet of the hermeneutical process comes clearly into play.
Textual criticism plays a large role because of the necessity of reconstructing the texts to be interpreted: the parables of Jesus are texts
reconstructed by modern critical scholarship from the New Testament
and the recently discovered Gospel of Thomas. The importance of the
figure of Jesus himself guarantees great interest in a historical understanding of his actual message, so *historical criticism* of his parables
becomes important; the more so since the parables are a most distinctive feature of that message, and today they represent our best source
for reconstructing it. *Literary criticism* is important because the parables are very distinctive texts from the standpoint of language and
literary form. At their heart lies metaphor and the use of metaphor to
challenge the hearer to a new apprehension of reality. But that metaphor is characteristically extended into a narrative, and that narrative
is realistic, so that we must consider not only metaphor and the function of metaphorical language, but also the force of realistic narrative.
Then the parables have been reinterpreted as exemplary stories, as
allegories, as teaching devices of various kinds, and presented as such
in the gospel texts. So literary criticism becomes important at every
stage of the interpretation of the parables. At the level of a historical
understanding we need to understand and appreciate the parables of

Jesus in accordance with their literary characteristics, and at the level of interpretation into the present of the interpreter these characteristics will become very important indeed. The modern interpretation of the parables of Jesus begins with the recognition of a distinction between the literary forms of allegory and parable, and it has continued with the exploration of similitude, example story, metaphor, and metaphor extended to narrative. In considering the parables as narratives we get involved in plot, recognition scenes, the function of characters, *actants* and *actantiel* analysis, and so on almost endlessly. Finally, the ultimate concern of all the interpreters of the parables has been to enter into *dialogue with the texts themselves* and the interpretation of the parables explores the myriad possibilities in this regard. If there is a hermeneutical option that has not been explored in connection with the parables then I, at any rate, would find it hard to say what that option might be!

The interpreters of the parables of Jesus to be discussed in this study have been chosen with some care. We begin with *Joachim Jeremias*[1] because he sums up the work of his two most important predecessors, Adolf Jülicher and C. H. Dodd. We then turn to the "new hermeneutic," represented in parable interpretation by *Ernst Fuchs* and his pupils *Eta Linnemann and Eberhard Jüngel.* This will necessitate further discussion of Bultmann's hermeneutical method, because Fuchs is self-consciously attempting to go beyond Bultmann, his own teacher. From Europe we will then turn to America, where the most important recent developments in parable interpretation have taken place.

The American work really begins with *Amos Wilder,* a truly seminal figure. A major New Testament scholar as well as a creative literary artist and an experienced literary critic, Wilder was uniquely equipped to point the way forward to an interpretation of the parables that would utilize creatively the insights of both New Testament and more general literary scholarship. He profoundly influenced the generation of scholars currently active in parable interpretation in America. Of these we shall discuss *Robert Funk,* who took the first step along the way Wilder had pointed out; *Dan Via,* who published the first major interpretation of the parables which made self-conscious use of the insights of general literary scholarship; and *Dominic Crossan,* who brought to the parables an appreciation in depth of poetry and poetic criticism. Finally we will turn to the Parables Seminar organized by the

Society of Biblical Literature, a seminar in which all the major students and interpreters of the parables in America are involved, under the leadership of Dominic Crossan. The seminar has now been working for two years, and the results of its work so far have been published in the first two issues of the new, experimental journal being published by the SBL, *Semeia* (vols. 1 and 2, both 1974). These two issues of *Semeia* will be the focus of our concern.

This selection encompasses various hermeneutical possibilities. Jeremias is the archetypal historical critic in parable interpretation, while Fuchs and the other representatives of the "new hermeneutic" have a major concern for the dynamic interaction between interpreter and text, and between text and interpreter. The American work is concerned with author, text, and interpreter, with various combinations of particular emphases, and it supplies a degree of sophistication about language and literary form that is new in the discussion. In the SBL seminar the American scholars, among other things, take up the challenge of French structuralism in parable interpretation.

It will not be possible to discuss in detail the interpretation of the individual parables, but at the same time a sample of each interpreter's work should obviously be given. Where possible, therefore, we will give in some detail each scholar's interpretation of The Good Samaritan, because it has been discussed at length by almost all interpreters and because it was the focus of the second year's work of the SBL Parables Seminar.

A. JOACHIM JEREMIAS AND THE HISTORICAL INTERPRETATION OF THE PARABLES OF JESUS

Joachim Jeremias, emeritus professor of New Testament at the University of Göttingen, published the first edition of his *Die Gleichnisse Jesu* in 1947. For almost the next twenty years he continuously rewrote, revised, and expanded that book through edition after edition, the last major revision being the sixth German edition of 1962, which took account of the newly discovered Gospel of Thomas. There was an English translation of the third German edition in 1954, and there is now an English translation of the sixth German edition: J. Jeremias, *The Parables of Jesus* (revised edition; New York: Scribner's, 1963; third rev. ed.; London: SCM Press, 1972). As it developed through its various editions this book became the most widely read book on the parables, and today it is the essential starting point for parable re-search. It represents a watershed in the development of the discussion, taking up into itself, as mentioned above, the work of the two most important previous contributors, Adolf Jülicher and C. H. Dodd, and bringing to a successful conclusion the first phase of the discussion, the establishment of the texts to be interpreted. It also represents the greatest possible concentration of interest on a historical understanding of the parables. Jeremias is often affectionately referred to as the arche-typal "old quester";[2] certainly it would be difficult to imagine a more dedicated concern for recovering the parables in the form in which Jesus told them, and for interpreting them in terms of their original historical context in his ministry in first-century Palestine.

Jeremias's point of departure is the epoch-making work of Adolf Jülicher, *Die Gleichnisreden Jesu*.[3] For centuries, beginning in the New Testament itself and continuing from that moment onward, the parables of Jesus were treated as allegories; that is, they were treated as deliberately mysterious pictures or stories, every feature of which referred to something other than itself. In order to interpret an alle-gory, one needed the key to identifying the various elements. The insider, possessing the key, could identify the elements and hence grasp and express the meaning of the allegory in non-allegorical lan-guage. The outsider, on the other hand, did not possess the key, and hence for him the allegory remained forever a mystery. A parable, Jülicher claimed, was not like this. A parable was a vivid and simple picture or story the meaning of which was self-evident to the hearer or reader.

The distinction between allegory and parable, and a grasp of the fundamental nature of both, is essential to the interpretation of the parables. It was Jülicher who first made the distinction, and who, further, demonstrated that the parables of Jesus were parables and not allegories. In the moment that he did this the modern interpretation of the parables of Jesus began, and, what is more, the whole modern interpretation of the parables has continued to wrestle with the distinc-tion, as it has continued to seek to understand the actual nature of a parable as a literary entity. Jülicher pioneered both in arguing that the parables of Jesus were parables and not allegories, and also in seeking to understand the parable as a literary entity. But the whole matter has turned out to be much more complex than anyone could have imagined, and Jülicher's categories have long since been overtaken by the discussion. We may therefore treat Jülicher's work in this connection rather briefly.

Jülicher's method of arguing against understanding the parables of Jesus as allegories was devastatingly simple: he wrote a one-hundred-and-twenty-page "history of the interpretation of the parables of Jesus."[4] Beginning with the apostolic fathers and continuing into his own day he showed relentlessly how many and varied the possible interpretations were when the hermeneutical method was that of identifying the referents of the various elements in the stories which Jesus told. As Jeremias puts it: "It is positively alarming to read in his *History of the Interpretation of the Parables of Jesus* the story of the centuries of distortion and ill-usage which the parables have suffered through allegorical interpretation."[5] The fundamental point Jülicher makes, and it is a good one, is that the parables Jesus told give the impression of being vivid and understandable. Moreover, historically speaking, Jesus seems to have been one who was heard gladly and understood readily; the idea that his parables are esoteric and mysterious, needing a key to be understood, is foreign to everything we know about him. His parables are vivid, simple pictures, taken from real life.

With regard to the fact that the parables of Jesus were not allegories, Jülicher's point was well taken, and the subsequent discussion has only strengthened it.[6] With regard to the nature of a parable as a literary entity, however, Jülicher only scratched the surface of what turned out to be an extraordinarily complex issue. He took his point of departure from Aristotle's *Rhetoric*[7] and argued that the fundamental element in a parable was a comparison. In a parable two conceptions were set down side by side and compared with one another; there was a *tertium comparationis*, a point of comparison between the two which related the one to the other; hence something learned from the one could be applied to the other. A parable is essentially instructional in nature; one learns from something that is known or usual and then applies it, through the point of comparison, to the unknown or unusual with which it may logically be compared, thereby learning something new. A parable consists of two parts, the *matter* (*Sache*) which is the real concern of the parabolist, and the *picture* (*Bild*) with which it may be compared. The picture does not need to be interpreted, it is drawn from the world of the known and the familiar, and its meaning is self-evident. The picture needs to be applied to the matter, which it will be found to illuminate. "The pictorial element in the parable is not intended to be *interpreted* but to be *applied,* so that something may be learnt."[8] The verbal picture offers the hearer something he knows, something with which he is familiar, and the parable then requires "that he take the central idea or dominant theme from the known or familiar picture and apply it to the comparable matter that up to that moment was unclear to him."[9]

Before leaving Jülicher we will give, as an example, his interpretation of The Good Samaritan, which we will offer in contrast to an allegory. Augustine interpreted The Good Samaritan as an allegory, in which *the traveler* was Adam and *Jerusalem* the heavenly city of peace, "from whose blessedness Adam fell." *Jericho* is the moon, signifying our mortality; *the thieves* are the devil and his angels, who *strip* the traveler of his immortality, *beat him* by persuading him to sin, and *leave him half-dead* in his sinful state. The *priest* and *Levite* represent the ministry of the Old Testament, "which could profit nothing for salvation." The *Samaritan* is "the Lord Himself" and the various instruments of his charity are aspects of the Christian faith. The *morrow* is the resurrection of the Lord; the *two pence* are the precepts of love, or the promise of this life and the life to come; the *innkeeper* is the Apostle Paul, and so on.[10]

Jülicher understood The Good Samaritan to be an "exemplary story";[11] it is a story "epitomizing a religious conception of unquestionable universal validity."[12] The story itself is extraordinarily realistic. One literally goes *down* to Jericho from Jerusalem; that Jericho road was notoriously dangerous for travelers because it passed through hilly, desert terrain made to measure for outlaws and robbers. Priests and temple officials, normally somewhat rare in the community, would be found frequently on roads near Jerusalem. Oil and wine were commonly carried by travelers for emergency use, as in this instance. Strangely enough, in view of what was to come in later exegesis, Jülicher does not make much of the contrast between priest and Levite on the one hand, and Samaritan on the other; although he does note that a Samaritan was a "despised heretic," "a half-heathen" in the eyes of the Jews, and he suggests that the "he that showed mercy on him" in verse 37 is a circumlocution for "neighbor." A "fanatical Jew," he notes, would not call a Samaritan a neighbor.

What is Jesus teaching by means of this vivid, realistic story? It is not that he intended simply to extol a "half-heathen" Samaritan as being better than some Jews; that would be a contradiction of the normal concern which Jesus showed for maintaining the religious integrity of Judaism. Rather, Jesus is concerned to extol even a Samaritan who acts in love over a priest who does not do so—just as in Matt. 21:28–32 he extols penitent tax collectors and harlots over unrepentant high priests and elders.[13] In the story of the Good Samaritan Jesus is developing his ideal of a "neighbor," and the point he intends to make is the following: "The self-sacrificial act of love is of the highest value in the eyes of God and men; no privilege of position or birth can take its place. The compassionate man, even though he is a Samaritan, is more deserving of blessing than the selfish Jewish Temple official."[14]

We have noted that Jülicher's understanding of the function of the parable is essentially pedagogical in nature. The parable is designed as an aid to understanding; it serves to increase the hearer's fund of knowledge.[15] This understanding of the parable as a literary form is drawn from the schoolroom of classical antiquity, and Jülicher himself was often reproached for this. Paul Fiebig especially challenged Jülicher's understanding of the nature of parable, on the grounds that such an understanding drawn from classical antiquity was too remote from Jesus himself. Jesus taught in the context of ancient Judaism, in which the parable was a frequently used literary form; we must therefore seek in the ancient Jewish use of parables an understanding of parable as a literary form which will serve as an introduction to the parables of Jesus. Fiebig himself summed up his challenge to Jülicher in the title of a book he wrote, *The Parables of Jesus in the Light of the Rabbinic Parables of the New Testament Period* (1912).[16] Fiebig's point is well taken. It is not so much that the schoolroom of classical antiquity is too remote from the parables of Jesus, as it is that Aristotle's categories were ultimately to be found inappropriate to an understanding of the parables of Jesus. The rabbinical parables to which Fiebig pointed not only stood in closer cultural proximity to Jesus—and, what is probably even more important, to the early Christian communities using the parables—they were also closer to the parables of Jesus in literary form and function. In this respect Jeremias follows Fiebig rather than Jülicher, as we shall see. But Jülicher took the first steps toward an understanding of the parable as a literary form, and for this reason he is important.

Jülicher saw the parables of Jesus as essentially instructional in nature; what did they give instruction about? The answer to that question is obvious: Jesus' understanding of the Kingdom of God. The parables tell us how Jesus thought of the Kingdom of God, *"wie Christus das Reich Gottes sich gedacht hat."*[17] But Jesus turns out to be very much a late nineteenth-century German liberal, for this Kingdom of God is "a fellowship in God . . . a fellowship of brothers and sisters under the protection of their father," a fellowship already at work "in seeking and finding the lost . . . already enjoying in full measure the gifts of God, forgiveness, loving kindness, peace, joy, security," a fellowship in which "spiritual effort and endeavour is demanded of all its members. . . ."[18] Jülicher has read his Ritschl; it seems doubtful whether he has read Johannes Weiss!

Given this understanding of the Kingdom of God, and given, further, the understanding of the parables as vivid and simple *pictures* designed to illuminate the Kingdom as *matter*, then it follows as does the night the day that the parables will offer their hearers general moral and spiritual instruction. And, so they do, through all the six hundred pages of the second volume of Jülicher's work. I may quote a summary I have previously published.

The House Built on Sand (Matt. 7:24–27) has the point that hearing and not doing in the case of Jesus' message is as senseless as building a house without bothering about the foundations (II, p. 266). The Friend at Midnight (Luke 11:5–8) is intended to encourage the hearers to constancy in prayer (II, p. 276), as is The Widow and the Unjust Judge (Luke 18:1–8; II, p. 288). The Great Supper (Matt. 22:1–14) makes the point that as with the feast-giver, so with God; if Jesus' first hearers do not respond, then others will be given the opportunity (II, p. 432). The Laborers in the Vineyard (Matt. 20:1–16) is concerned with the fact that God has one salvation for all mankind, "for high priest and aristocrat, for tax collector and prostitute" (II, p. 467). The Sower (Mark 4:3–9, 14–20) is a story to which the hearers would have responded with the recognition that such is indeed the way it is in sowing and harvesting; as they would also have readily made the proper application that it is this way too with the word of God in men's hearts (II, p. 536). The Good Samaritan (Luke 10:29–37) teaches that a self-sacrificial act of love is the most valuable thing in the eyes of man and of God. No privilege of office or birth can take its place (II, p. 596).[19]

So far as Jeremias is concerned, and indeed so far as the subsequent discussion as a whole is concerned, the important thing about Jülicher is the fact that he raised the question of the nature of the parables of Jesus as literary entities, and in his demonstration that they were not allegories he laid the foundation stone for their modern interpretation. In regard to the nature of the parables of Jesus at the literary level Jeremias accepted wholeheartedly Jülicher's contention that they were not allegories, and he accepted, further, the contention that they were vivid, simple pictures and stories designed to make a single point. What he refused to accept from Jülicher, however, was that that point was a general moral principle. But one must remember what had happened between 1888 and 1947 in connection with the understanding of Kingdom of God in the message of Jesus: Johannes Weiss and the first fifty years of the discussion set off by his book on the proclamation of Jesus had happened. We covered this discussion briefly in the first study in this volume.[20]

It is obvious that a discussion of the parables of Jesus will be deeply affected by the understanding of Kingdom of God in the message of Jesus, since the *matter* (*Sache*) with which the parables are concerned is the Kingdom of God. Of that there is no doubt in any interpreter's mind. We saw already how crucially the late nineteenth-century liberal theological understanding of Kingdom of God affected Jülicher's interpretation of the parables. Having decided on literary grounds that each of the parables was designed to make one point in relationship to the Kingdom of God, he then let his understanding of the nature of that Kingdom lead him to understand the nature of that point as general moral or spiritual instruction. But between Jülicher and Jeremias, as we said immediately above, a great deal had happened in the discussion of Kingdom of God in the message of Jesus; in particular, so far as Jeremias was concerned, C. H. Dodd had published in 1935 his book *The Parables of the Kingdom*.[21] As we pointed out in the discussion of this book in our first study, this was important because it introduced the parables into the discussion of the Kingdom in the message of Jesus.[22] But it also had the reverse effect: it introduced the Kingdom of God into the discussion of the parables. After Dodd one could not but be aware, not only of how deeply one's interpretation of the parables affected one's understanding of the Kingdom of God in the message of Jesus, but also of how deeply one's understanding of the Kingdom affected one's interpretation of the parables. After Dodd any interpreter of the parables had to become self-conscious about his understanding of Jesus' use of Kingdom of God.

Certainly Jeremias became self-conscious about this. He modified Dodd's "realized eschatology" to "eschatology in the process of realization," as we noted above,[23] and he understood this as the key to understanding the parables. The parables are full of "the recognition of 'an eschatology that is in the process of realization.' " The one note that sounds through them all is that "the hour of fulfillment is come."[24] But Jeremias took more from Dodd than his insistence that an understanding of the eschatology of Jesus was an essential key to the interpretation of the parables; he also took from Dodd a claim that the parables had to be interpreted in terms of their historical context in the ministry of Jesus.

Dodd had claimed that a parable must be interpreted in terms of what the form critics called the "setting in life" (*Sitz im Leben*), except that the "setting in life" so far as the parables were concerned was not that provided by the situation in the early church, as it was in the case of the sayings which interested the form critics. "We shall sometimes have to remove a parable from its setting in the life and thought of the Church, as represented by the gospels, and make an attempt to reconstruct its original setting in the life of Jesus."[25] Dodd pursues this theme through a whole chapter of his book,[26] seeing some parables as related to Jesus' challenge to his hearers in view of the coming of the Kingdom in his own ministry, others relating to the particular situation of his disciples in relationship to the Kingdom, others relating to a major feature of the coming of the Kingdom, that is, the "unprecedented concern for the 'lost,' " and so on. In this respect Jeremias follows Dodd enthusiastically, relating parable after parable to hypothetical situations in the ministry of Jesus, situations of Jesus confronted by eager hearers, by hostile opponents, by questioning disciples, and so on.

I have said that these are *hypothetical* situations. We have very little firm historical knowledge of the situation of the ministry of Jesus, so any discussion of Jesus and his hearers, opponents or disciples, and the situation between them, is necessary hypothetical. But there is also such a thing as reasonable extrapolation from such knowledge as we do have, so too much should not be made of the fact that any "setting in the life of Jesus" is necessarily hypothetical. This is not in itself a valid argument against the insistence of Dodd and Jeremias that the parables of Jesus should be interpreted in the context of such a setting.

Dodd made two further points about the parables, both at the level of a literary concern. The first of these can be stated briefly; it has to do with the *realism* of the parables. Jülicher had claimed that the parables were vivid, simple stories taken from real life, and we noted how much emphasis he put upon the realism of the narrative of The Good Samaritan. Dodd develops this emphasis very strongly. "In the parables in the gospels," he says, "all is true to nature and to life. . . . Each similitude or story is a perfect picture of something that can be observed in the world of our experience. . . . The actions of the persons in the stories are in character; they are either such as anyone would recognize as natural in the circumstances, or, if they are surprising, the point of the parable is that such actions *are* surprising."[27] If the parables are taken as a whole, "their realism is remarkable." They give "a singularly complete and convincing picture . . . of life in a small provincial town— probably a more complete picture of *petit-bourgeois* and peasant life than we possess for any other province of the Roman Empire except Egypt, where papyri come to our aid."[28]

The second point which Dodd makes at the literary level is more complex. He offers a very important discussion of the linguistic characteristics and literary form of the parables, a discussion that was to be very important to Robert Funk, and through him to contemporary work on the parables in America.[29] At the heart of the parable, claims Dodd, there is a metaphor or simile "drawn from nature or common life, arresting the hearer by its vividness or strangeness."[30] Such metaphors or similes have a very particular *function*; they leave the mind in sufficient doubt about their precise application "to tease it into active thought."[31] The metaphor can be elaborated into a picture, by the addition of details. "Thus: 'They do not light a lamp and put it under a meal-tub, but on a lampstand; and then it gives light to all in the house'; 'No one sews a patch of unshrunk cloth on an old coat, else the patch pulls away from it—the new from the old—and there is a worse tear.'" Such a metaphor elaborated into a picture is the simplest form of parable, the Jülicher-Bultmann *similitude*. But the metaphor or simile can be further elaborated, developed into a story instead of a picture, "the additional details serving to develop a situation." These are the Jülicher-Bultmann *parables*, and they can vary in length from The Hid Treasure and The Pearl of Great Price to The Prodigal Son and The Laborers in the Vineyard. Dodd does not distinguish exemplary stories from parables, and properly so. From a literary standpoint The Good Samaritan and The Prodigal Son are equally metaphor extended into narrative, to distinguish them as exemplary story and parable respectively is to make a distinction based on their supposed function on the lips of Jesus. But such a supposition is not necessarily correct and, in any case, the distinction is not being made on grounds of language or literary form. In Dodd's distinction among metaphor, metaphor developed into a picture (*similitude*), and metaphor or simile developed into a story (*parable*), Dodd himself notes that no line can be drawn among them with any precision, "One class melts into another," and, "in all of them we have nothing but the elaboration of a single comparison." Moreover, they all *function* in the same way; they are all designed "to catch the imagination"; any details given as the metaphor is elaborated are "details . . . designed to set the situation in the clearest possible light."[32]

Dodd's discussion of the relationship among metaphor, similitude, and parable was extremely important, as was also his concern for the function of metaphor "to tease the mind into active thought," and his recognition of the fact that the elaborated metaphors of the parables were designed "to catch the imagination." Dodd, indeed, was stronger on the literary aspect of the parables than any other participant in the discussion before Amos Wilder and the younger, contemporary American scholars. But then, as I pointed out above, that discussion is in part built upon a re-appreciation of Dodd's insights. Being strong on the literary aspects of the discussion of the parables, Dodd appreciated the force of the distinction between parable and allegory, for this is a literary distinction. He distinguishes between parables as "the natural expression of a mind that sees truth in concrete pictures rather than conceives it in abstractions," and allegories as "allegorical mystifications"[33]

Before turning to a summary of Jeremias's contribution to the discussion of the interpretation of the parables of Jesus, we must make one further preliminary point. In our discussion of Jülicher above we pointed out that he ignored the use of parables in ancient Judaism, and that Paul Fiebig challenged him on this point. Now Jeremias does not discuss this point at all; he sees absolutely no need to do so. Jeremias assumes that one must come to the parables of Jesus from an intensive study of the use of parables in ancient Judaism, especially from an intensive study of the use of parables by the rabbis representing the earlier phases of the Jewish rabbinical literature, those most nearly contemporary with Jesus. Jeremias has conducted such a study himself;[34] that much is evident from every page of his book, and this is an important aspect of his historical approach to the parables.

We may now summarize Jeremias's contribution to the discussion of the interpretation of the parables of Jesus, beginning under the rubric of *textual criticism*. It is here that we find the first aspect of Jeremias's contribution to the discussion, for it is to Jeremias above all others that we owe our present ability to reconstruct the parables very much in the form in which Jesus told them. Indeed, when we talk of interpreting the parables of Jesus today we mean interpreting the parables as Jeremias has reconstructed them, either personally or through his influence on others who have followed the method he developed.

Jeremias begins by recognizing that the parables of Jesus have been reinterpreted in the tradition of the Christian communities, and that they have been changed very considerably in the process of transmission from their first telling to their being written down in the sources in which the evangelists find them. Today we would add that they have also been further edited by the evangelists themselves as they become integral parts of the texts of the various gospels. This process of editing, reinterpreting, changing, and adapting the texts of the parables was not a random, haphazard process. Rather it followed rules which we can reconstruct; it was a procedure the details of which we can work out. For example, there were certain definite methods by means of which reinterpretation has been carried out. First there is the act of allegorization: an allegorizing interpretation can be added. A good example of this is The Sower, Mark 4:3–9, where the allegorizing interpretation, verses 14–20, has been added as the parable was transmitted in the early Christian communities. Allegorization was the favorite method of reinterpretation of the parables of Jesus in the early Christian communities, and sometimes this was carried out in a second way, by adding allegorizing touches within the parable itself. A good example of this is The Great Supper, Matt. 22:1–14 = Luke 14:16–24, where the references to the killing of the servants and to the king sending his army in Matt. 22:6–7 are references to the fate of Jesus and the prophets, and to the fall of Jerusalem; they make the story an allegory. A third method of reinterpretation was to add moralizing conclusions, and a good example of this is The Unjust Steward, Luke 16:1–9, where verses 8 and 9 represent a series of sermon notes by early Christian preachers almost desperately trying to make a wholly reprehensible character into a moral example. A fourth method of reinterpretation was to give the parable a setting such as it might have had if it were to be found in the context of Jewish wisdom literature. The prime example here is The Good Samaritan, Luke 10:25–37, where the setting, verses 25–29, makes the parable an exemplary story illustrating the principles of neighborliness. This is how untold exegetes have read the parable, beginning with the exegetes of earliest Christianity, but the setting of the story has been supplied as an act of interpretation and is not integral to the parable itself.

In addition to such definite methods of reinterpretation there were also other recognizable factors at work affecting the text of the parables as they were transmitted in the tradition of the early Christian communities. For example, language: Jesus had taught in Aramaic whereas the church transmitted the text of the parables in Greek. Or, again, the change of audience: from Palestine to the Hellenistic world, and from Jews confronted by the message of the Kingdom of God to Christians confronting the delay of the Parousia or the challenge of the Gentile mission. There was, further, the natural process of embellishment as the stories were told and retold. Such observable factors as these, together with knowledge of the various methods of reinterpretation indicated above, made it possible for Jeremias to reconstruct enough of the history of the transmission of the text of the parables from the oral form of Jesus' message to the written form of their presentation in the gospels to enable him convincingly to reconstruct the original form of the parables.

I need to emphasize the fact that Jeremias was spectacularly successful in his attempt to retrace the stages of the transmission of the parables of Jesus from their present form in the gospels, and that to all intents and purposes the current discussion of the parables of Jesus is a discussion of the parables of Jesus as Jeremias has reconstructed them. Of course, there is a discussion of details, but these are comparatively minor, and what is more important such a discussion is always carried on in terms of Jeremias's characteristic methodology. There are differences of opinion about one parable or another, or about details within a given parable, but it is Jeremias who has taught us all to reconstruct the parables of Jesus, and today the parables of Jesus are pretty much what Jeremias says they are, or what they are said to be by scholars using Jeremias's characteristic method. Today we would add a concern for the final stage of editing the texts and settings of the parables carried out by the evangelists themselves, and a concern for the logic of the various kinds of narrative represented in our texts, e.g., discourse and story,[35] but this only adds concerns taught us by redaction criticism and structuralism; it does not change the fundamental thrust of the Jeremias methodology.

A second aspect of Jeremias's contribution to the interpretation of the parables may be discussed under the rubric of *historical criticism,* and here we will see a characteristic strength and also a characteristic weakness of his work. Moreover the strength and weakness stem from the same root, the root of his deep and abiding concern for the message of the historical Jesus. For Jeremias the whole purpose of the scholarly interpretation of the parables of Jesus is to allow the man of another time and place to hear the voice of Jesus as Jesus' contemporaries heard that voice. Jeremias is himself quite self-conscious about this. In the foreword of his book he writes: "It is to be hoped that the reader will perceive that the aim of the critical analysis contained in the second part of this book is nothing less than a return, as well grounded as possible, to the very words of Jesus himself. Only the Son of Man and his word can invest our message with full authority."[36] Moreover he constantly returns to this theme throughout the book. For example, "Our task is to return to the actual living voice of Jesus. How great the gain if we succeed in rediscovering here and there behind the veil the features of the Son of Man! To meet with him can alone give power to our preaching."[37] When Jeremias's students put together a *Festschrift* for his seventieth birthday they called it *Der Ruf Jesu und die Antwort der Gemeinde* (Göttingen: Vandenhoeck & Ruprecht, 1970). This choice of a title was a deliberate and happy one. Jeremias himself thinks consistently in terms of the challenge of Jesus and the response of the community, and he quite deliberately and consistently does not differentiate between the "community" of first-century Jews or of twentieth-century Germans or Americans. For Jeremias the essential religious discourse is always the discourse between Jesus of Nazareth and those who heard him, *and those who hear him.* "Those who hear him" today need all the apparatus of historical-critical scholarship to be able to do so, but Jeremias recognizes this and, in consequence of recognizing it, has spent his whole life in an effort to provide that necessary apparatus of historical-critical scholarship.

The strength stemming from this concern for the voice of the historical Jesus is the single-mindedness with which Jeremias has pursued his chosen task, and the contribution he has consequently been able to make to the historical understanding of the parables. He has investigated in depth the literature of ancient Judaism, especially the earlier rabbinic literature, so he brings to the parables a deep awareness of their most immediate literary context. He has spent a lifetime of research on Palestine and Judaism at the time of Jesus; he is able therefore to set the parables in their context in the ministry of Jesus, as Dodd had urged should be done. Perhaps most striking of all is the way in which he is able to identify the references and to catch the allusions in the parables. The parables of Jesus are *occasional* texts; they were directed toward a specific group of people on specific occasions and they assume a whole spectrum of history, culture, and experience shared by the parabolist and his hearers. Jülicher and Dodd had developed the thesis that the parables were realistic pictures and stories, drawn from life. But the life from which they were drawn is the *petit-bourgeois* and peasant life of Palestine in the early Roman Empire. If we are to understand those pictures and stories historically, therefore, we must understand that life from which they were drawn.

I would personally put a great deal of emphasis upon this last point. The parables of Jesus are pictures and stories drawn from *petit-bourgeois* and peasant life in Palestine under the early Roman emperors. They are not myths employing archetypal symbols; they are not fables exploiting the universal features of the human condition; they are not folk tales appealing to the collective experience of a people as a people. They are vivid and concrete pictures and stories drawn from the details of a particular situation at a given time and in a given place. They are occasional, transitory, essentially fleeting snapshots of life. At times, as in the home-coming scene of The Prodigal Son, they are elevated to a more universal frame of reference, but that is only an infrequent feature; it is *not* an essential feature of the parables as such. Even The Prodigal Son is misunderstood if it is not read in terms of the economic realities of life in Palestine, of the particularities of the ancient Jewish system of inheritance, and of the cultural dangers of life in the Diaspora. By their very nature as texts the parables of Jesus demand this kind of information a hundred times over if they are to be understood historically, and it is one of Jeremias's great contributions to the discussion that over and over again he provides exactly this kind of information.

The weakness stemming from Jeremias's concern for the voice of the historical Jesus is that ultimately he is not concerned with the parables as texts with an integrity of their own, needing to be interpreted in their own right. His ultimate concern is the message of Jesus as a whole, and the interpretation of the parables is for Jeremias only a means to the end of reconstructing this message. For all the time and effort he has spent on the interpretation of the parables he is really only interested in them as contributing to an overall understanding of the message of Jesus. He does not respect their integrity as texts.

The most immediate result of this overriding concern for the message of Jesus as a whole is that Jeremias presents his interpretation of the parables under a series of rubrics which together make up "the message of the parables." The rubrics are as follows:

> Now Is the Day of Salvation
> God's Mercy for Sinners
> The Great Assurance
> The Imminence of Catastrophe
> It May Be Too Late
> The Challenge of the Hour
> Realized Discipleship
> The Via Dolorosa and Exaltation of
>   the Son of Man
> The Consummation

One is tempted to say that what for Jülicher was a general moral principle has tended to become for Jeremias a rubric under which to consider an aspect of the message of Jesus. One is further tempted to remark that whereas a summary of Jülicher's general moral principles looks very much like a manifesto of nineteenth-century theological liberalism, this list of rubrics looks very much like a summary of a rather conservative Lutheran piety. But none of that would be important. What is important is that the very nature of the parables of Jesus as texts forbids the reduction of their message to a series of general moral principles, or to a series of rubrics. Parables as parables do not have a "message." They tease the mind into ever new perceptions of reality; they startle the imagination; they function like symbols in that they "give rise to thought."

Inherent in what I have just said is the fact that I regard Jeremias's contribution to the discussion of the parables to be at the levels of *textual criticism* and of *historical criticism.* At the level of *literary criticism* Jeremias fully appreciated the nature of the parables as "occasional" texts, but he could not see the way the parables function as metaphor or as metaphor extended to picture or to narrative. His overriding concern for the "message" of the parables as a means for arriving at the "message" of the historical Jesus hindered him too greatly. Similarly, that same overriding concern hindered him from exploring the dynamic interaction between text and interpreter which I tend to call "hermeneutics proper." For all that he could often visualize the dynamics of the interaction between the parables and their original hearers, he could see them today only in the context of coming to appreciate the message of Jesus as a whole. In its own way that is an honorable and most important endeavor, but it is not a hermeneutics of the parables, because it does not sufficiently respect the integrity of the parables of Jesus as texts.

We will conclude this discussion of Jeremias by giving as an example his interpretation of The Good Samaritan.[38] This is subsumed under the rubric "Realized Discipleship," and is therefore taken to be one of a group of parables of which the other members are The Hid Treasure and The Pearl of Great Price (Matt. 13:44–46), The Great Fish (Thom. 81:28–82:3), The Sentence at the Last Judgment (Matt. 25:31–46),[39] and The Unmerciful Servant (Matt. 18:23–35). The message of this group of parables is concerned with the quality of life which has been overmastered by the great joy, the boundless love experienced as the Kingdom of God, the quality of a life of preparedness to respond to that love. The Good Samaritan belongs here: "The example of the despised half-breed was intended to teach him [the questioner] that no human being was beyond the range of his charity," to show him that "the law of love called him to be ready to give his life for another's need."[40] Jeremias thinks of the parable as an exemplary story.

Jeremias sees the setting of the story, Luke 10:25–29, 36–37, as authentic, because it reflects so accurately the cultural possibilities of first-century Jewish Palestine. But this, I would claim, does not necessarily follow. It is the tradition that has supplied this setting and the tradition is a cultural tradition within first-century Jewish Palestine. As had Jülicher before him, Jeremias emphasizes the realism of the story with regard to journey, road, and robbers. He discusses the possible motivation of the priest and Levite in avoiding the wounded man and determines that they were not motivated by ritual considerations, but by purely personal considerations of safety. Jeremias then comes to what is for him the crux of the story. "According to the triadic form of popular stories, the audience would now have expected a third character, namely, after the priest and the Levite, an Israelite layman; they would hence have expected the parable to have an anti-clerical point. It would have been completely unexpected and disconcerting for them to hear that the third character, who fulfilled the law of love, was a Samaritan."[41] Jeremias goes into details of the deteriorating relationships between Jews and Samaritans under the Roman occupation, and in this way he reaches the message of the story. "It is clear that Jesus had intentionally chosen an extreme example; by comparing the failure of the ministers of God with the unselfishness of the hated Samaritan, his hearers should be able to measure the absolute and unlimited nature of the duty of love."[42] Turning from the hearers in general to the questioner in particular Jeremias draws the lesson we quoted above. "The example of the despised half-breed was intended to teach him that no human being was beyond the range of his charity. The law of love called him to be ready at any time to give his life for another's need."

B. THE "NEW HERMENEUTIC" AND THE PARABLES OF JESUS

1. Ernst Fuchs: The Parable as Sprachereignis

Ernst Fuchs was Bultmann's pupil, and his successor to the New Testament chair at Marburg, from which he has recently retired. Together with Gerhard Ebeling, he is the leader of a strong movement in German language theology, the so-called new hermeneutic.[43] He is not only a pupil of Bultmann, he is concerned also to go beyond Bultmann, especially in his understanding of hermeneutics. Fuchs is self-consciously a *post*-Bultmannian.

✓The key element in Fuchs's hermeneutics is the idea of a *Sprachereignis* (language event), and it is one of the two points at which he is consciously concerned to go beyond Bultmann.[44] As we saw in our previous discussion of Bultmann,[45] Bultmann undertakes to bridge the gulf between the mythological language of Jesus and the New Testament on the one hand and modern technological man on the other. He bridges this gulf by means of a hermeneutical method which interprets that language in terms of a concern for human existence in the world. Such a concern, Bultmann held, was the common ground between Jesus and the New Testament on the one hand, and modern technological man on the other. Hence the gulf could now be bridged by means of a recognition of this commonality of concern. Moreover, the bridge could be the more readily built by expressing the message of Jesus and the New Testament in terms of an existentialist philosophy, because modern technological man could analyze his existence in the world by using that same philosophy.

This is a bald and all too brief summary of Bultmann's existentialist hermeneutics as I understand it, and as I tried to express it in my earlier discussion above. But before I turn from Bultmann to Fuchs there is another point about Bultmann's position to be considered: the role he ascribes to the message of Jesus as he addresses modern technological man's existence in the world.[46] By means of existentialist philosophy, Bultmann considers human existence in the world as being possible at two levels: one can live in the world at the level of *inauthentic* or at the level of *authentic* existence. At this point he is consciously indebted to Martin Heidegger, and to the analysis of human existence carried out by Heidegger in the early nineteen twenties and published in *Sein und Zeit* (1926).[47]

Heidegger concerns himself with two things which are threats to all human existence: *care* and *death*. *Care* is the necessity to wrestle constantly with the concrete immediacies and problems of life in the world, and the temptation to abandon oneself to those immediacies and problems, to choose that world as one's home and to abandon oneself to it. *Death* is the end of being, and it is at the same time the one inescapable possibility of human existence. The "being" of man is necessarily a "being-unto-death." Life itself is a constant flight from death. The nature of life in the world is such that it is characterized by care and the threat of death; everyday existence in the world is bedeviled by care and shot through and through with the necessity to flee from death. This everyday existence in the world is a fallen existence: it is inauthentic existence.

But man in the world is confronted by the possibility of authentic existence, and, moreover, he is free to choose the possibility of existing authentically. In that moment when he is confronted by death and shattered by its inevitable prospect, he can resolve to accept his existence in the world as being bounded by death. What happens in this moment of decision is that man chooses resolutely to accept the certainty of death and the nothingness of human existence. In doing this he achieves authentic existence because he now has no necessity to delude himself about the nature of his existence in the world. We may say that he comes to know that his existence in the world is bounded by death and limited by the facts of life; in the resolve to accept this he finds the power to go through with it.

Bultmann accepts the Heideggerian distinctions between inauthentic and authentic existence, but not the possibility of achieving authentic existence on the basis of a resolute decision to accept the inevitable. He calls this "a resolution of despair."[48] At the crucial point of the transition from inauthentic to authentic existence Bultmann abandons Heidegger and makes what he regards as the "affirmation of faith," namely, that authentic existence is possible only in response to an encounter with the Word of God. Authentic existence is a new understanding of the self which brings with it the possibility of a new authentic existence for the self in the world, and this possibility is only present in faith and to faith. Faith, in turn, is to be found only in response to the kerygma, the proclamation of Jesus by the church. A characteristic statement of this viewpoint is the following paragraph.

In the New Testament faith is not understood as a self-understanding[49] arising spontaneously out of human existence but as an understanding made possible by God, opened up by his dealing with men. Faith is not choosing to understand one's self in one of several possible ways that are universally available to man but is man's response to God's word which encounters him in the proclamation of Jesus Christ. It is *faith in the kerygma*, which tells of God's dealing in the man Jesus of Nazareth.[50]

Bultmann is, then, ultimately concerned with *faith*, i.e., Christian faith, which alone makes possible the transition from inauthentic to authentic existence. This faith is "faith in the kerygma," in the proclamation of the church "which tells of God's dealing in the man Jesus of Nazareth." In light of these considerations we can now turn to Bultmann's understanding of the role of the message of the historical Jesus in all this. Briefly, Bultmann regards the message of Jesus, existentially understood, as challenging modern technological man at the level of his understanding of his existence in the world, that is, as challenging the self at the level of self-understanding. But this challenge cannot and does not make possible the transition from inauthentic to authentic existence; that possibility is strictly reserved for the challenge of the kerygma. In Lutheran terms, and Bultmann is very much a Lutheran, the message of Jesus is preparation for the gospel but not yet the gospel itself.

We may now turn from Bultmann to Fuchs, who deliberately departed from Bultmann both in respect to an understanding of hermeneutics and also in respect to the role ascribed to the historical Jesus in the Christian's coming to faith. One should perhaps remember that Fuchs is a leader in both of the two deliberately "post-Bultmannian" movements, in the "new quest"[51] as well as in the "new hermeneutic." In respect to hermeneutics the fundamental change lies in a consideration of language itself. Bultmann had tended to regard language as essentially a vehicle for transmitting an understanding of existence, as a means of conveying an "expression of life." Fuchs, on the other hand, is concerned with what in English came to be called the "performative" aspect of language.[52] He is concerned with language as "language event," with the power of language to bring into being something that was not there before the words were spoken. So Fuchs understands the parables of Jesus as a "language event." It is not that Jesus created new concepts, but rather that in the parables "Jesus' understanding of his situation 'enters language' in a special way." In the parables Jesus verbalizes his understanding of his own existence in the world in such a way that that understanding of existence is now available as a possibility for the hearers. "Without doubt Jesus' parables summon to decision.

. . . Like the man who found the treasure, or the pearl merchant who found the one pearl of great price, the hearer must stake all on one thing—that he can win the future which Jesus proclaims to him."[53]

Fuchs is particularly interested in the parables precisely because, as "language events," they both verbalize Jesus' understanding of his own situation in the world and before God, and they also create the possibility of the hearer's sharing that situation.

[The parables] simply portray the new situation [of the hearers before God and in the world]. Between the present which they share with Jesus, and the future in which God is to accomplish his rule [*Basilein* = Kingdom], they find themselves, as between a tiny beginning and a magnificent end: that is the intention of the . . . [parable] of the mustard seed and the leaven. . . . But all of them, together with Jesus, move *within* this occurrence, when they understand and have faith. . . .

This is the decisive achievement of the parables of Jesus: whoever understands and goes this way moves already in a new context, in being before God. He can then relate God to himself in a relationship like that of the labourer who actually came too late to the generous lord of the vineyard. Thus Jesus intends to "bring God into language". . . . Jesus' proclamation bestows on these people "freedom for the word."[54]

Bultmann would have approached a parable with questions regarding the parable's understanding of existence, and, further, he would have regarded that understanding of existence as challenging that of the hearer, or interpreter, but not as mediating the possibility of authentic existence to the hearer, or to the interpreter.[55] But Fuchs sees the parables as verbalizing Jesus' own understanding of existence in such a way that the parable mediates the possibility of sharing Jesus' understanding of existence, both to the immediate hearer and also to the subsequent interpreter.[56]

Fuchs speaks of "Jesus' understanding of his situation," and this brings us to the second point at which Fuchs deliberately goes beyond Bultmann. Bultmann resolutely refused to speak of Jesus' understanding of his own situation, of his understanding of his existence, or indeed of anything else that depended upon a claim to know something of the thought processes of Jesus. This, to Bultmann, was an unwarrantable psychologizing about Jesus.[57] Fuchs, however, is fully prepared to make such statements.

In many ways Fuchs reminds one of the older theological liberalism with its interest in the religion of Jesus, except that now it is not the religion of Jesus which matters but his faith. Fuchs really is concerned with a personal act of faith on the part of Jesus, an act of faith in God in the concrete historical situation of being confronted by the fate of John the Baptist.

Jesus himself did of necessity face a problem similar to the one his disciples faced after his death. Jesus had lived through the experience of the violent death of the Baptist. But if at the time of his own baptism Jesus without doubt recognized the gravity of eschatological judgment implied in the Baptist's message, then after the Baptist's death he would have to decide what this death meant for him.[58]

We need to make one further point about Fuchs's understanding of the nature of the literary form of the parables, and then we will be in a position to make a summary statement about Fuchs and his interpretation of the parables. He constantly refers to the parables as similitudes and as constantly talks about the *tertium comparationis.* He conceives of them as essentially a setting of two things side by side—e.g., the Kingdom of God and the finding of the treasure in the field, Matt. 13:44—which have a point of comparison between them through which the message of the parable is disclosed. We can see this in the following sample of Fuchs's work, his interpretation of The Mustard Seed.

The following *scopus* would emerge: God's miracle is accommodated to our need, the great to the little, the saviour to the one to be saved, the judge to the sinner, etc. The *tertium comparationis* would not be the equation, "small origin: vast results," but rather the inverse scheme, "*small stake: vast yield.*" The poetic means of expression and the choice of material are still, then, appropriate to Jewish linguistic style. The introductory double question indicates the need for caution in assessing the comparison, and the pious conclusion justifies the paradox of the comparison. But the similitude is no longer a pious address, nor is it a toying with irony; it has the effect of a sudden flash of lightning that illumines the night. It is now irresistible and self-sufficient. It has become a text, a preaching text. It gives to these people a context for which they could *not* hope, *nor* even reckon with. This is why it has indeed something miraculous about it: what no one sees, he already hears: his call through God. He who has ears to hear, let him hear.[59]

Fully recognizing the grave risk of oversimplification I would summarize Fuchs's position as follows. He begins with a concern for Jesus as the author of the parables and a particular concern for Jesus' *faith,* for the decision he made for God and his Kingdom when confronted by the fate of the Baptist. It is this decision of faith and its consequences—Jesus' relationship to God and his Kingdom, or, Jesus' understanding of time—which comes to language in the parables as they come to be *Sprachereignisse*. At the literary level the parable functions through its characteristic as a similitude with a *tertium comparationis*. If the hearer has ears to hear then the message can become a *Sprachereignis*, and the faith venture of Jesus can become the faith venture of the believer. That, or something very like it, would be my understanding of the Fuchs position, but I find him so difficult to follow that it may well be a misunderstanding, as well as an oversimplification.

In attempting to understand Fuchs and his interpretation of the parables, however, one is not limited to the work of Fuchs himself. Two of his pupils, Eta Linnemann and Eberhard Jüngel, addressed themselves at length to the parables of Jesus in self-conscious attempts to develop and apply the insights of their teacher. We turn first to Eta Linnemann who wrote a book in which she specifically discusses "the parables as 'Language Event.' "[60]

2. Eta Linnemann: Jesus of the Parables

Linnemann understands a successful parable as an event that decisively alters a situation, creating possibilities that did not exist before in the situation of the one addressed by the parable. Moreover the parable not only creates this new possibility, it also compels the making of a decision with regard to it. In the parable is "the moment of truth." Jesus' addressing his hearers by means of parables offers the possibility of achieving a new existence. "Jesus, by compelling his listeners to a decision through telling a parable, gives them the possibility of making a change of existence, of understanding themselves anew from the depths up, of achieving a 'new life.' "[61] The parables of Jesus present this possibility because "something decisive happens here through what is said."[62] Language, however, is subject to historical change, and language which created a language event in one historical situation may not do so in another. "The parables of Jesus have been passed down to us, but the 'language event' they effected cannot be passed down."[63] Although the language event of the parables cannot be transmitted it can be made intelligible, and it is the task of interpretation to make the language-event character of the parables to their original hearers intelligible to later readers. Not only can the language-event character of the parables be made intelligible, it can be repeated, and this happens in Christian preaching. "Preaching repeats the *event* that happened to Jesus' listeners through the parables of Jesus. It is the word . . . that alone makes this change of existence possible for man, that helps him from unbelief to faith."[64]

But Linnemann does more than discuss the parables as "language event"; she also offers a detailed exegesis of a number of them: The Good Samaritan, The Pharisee and the Tax-Collector, The Lost Sheep and The Lost Coin, The Prodigal Son, The Laborers in the Vineyard, The Great Supper, The Unique Opportunity (i.e., The Treasure and The Pearl), The Unmerciful Servant, The Sower, The Unjust Judge, The Wise and Foolish Virgins. We will look in some detail at her exegesis of The Good Samaritan, Luke 10:25–37.[65]

The exegesis begins with what is in effect a retelling of the story with a running commentary explaining things to the modern reader.

> Jesus uses the story of the Good Samaritan to answer the question of the scribe: "Who is my neighbour?" [The scribe] addresses Jesus as "Master," that is, "Rabbi," and so recognizes him as of equal status. He puts the question to him, as was then customary to test a strange Rabbi's knowledge. . . . The road from high-lying Jerusalem to Jericho down the Jordan valley leads through an uninhabited rocky wilderness and is notorious even to this day for attacks by robbers. . . . Priest and Levite go by without bothering about the victim. . . . What matters is the contrast between the attitude of these cult officials and that of the Samaritan. . . . It was, however, surprising and offensive for Jesus' hearers that it should be a Samaritan that was given the role of the merciful man. . . .

Linnemann continues in this vein through the story; then she gives her interpretation of the parable as a whole, which we will quote at length.

> Jesus uses the story of the good Samaritan to bring the question of the neighbour to the right place . . . he calls man forth from the place where he views the world simply as one that is basically controlled by a law that is as complete as possible, and on to the movement of authentic living.
>
> The story certainly leaves no doubt that what really matters is to act as the Samaritan did; and our conscience says a clear "yes" to this. . . . [We must] let ourselves be governed completely by the need of the man who confronts us. And that is not a thing that can be "done." As soon as we let ourselves be called out of the shell we have made of the world into the unprotected life

of real encounter, we shall unquestionably make the discovery that we are exposed to the possibility of failing in life, in fact are always doing so already. Then the question about our lives makes us realize that we can no longer ourselves provide the answer to it. . . . Perhaps one must say that only when this question of our lives finds an answer does life truly continue in real encounter, and that in Christian preaching what is at stake is precisely the answer to this question.[66]

This is interesting as an example of the kind of interpretation demanded by the "new hermeneutic" and its understanding of the parables as "language event." Linnemann had defined this as requiring that the language-event character of the parable in the situation of Jesus and his hearers should be made intelligible, so that it might then be repeated in Christian preaching. She now follows this hermeneutical process in the case of this parable by speaking of Jesus' using the story to "call man forth" from "inauthentic existence" and on to "authentic living," and by speaking of Christian preaching wherein we find the "real encounters" which provide the answer to the "question of our lives."

Linnemann follows this same hermeneutical process in the case of the other parables, although she is usually not so concerned with the possibility of repeating the language event in Christian preaching as she is in the case of The Good Samaritan. In The Pharisee and the Tax-collector, Luke 18:9–14, Jesus' verdict, "I say to you, this man went down to his house as a righteous man, not that one,"[67] reflects Jesus' own decision to "stake all on" the grace of God, a decision reflected in his preparedness to hold table-fellowship with tax-collectors and sinners. "Jesus wants to win the agreement of his listeners for his decision . . . but they can allow Jesus to be right only if they go through a radical conversion." In The Lost Sheep and The Lost Coin Jesus tells his contemporaries that repentance is "an event coming from God, the arrival of his Kingdom," and that "here and now in these objectionable table companions this deed of God has happened. . . . To come to agree with Jesus his listeners had to alter their ideas radically." The Prodigal Son also has reference to Jesus' table-fellowship with tax-collectors and sinners. "The reproach brought by the Pharisees was, 'How can you celebrate with such people?' Jesus' answer runs, 'The lost is found. This must be celebrated. I am joining in celebrating God's feast. And what are you doing?' " "Jesus' action turns the world upside

down, because it disturbs its orders. . . ." The Laborers in the Vineyard
is directed to a situation in which "Jesus stands before his listeners as
one who disturbs God's order," and the story is intended to convince
the listeners that they are in fact protesting against an "appearance of
goodness," that is, against a manifestation of goodness, against "an
epiphany, an appearance of God." The parable "connects the appearance of goodness with the Kingdom of God, which is now arriving."
The Great Supper is Jesus' response to the expectation of the Kingdom
of God, under the imagery of a banquet, as an event in the future, and
it is concerned to show "that the meal has already begun." The Kingdom is present opportunity for those who respond, just as we are
challenged "to have faith in the Gospel which invites to God's feast
now, and to act accordingly." The Hid Treasure and The Pearl of
Great Price together present "the unique opportunity"; they show Jesus
challenging his hearers, not simply to wait "until the nearness of God
had become visible in the reversal of the whole of life . . . [but] to take
seriously this nearness of God here and now."[68]

In general it must be admitted that Linnemann's interpretations of
the parables are not so striking, or so convincing, as her theoretical
discussion leads one to expect. The interest in the "language-event"
character of the parables is certainly justifiable, and it is an interesting
insight to think of hermeneutics in terms of making intelligible the
parable as language event in the situation of Jesus and his hearers, and
then, further, in terms of repeating the parable as language event
under certain subsequent conditions. In the interpretation of The Good
Samaritan this hermeneutical process shows promise, but the interpretation of the other parables does not live up to this promise. In practice
Linnemann has advanced over Jeremias only in stressing the "event"
character of the things from the ministry of Jesus that she finds reflected in the parables, or toward which she sees the parables as directed; and Jeremias would be happy, I am sure, to support her in most
of what she has said. Apart from stressing the "event" character of
repentance, or the table-fellowship with tax-collectors and sinners,
Linnemann moves the discussion forward in her appreciation of the
extremely radical thrust of the parables. In speaking of Jesus' demand-
ing that his listeners "alter their ideas radically," or of his turning "the
world upside down," or of him as "one who disturbs God's order," she
is sounding a note that is being heard a great deal in the current

American discussion, especially from Dominic Crossan. But in general her interpretation in practice does not live up to its promise in theory, and there is good reason for this: Linnemann has not paid sufficient attention to the literary-critical element in the hermeneutical process. But this is a problem she inherited from her teacher, so we will take it up below, when we comment critically on "the new hermeneutic and the parables of Jesus." Next, however, we turn to the second pupil of Ernst Fuchs to address himself to the parables, Eberhard Jüngel.

3. Eberhard Jüngel: Paulus und Jesus[69]

Jüngel's concern is to compare the Pauline doctrine of justification by faith with the proclamation of Jesus, and his interest in the parables is as the key to understanding the proclamation of Jesus as a whole. We will limit our concern, however, to his discussion of the parables. He reviews the previous discussion of the parables by Jülicher (under the rubric "The Aristotelian Approach to the Interpretation of the Parables"), Bultmann ("The Form-Critical Approach to the Analysis and Understanding of the Parables"), Dodd and Jeremias ("The Historicizing Approach to an Eschatological Interpretation of the Parables [!]"), and by Ernst Lohmeyer[70] and Ernst Fuchs ("The Hermeneutical Approach to an Eschatological Interpretation of the Parables"). I have been conscious of this review of the discussion in what I myself have written above, especially in connection with Jülicher,[71] but my interest now is in Jüngel's own views so I will not discuss his review of the discussion but rather turn immediately to the conclusions he draws from it. He draws twelve (!) conclusions,[72] of which the first five are the most important.

1. The proclamation of Jesus is to be understood as "language event." We may not distinguish between an outer mythological "form" and an inner existentialist (existentiale) "intent" as Bultmann's demythologizing program does.[73]
2. What is true of the proclamation of Jesus in general is certainly true of the parables in particular. The Kingdom of God is *not a theme* with which the parables are concerned.[74]
3. "From this we can establish a guiding principle for parable interpretation: *The Parables of Jesus bring the Kingdom of God into language (zur Sprache) as parable*."[75]
4. The literary understanding of parables in terms of "matter," "picture," and "*tertium comparationis*" (stemming from Jülicher) is misleading in that

it takes us into the schoolroom whereas the concern of the parables is not to teach us lessons but to confront us with ultimacy.[76]

5. The parables are a *collection* of pictures and stories which constantly have a single point of reference, a point of reference to human existence. "If the parables are concerned with the Kingdom of God, then human existence has its point in the *extra nos* of the Kingdom of God."[77]

The remaining seven points are not of the same interest or importance as these first five.[78] But these first five points offer a number of most challenging insights. If I may put some of these in my own words, then Jüngel challenges us to do justice to the integrity of the parable as a literary form and not, for example, to draw a non-parabolic "message" from it, whether moral, theological, existentialist, or some other kind. He challenges us, further, to seek an appropriate way of approach to the parables, claiming—in my view rightly—that the way pioneered by Jülicher with its distinction between *matter* (*Sache*) and *picture* (*Bild*) and its *tertium comparationis* was inappropriate. This point was a particular challenge to Jüngel's own teacher, Fuchs, who had made extensive use of this method of approach. But clearly for Jüngel himself the most important point of all is his italicized claim that the *parables of Jesus bring the Kingdom of God zur Sprache as parable*. Now I am not at all sure what that means, but Jüngel offers us a discussion of "The Kingdom of God as Parable"[79] in which he interprets a whole series of parables from this perspective and to which I now turn.

Jüngel begins his discussion of "the Kingdom of God as parable" by interpreting The Hid Treasure and The Pearl of Great Price (Matt. 13:44–46). These are understood as challenges to the hearer to allow himself to be drawn into the parables so that he who seeks the Kingdom may suddenly discover himself to have been "found" by it.

The truth is that the attitude and actions of the lucky finder are so dominated by the overwhelming value of that which is found that the apparently *passive* element (that which is found) becomes the active element, over against which the attitude and activity of the finder demanded by the discovery, that is, the apparently active element, can only be regarded as a passivity corresponding to that active element; it becomes a "non-action" which "corresponds to the action of God"—because God has already acted![80]

This interpretation makes the parable very much a paradigm of the activity of God and the response of man, a paradigm of the relationship between God and man. Jüngel's interpretation of other parables follows this same pattern, often in language very reminiscent of a sermon. The Dragnet (Matt. 13:47–48) concerns the gathering and the sorting of fish; its point is that the people "gathered" by the proclamation of Jesus are challenged to decision in prospect of the "sorting" to be expected in relationship to the coming of the Kingdom of God. Jesus "*guarantees* his hearers an opportunity for decision."[81] The Seed Growing by Itself (Mark 4:26–29) is another guarantee by Jesus to his hearers. The proclamation of the Kingdom of God by Jesus in this parable establishes the present of his hearers as a time free *from* the past (the time of sowing) and free *for* the future (the time of harvest). It is guaranteed as a time of hearing, and hence of the opportunity for decision.[82] In The Mustard Seed (Mark 4:30–32) Jesus leads his hearers to consider the present in light of the "wonderful future of the Kingdom (of God)." But there is more to the matter than that because "the power of the coming Kingdom of God is already present in this parable (*ist im diesem Gleichnis da*)." Jesus himself is so convinced that the power of God is at work in the present that he "dares, by means of the parable of the Mustard Seed, to gather men together, to summon them for the Kingdom (*für die Basileia zu berufen*),[83] so that those who are summoned for the Kingdom then belong themselves to the beginning of that wonderful end."[84]

Jüngel offers an interpretation of other parables—The Importunate Friend (Luke 11:5–8), The Unjust Steward (Luke 16:1–7), The Prodigal son (Luke 15:11–32), The Laborers in the Vineyard (Matt. 20:1–15)[85]—but we will discuss further only his interpretation of The Good Samaritan (Luke 10:30–35).[86]

Jüngel understands The Good Samaritan as an exemplary story,[87] and he interprets it without reference to its context, the lawyer's question, which he regards as secondary. The story turns on the contrast between the unloving Jew and the loving Samaritan, as both are related to the man in need of love. Priest, Levite, and Samaritan all experience *need-of-love* (*Liebebedürftigkeit*) as an *event* (*Ereignis*), but the priest and Levite ignore it while the Samaritan responds to it. The contrast between the Samaritan and the Jews becomes the more emphatic when one remembers that, according to rabbinical teaching, no Jew could accept an act of almsgiving or of love from a Samaritan because to do so would delay the redemption of Israel. As a story The

Good Samaritan is concerned with fulfilling and not fulfilling the Jewish law of loving the neighbor.[88] It shows the Jewish priest and Levite, bound by that law, as not fulfilling it, although it is for them the law of God, while it shows the Samaritan, not bound by that law, fulfilling it as the natural law of man's conscience. The exemplary story shows *to us* Jesus as a preacher of the law interpreting the law as fulfilled in an event of love occasioned by an event of need-for-love. Jesus can do this "because he is speaking out of the experience of the love of God as an event." By its power as analogy the exemplary story confronts *us* with the love of God as an event as it directs our attention toward the need-for-love of our fellow men. As Jüngel interprets the parable, Jesus, the preacher of the law to his contemporaries, becomes Jesus, the preacher of the law to us. Jüngel bridges the hermeneutical gulf by means of the sermon!

4. The "New Hermeneutic" and the Parables of Jesus

Having discussed Fuchs, Linnemann, and Jüngel separately, I now turn to some reflections on them as a group of scholars concerned to interpret the parables according to the interpretative method of the "new hermeneutic." I will offer these reflections under the various rubrics I am using throughout this study.

At the level of *textual criticism* the group has little to offer. Insofar as it is a matter of concern at all they follow the methods which Jeremias had made traditional. But it is difficult to interpret the text of a parable without reference to its gospel context even when one recognizes that the context is secondary and hence irrelevant. Linnemann interpreted The Good Samaritan in the context of the lawyer's question, while Jüngel saw it as a sermon on the text of the Jewish legal maxim involved in the discussion leading up to the question, even though he specifically recognized that context as secondary. The problem seems to be that some of the settings are apposite—The Good Samaritan as relating to an interpretation of Deut. 6:5 and Lev. 19:18; The Prodigal Son as relating to a dispute about table-fellowship with tax-collectors and sinners—and at the same time representative of the situation of the ministry of Jesus as it must have been. Jesus no doubt debated aspects of the law and there was certainly dispute about his eating with the outcast, and the tendency is to accept the setting as actual at the historical level even though we know it to be secondary at the literal level.

We shall see that the SBL Parables Seminar became very much aware of this problem in connection with The Good Samaritan.

As for *historical criticism*, the work of both Fuchs and Linnemann is very interesting. Fuchs has a good definition of historical-critical method. He is concerned to reach the *intention* of the text with the help of the varied aids: "the furthering of the history of word meanings with the aid of lexicons, grammar, literary and style criticism and parallel materials; research into the historical circumstances which produced the text; comparative examinations of the history of ideas and of the history of religion, etc."[89] Linnemann's running commentaries on the parables present an excellent historical understanding of the text, building on the foundations Jeremias had laid and working quite in his style. Jüngel also provides some useful information, especially the fact, important to the interpretation of The Good Samaritan, that, according to rabbinical teaching, for an Israelite to accept alms from a Samaritan was to delay the redemption of Israel.

But the most important aspect of the work of this group of scholars at the historical level is their concern for Jesus as the author of the parables. Fuchs sees a very close relationship between personal decisions which Jesus made and the parables which he taught, and Linnemann follows him closely in this.[90] As we have seen, Fuchs is fully prepared to speak of Jesus' personal faith, and of that faith as reached by resolute decision in face of the fate of the Baptist, while Linnemann echoes this preparedness to speak of Jesus' personal decisions in her interpretation of The Pharisee and the Tax-collector as reflecting Jesus' decision to stake all on the grace of God. One can dismiss this as unwarrantable psychologizing about Jesus, as Bultmann did, but then Fuchs and Linnemann could retort that this is not a case of psychologizing about Jesus but of recognizing that a person is necessarily involved in his word, that the message necessarily involves the messenger, that a challenge to decision necessarily reflects a decision already made by the challenger.[91] But Fuchs's concern for the parables as verbalizations of Jesus' understanding of his own situation in the world and before God is not to be dismissed lightly. In the American discussion this concern was voiced by Amos Wilder,[92] in terms different from and more persuasive than those of Fuchs, and it remains as an issue to be faced in the discussion of the interpretation of the parables of Jesus.

As I indicated at the close of my discussion of Linnemann's book above, the "new hermeneutic" is most vulnerable at the level of _literary criticism_. The concern of the movement for literary form and language is very real but idiosyncratic. We need to state this judgment with some care—if we are both to appreciate the importance of what the movement was trying to do, and also to see why it must ultimately be judged to have failed. The movement attracted attention, and showed real promise, precisely because of its concern for literary form and language; to understand the reason for its failure is therefore to take a long step forward in one's understanding of hermeneutics, and in the function of literary criticism in the hermeneutical process. In what follows I shall be particularly dependent upon the presentation of the "new hermeneutic" and its understanding of parable interpretation in James M. Robinson's contribution to the Colwell _Festschrift_, "Jesus' Parables as God Happening."[93]

We have seen that Fuchs is concerned with the _tertium comparationis_ of the parables. He is concerned with the fact that a parable compares one set of concepts to another, that it permits, and indeed demands, a rational judgment with regard to the better known set of concepts that must then be applied, by analogy, to the lesser known. Robinson puts this very well.

The internal relationship or organization clearly discernible in the one set of concepts clarifies by analogy the relation only dimly sensed in the other set. The relationship of A to B is analogous to and hence clarifying for that of C to D. We have to do with the classical _analogia proportionalitatis_ or _analogia relationis_. The proportionateness of the two sets of concepts means that they share one judgment, the _tertium comparationis_, the single point of the parable. Thus the parable is one of the forms of rational argument, making use of the point of a picture to argue for an equivalent point in another dimension of reality. This means that the parable has a "picture half" (the language of the parable) and a "material half" (the "higher" or "spiritual" dimension, e.g., the Kingdom of God).[94]

The essential point in this, as in the work of Jülicher from which it is drawn, is that the parable functions by comparison; one thing is compared to another, "The Kingdom of God is like . . ." But the conclusion that the parable is therefore "one of the forms of rational argument, making use of the point of a picture to argue for an equivalent point in another dimension of reality" is dependent upon the use of Aristotelian categories to understand the element of comparison in the parables. It is dependent upon the assumption that the parables of Jesus are "forms of rational argument," and this is a very questionable assumption. One look at the use of parables by the ancient Jewish rabbis, a look Jülicher had not taken, shows parables being used to explicate or illustrate an aspect of the law, or as weapons of attack or defense in controversies concerning its interpretation. The breadth and variety of the use of parables in ancient Judaism raises serious doubts about the validity of Jülicher's understanding as it was followed and developed by Fuchs and Robinson.

Much more important than this, however, is the fact pointed out by Jüngel,[95] namely, that this understanding of the nature of the parable is at variance with the fundamental insight of the "new hermeneutic" itself. The "new hermeneutic" was concerned with the parable as the disclosure of ultimacy, and this is a very different thing from the parable as a form of rational argument. The fundamental insight of the "new hermeneutic" itself should have led to a consideration of a form of language which uses comparison but which can serve as a vehicle for the disclosure of ultimacy; it should have led to a consideration of the nature, function, and power of *metaphor*. But this could not be, because the practitioners of the "new hermeneutic" were not literary scholars, nor were they in conversation with literary scholars. So the development of this insight had to wait until the discussion moved to America, and it had to wait particularly for Robert Funk, who was in conversation with literary scholars.

The practitioners of the "new hermeneutic" moved most naturally from New Testament scholarship to philosophy and theology, rather than to literary scholarship. So they sought to understand the impact of the parables of Jesus as a "language event" or "God happening" on the basis of two considerations beyond the essential first step of seeing the parable functioning by means of comparison: an insight from the later work of the German philosopher Heidegger concerning the power of language to disclose being, and a theological conviction that in Jesus himself—and hence in his characteristic language, the parables—the ultimate disclosure of being is to be found.

Heidegger came to concern himself with language as having a primordial function, a function whereby the subject matter of the language comes to encounter man in language.[96] Heidegger's model is poetic language. "He takes a text from Hölderlin:

> Full of merit, and yet poetically, dwells Man on this earth.

What is man as poet? 'Poetry is the act of establishing by the word and in the word.' The poet names being and so brings it to stand."[97] It is not that the poet creates being, but rather that the poet allows being to speak through him. In language at this level "being itself is at stake."[98] But then man himself is at stake, since man lives out of his relationship to the ultimate reality which discloses itself in language: "Language is the means by which man exists historically,"[99] because he exists historically (i.e., in his concrete historicality—remember, Heidegger is also the existentialist of *Sein und Zeit* who influenced Bultmann), out of his relationship to the ultimate reality, being, and because "language is the house of being."[100]

One tends to think of Heidegger in the Black Forest, leading the life of a recluse, "meditating in silence, pondering language, and exhibiting an increasing tendency to the poetic mode."[101] But there can be no doubt of the validity of his insight that reality with a power to shape men's lives, with the ability to transform men's perceptions of meaning in existence, can and does disclose itself in certain kinds of language, especially in the primordial language of the poet. But this point, again, has ramifications at the level of literary criticism. If poetic language is, or can be, primordial language with the power to disclose being, then Heidegger will not have been the first to notice this. Poets and critics of poetry will have "noticed" it also; indeed they can be expected to have explored this aspect of language both creatively and critically.[102] The next step from this insight should therefore have been a step toward poets and critics of poetry, to learn how far and in what ways they could help us to understand this dimension of language, a dimension new to us as New Testament scholars, but not to them. But the "new hermeneutic" is primarily a Christian theological movement, so the next step taken was not one toward a better understanding of the power of poetic language to mediate an ultimate reality, to disclose being. Rather it was a step toward Jesus, an immediate attempt to use the insight the better to understand Jesus as the revelation of God, as the primal discloser of being, and to understand his language as the language in which "God's reign is inescapable, as invitation and challenge, grace and judgment," as the language "in which God's reign happens as reality's true possibility."[103] And this step was taken in connection with the parables because, as Fuchs sees the matter, "it is his parables that are typical of Jesus . . . in the parables Jesus' understanding of his situation 'enters language' in a special way. . . . Like the man who found treasure, or the pearl merchant who found the one pearl of great price, the hearer must stake all on one thing—that he win the future which Jesus proclaims to him."[104]

I do not dispute the right of Fuchs and the other practitioners of the "new hermeneutic" to have as their primary concern Jesus as the one who discloses the reality by means of which alone "a sinner . . . [may flee] for refuge to that God from whose judgment he had previously to flee in fear,"[105] and to consider the parables as, therefore, "God's advent in language."[106] But to one whose primary concern is to develop a hermeneutical theory by means of which the parables may be interpreted both in terms of their historical meaning on the lips of Jesus, and also in terms of their potential meaning for subsequent and different readers and situations, it does seem to me to take some short cuts; the "new hermeneutic" ignores many literary-critical steps along the way that ought most carefully to be explored. Fuchs and his colleagues are too quick to get to the sermon, too anxious to see the sermon as the ultimate model for the interpretation of the parables.

This brings me to the fourth and final element in the hermeneutical process, the act of interpretation itself, the dynamic *interaction between text and interpreter that is hermeneutics itself.* In point of concern for this the "new hermeneutic" can certainly not be faulted. Fuchs and his pupils build on Bultmann's understanding of hermeneutics as dialogue between text and interpreter, and they emphasize very strongly that it is a dialogue in which the interpreter interprets the text and the text the interpreter. Indeed they emphasize this latter aspect of the matter even more strongly than Bultmann had done. For Fuchs the text is not the servant of an understanding of existence which can be derived from it by the hermeneutical process of demythologizing; rather it is "a master that directs us into the language-character of our existence, in which we exist 'before God.' "[107] Funk puts the matter as follows. "Since Bultmann is exercised over the opaqueness of biblical language, he wants to demythologize it. For Fuchs and Ebeling, however, what requires demythologizing is not so much the language of the text as modern man. Modern man is to be interpreted by the text, not the text by modern man."[108] But the problem is the omnipresent model of the sermon. The text of the parables addresses modern man as do the words of a preacher, upon whose lips the words of a man become the word of God because this is what happens in true preaching.

Fuchs is quite self-conscious about the primacy of a concern for preaching. In the Preface to his *Studies of the Historical Jesus* he writes:

How can the very texts, which have become the sources for the analysis of the historical-critical method, again become the texts of a sermon? What do we have to do at our desks, if we want later to set the text in front of us in the pulpit? . . . We do not abandon the historical question. However, we do guard against the naive opinion that it might be possible to understand the New Testament without reflecting on its purpose. That purpose is preaching; at least it included preaching.[109]

As was the case in my discussion of Fuchs and the "new hermeneutic" under the rubric of literary criticism, I am not at all concerned to dispute Fuchs's right to understand the hermeneutical task in this way. But it does seem to me that, as was the case in his concern for Jesus as revealer of ultimate reality, he turns too rapidly to the model of the sermon. He hears the parables of Jesus, historically, as *sermons* addressed by Jesus to his own contemporaries, and for this reason he can use language concerning them that is hard to justify on grounds of historical or literary criticism. In his exegesis of The Mustard Seed, for example, he can say that the similitude "has become a text, a preaching text," which gives to the original hearers of Jesus "a context for which they could *not* hope, *nor* even reckon with." There is "something miraculous about it: what no one sees, he already hears: his call through God."[110] Now no historical or literary critic could make a statement like that, as a historian or literary critic, but Fuchs can and does make a hundred statements like that, because for him the sermon is the dominant hermeneutical model. Moreover, he teaches his pupils to think in this way. We saw above how Jüngel, for example, can view The Good Samaritan as a sermon preached by Jesus to his contemporaries on a Jewish legal text, and then move immediately to considering it as a sermon preached by Jesus to us, the twentieth-century readers and interpreters.

The "new hermeneutic" is a hermeneutical method dominated by the model of the sermon. The parables of Jesus are thought of as sermons preached by Jesus to his contemporaries, and hence we find language used which is natural to the context of a preacher and his congregation —decisions which have been made by the preacher and which he challenges his congregation to make in turn; the present as challenge and opportunity in prospect of the future as God's future, and so on. But this language is only proper in reference to Jesus if the sermon is the proper model for understanding him at the historical level. It is by no means self-evident to me that this is in fact the case. In the "new hermeneutic" the sermon also serves as the model in the act of interpretation itself. The beginning of the hermeneutical process is the act of Jesus preaching a sermon to his contemporaries; the end of the hermeneutical process is Fuchs, Linnemann, and Jüngel preaching a sermon to their contemporaries, a sermon which has Jesus' sermon as a text. The sermon is the ubiquitous model for every stage of the hermeneutical process. It is by no means self-evident to me that this should be the case.

C. AMOS WILDER, EARLY CHRISTIAN RHETORIC: THE LANGUAGE OF THE GOSPEL

In Europe, Joachim Jeremias brought to a climax a period of work on the parables of Jesus that had begun with Jülicher's demonstration that they were indeed parables and not allegories, and Ernst Fuchs and the "new hermeneutic" went on to explore the challenge of the parables as "language-event." The unfinished business in all this comes under the rubric of *literary criticism,* for, as I argued above, the weakness in the treatment of the parables thus far had been pre-eminently a weakness at the level of literary criticism. After Fuchs and the "new hermeneutic," interest in the discussion shifts to America, where the weakness of the European approach was recognized, attempts were made to remedy it, and a whole new discussion got under way.

In the vanguard of the American work stands Amos Wilder, distinguished poet, literary critic, and New Testament scholar. As a New Testament scholar he fully appreciated the discussion among New Testament scholars; as a literary critic he was in a position to begin to remedy the deficiency in that discussion at the level of literary criticism; while as a poet he was able to appreciate both the creative force of poetry as primordial language, and the dynamics of the relationship between the poet's own vision and that which comes to expression in his words. A further thing about Wilder that matters very much is his influence on younger American scholars. All the American scholars contributing to the current discussion of the interpretation of the parables have been deeply influenced by him.

The work of Wilder's which concerns us here is his book, *Early Christian Rhetoric: The Language of the Gospel.*[111] This book offers only a brief discussion of the parables,[112] but it proved to be seminal because of the combination of insights and skills he brought to the interpretation of the parables. For the first time a scholar looked at the parables who, on the one hand, fully appreciated the results of the discussion among New Testament scholars, while, on the other hand, was able to bring insights from the worlds of literary creativity and of literary criticism.

Wilder enters the discussion at the level of literary criticism, concerned with the literary features of the parables, but moving backward from there to a historical concern as he attempts to understand the creative vision of their author, Jesus, and moving forward from there toward the interpreter as he attempts to understand the particular, distinctive impact of the literary form and language of the parables. He begins by distinguishing various kinds of parables. "Some of the parables are straight narratives about a given individual case, ending with an application: The Good Samaritan, The Rich Fool. . . . Here we have 'example stories,' not symbolic narrative. The point in these cases is that we should go and do likewise, or take warning by a given example." But then there are also parables like that of the Lost Sheep, where "the upshot is not that we should or should not go and do likewise." Here we have rather "an extended image—the shepherd's retrieval of the lost sheep and his joy—a narrative image which reveals rather than exemplifies."[113]

This distinction between the parable as exemplary story and the parable as revelatory image is an important one, and Wilder, having made it, goes on to emphasize that "it is this revelatory character of Jesus' parables which is to be stressed," quoting with approval Günther Bornkamm's dictum, "the parables are the preaching itself," and claiming that Jesus used "extended images to unveil mysteries . . . above all to mediate reality and life."[114] Moreover, he claims the support of modern literary criticism in this, making a most important distinction between a simile and a metaphor in the process. "This understanding of Jesus' figures of speech is supported by our modern discussion of the metaphor in literary criticism. A simile sets one thing over against another: the less known is clarified by the better known. But in the metaphor we have an image with a certain shock to the imagination which directly conveys a vision of what is signified."[115] What the previous discussion had differentiated as similitude and parable is here identified, not as simile, but as metaphor. The similitude is a metaphor, and the parable is an extended metaphor. The idea of a comparison which clarifies is abandoned in favor of the metaphor which reveals. That metaphor can be simple or extended but it is always essentially a revelatory image. But Wilder recognizes that even with this emphasis as central, there still is reason to acknowledge that Jesus also taught "teaching parables and polemic-parables, like those of the Prodigal Son or the Workers in the Vineyard in which the revelatory-image is used to justify and defend Jesus' mission. . . . The larger observation is that Jesus uses figures of speech in an immense variety of ways."[116] But the idea of the parable as revelatory image remains central.

Another literary aspect of the parables which concerns Wilder is their realism. They are "human and realistic"; one may even speak of their "secularity." In these parables a shepherd is an actual shepherd and not "a flash-back to God as the Shepherd of Israel."[117] The realism and actuality of the parables are important because they command the attention of the listeners at the level of the actuality of their everyday existence. "[Jesus] is leading men to make a judgment and to come to a decision. The stories are so told as to compel men to see things as they are, by analogy indeed. Sluggish or dormant awareness and conscience are thus aroused. The parables make men give attention, come alive and face things. And they do this by evoking men's everyday experience."[118] Or, again, "the parables of Jesus, in addition to their revelatory character, are shaped more consistently towards a direct personal appeal or challenge, and their sobriety of style and sharpness of focus serve well the fatefulness of the issue in view."[119]

Against the background of these considerations Wilder turns to a discussion of the "parables of the Kingdom": The Sower, Seed Growing of Itself, Mustard Seed, from Mark 4; The Leaven, Hid Treasure, Pearl of Great Price, from Matthew 13.[120] These are to be counted as authentic parables of Jesus. "The characteristic design, the tight form of these utterances helped to guarantee them against change and supplementation. A coherent image-story is resistant to change. . . . The parables of Jesus have an organic unity and coherence."[121] But there is a further criterion for the authenticity of these parables, and it is a characteristic which they share with other forms of Jesus' speech. Jesus used various forms of speech; he "used trope and metaphor in the most varied way," but there is always the same element of "force" and "significance" in his imagery. In this connection Wilder makes a statement that is important, both in connection with understanding the natural force of the parables, and also in providing the link between the parables and the use by Jesus of the symbol, Kingdom of God, in other forms of speech.

In the parables we have action-images. But these are only one kind of metaphor, extended metaphor. Jesus' communication, just because it is fresh and dynamic, is necessarily plastic. Now we know that a true metaphor or symbol is more than a sign, it is a bearer of the reality to which it refers. The hearer not only learns about that reality, he participates in it. He is invaded by it. Here lies the power and fatefulness of art. Jesus' speech had the character not of instruction and ideas but of compelling imagination, of spell, of mythical shock and transformation.[122]

"A true metaphor or symbol is more than a sign, it is a bearer of the reality to which it refers." These words are the essential clue to understanding both the symbolic language of the Kingdom sayings and the metaphorical language of the parables on the lips of Jesus. But there is a further point about this language which is important to Wilder, and that is its relationship to the vision of the poet using it. Such language is not used idly; the poet who turns to symbol and metaphor does so because of some vision of reality which demands expression, and which can only find expression in such evocative or mind-teasing language. So it is with the parables of Jesus, as Wilder understands them. They are not "homiletic illustration drawn from nature." The Sower (Mark 4:3–8) "is not just an example of what happens every day offered as an encouragement," nor is The Seed Growing of Itself (Mark 4:26–28) to be taken in such "a banal sense." Their real authority and power emerge when we see them "in Jesus' own situation," that is, in the situation of Jesus addressing his disciples, in the situation of Jesus seeking to impart to his disciples "his own vision by the power of metaphor."[123]

The secret of the power of the parables of the Kingdom then, as Jesus addressed them to his listeners in their original historical situation, lies not only in their reality-bearing power as metaphor, but also in the fact that the reality they bear is that of Jesus' own faith. "It is Jesus' own certain faith that paints in the feature of the great harvest. The formal felicity and coherence of these parables reflect the intensity of his own vision."[124] But this is not only the secret of the power of the parables in the original situation of Jesus using them as he addresses his hearers; it is also the secret of their power as we seek to interpret them in a later day and a different situation. "For us, too, to find the meaning of the parable we must identify ourselves with that inner secret of Jesus' faith and faithfulness."[125] In this context Wilder quotes Fuchs. "The distinctive feature in the teaching aspect of Jesus' proclamation is the analogical power with which tacitly he sets forth himself, his own obedience, as a measure for the attention of his disciples."[126]

The fact that Wilder can quote Fuchs in this context shows that he is close to him in his fundamental concern for Jesus, and for the highly personal aspects of the message of Jesus. But this should not be allowed to obscure the point that in fact Wilder and Fuchs are far apart at the very point at which they seem to be close: their interest in the highly personal aspects of the parables of Jesus. Fuchs is interested in Jesus as the supreme revelation of God to man, and hence as the one who actualized the possibility of faith in his own experience, and who verbalized the possibility of faith for his hearers in his parables. Wilder, on the other hand, is interested in Jesus as a poet who imparted to his hearers his own vision of reality in the metaphorical language of his parables. But both are raising the question as to whether there is or is not an essential relationship between the author and the text of the parables as the interpreter seeks to interpret that text in a subsequent and quite different situation. They would both maintain that there is such a relationship, though on different grounds.

It is, I hope, evident that I regard Amos Wilder as enormously important in the discussion of both Kingdom of God and the parables in the message of Jesus. He is important because he taught us to see the significance of the literary factors in the Kingdom proclamation and the parables, the one as symbol and the other as metaphor. I have attempted to develop the former insight myself; the latter was developed in the subsequent American discussion of the parables.

D. ROBERT W. FUNK: THE PARABLE AS METAPHOR

By the early nineteen sixties the discussion of the interpretation of the parables had reached a stage where one could be definite about results and prospects. At the level of *textual criticism* the discussion was in good shape in that Jeremias had established the methodology for determining the text of the parables as told by Jesus, a methodology wherein development and refinement were possible but where the main lines to be followed were firmly established. Moreover, at this level two new factors were at work which were to be of great help: the discovering of the Gospel of Thomas, and the rise of redaction criticism. After 1959 the Coptic text and good translations of the Gospel of Thomas were readily available[127] and this gospel offered new versions of many of the parables of Jesus, versions, moreover, which seemed to represent a tradition which had diverged from that represented by the earlier canonical gospels.[128] Most parable interpreters came to hold the versions of the parables in Thomas to be independent of the versions in the canonical gospels and hence a valuable addition to our resources for reconstructing the original text of a given parable.[129] At the same time redaction criticism was developing as a discipline,[130] and this meant that scholars were becoming more sensitive to the editorial hand of the evangelist, both in the text of the parable and in the setting of the parable in the text of the gospel. With these two additional resources, and with the development and refinement of the characteristic Jeremias methodology, interpreters of the parables could be increasingly confident of the quality of the text they finally sat down with in the act of interpretation.

At the level of *historical criticism* also, the interpreter of the parables had good tools with which to work in the early nineteen sixties. A generation of form criticism had given life of Jesus research a fundamental understanding of the synoptic gospels and the traditions they use which made it possible to build on firmer ground than ever before, while the resurgence of interest in the "question of the historical Jesus" had set scholars particularly concerned with life of Jesus research basically to the task of building.[131] The interpreter of the parables therefore had firmer information about the ministry of Jesus and about the non-parabolic teaching than had been available before. Then there was the immense amount of work Jeremias had done in enabling us to listen to the parables with first-century Palestinian ears so far as the characters and situations depicted in them were concerned. All in all the interpreters were in a very good position with regard to reaching a historical understanding of the parables. As was the case at the textual level, they also had good tools with which to work at the level of historical understanding.

Things were, however, very different at the level of *literary criticism*. At this level Jülicher had begun with categories drawn from the schoolrooms of classical antiquity and had ended up with a series of lessons in morality. Jeremias had read the parables in the context of the use of parables by the rabbis of ancient Judaism and found that their principal concern was to illustrate, explicate, or defend the general message of Jesus, as the rabbis used parables to illustrate, explicate, or defend their interpretation of the law. The "new hermeneutic" had sounded a most important new note in challenging us to see the parables as "language event" or "God happening," but the inadequacies of this movement in literary scholarship, as well as its passion for the ubiquitous model of the sermon, prevented it from making any further progress.

The way forward here lay in returning to Dodd's original insight that at its simplest the parable "is a metaphor or simile drawn from nature or common life, arresting the hearer by its vividness or strangeness, and leaving the mind in sufficient doubt about its precise application to tease it into active thought."[132] This insight could serve as a point of departure, but it cried out for further development in terms of Wilder's insight that metaphor "is a bearer of the reality to which it refers," and in terms of the understanding of metaphor developed in literary scholarship. At the same time we should be aware of the insight of the "new hermeneutic" concerning the parable as "language event." All this is easy to see in retrospect; seeing it in prospect was a very different matter. It is Robert Funk's enormously important contribution to the discussion that he saw this in prospect, and that he carried this out in practice in a brilliant chapter on "The Parable as Metaphor" in his book *Language, Hermeneutic, and Word of God,* published in 1966.[133]

The chapter begins with Dodd's definition of the parable, quoted immediately above, which is analyzed into four points: "(1) the parable is a metaphor or simile which may (a) remain simple, (b) be elaborated into a picture, or (c) be expanded into a story; (2) the metaphor or simile is drawn from nature or common life; (3) the metaphor arrests the hearer by its vividness or strangeness; and (4) the application is left imprecise in order to tease the hearer into his own application."[134] Funk begins his development of this insight by concentrating on the fourth point: that the parable leaves the mind "in sufficient doubt about its precise application to tease it into active thought," which he takes to mean that the parable is not closed "until the listener is drawn into it as a participant."[135] This is very important since it links together two different literary features of the parables as having the same function. If the parable as metaphor draws the listener into it as participant then so does the parable as metaphor extended to narrative. When the metaphor is extended to narrative it is extended to *realistic* narrative, and realistic narrative also functions to draw the listener into it as participant. So it becomes a very important and deliberate feature of the parables of Jesus that they are designed, indeed they are doubly designed, to draw the listener into them as participant.

A further consequence of this same insight is that the parables can be seen to involve "a transference of judgment" on the part of the listener, inducing the listener "to make a judgment upon the situation set out in the parable and to apply that judgment, either explicitly or implicitly, to the matter at hand." In this the parables are to be distinguished from exemplary stories "where the application is evident in the example."[136]

A last consequence of this insight is that the parable must be regarded as open-ended so far as potentiality for meaning is concerned because to give the parable one particular application is to close off the possibility of the hearer's participation in the parable itself. Now the listener can only concern himself or herself with the meaning, a consequence of which is that "the parable, once the application has been made and reduced to didactic language, is expendable."[137] So if the parable is to continue to function by drawing the listener into it as participant, and by inviting a transference of judgment, then it must be kept open-ended; its potentiality of meaning is not to be exhausted by any one listener's apprehension of meaning, by any one act of transference of judgment. The parable is like the tensive symbol in that its potentiality of meaning is not exhausted by any one apprehension of that meaning.[138]

Dodd's definition had as its first point that a parable is a metaphor or simile. Funk now turns to this and begins to make an important distinction between the two, a distinction which will lead to the establishment of the conclusion that the parable is actually a metaphor and not a simile.

The distinction between simile and metaphor is that simile uses the prepositions "as" or "like" while metaphor uses only the verb "to be." "To say A is *like* B is a simile. . . . To say A *is* B is metaphor." But this is much more than a grammatical distinction; it is also a distinction in terms of essential function. In a simile "the less known is clarified by the better known," but in a metaphor "two discrete and not entirely comparable elements" are juxtaposed, and this juxtaposition "produces an impact upon the imagination and induces a vision of that which cannot be conveyed by prosaic or discursive speech." Another way of making this distinction is to go back to the point that a simile and a metaphor have in common "an element of comparison or analogy." But this element of comparison or analogy *functions* differently in a simile than it does in a metaphor. In a simile the element of comparison "is illustrative," but in a metaphor "it is creative of meaning."[139] This insight also enables us to see the relationship among simile, metaphor, and *symbol*. All three involve the element of comparison. If, in a simile, A is *like* B, and, in a metaphor, A *is* B, then, in symbolic language, B *represents* A.[140] "Symbolism is metaphor with the primary term suppressed."[141]

Obviously this is a most important point with regard to understanding both the parables of Jesus and also his use of the symbolic language of the Kingdom of God. If we may say or imply, "The Kingdom of God is *like* . . . ," then we have a simile: the Kingdom, or some aspect of a possible understanding of it, is being *illustrated*; the purpose of the parable is then pedagogical, or, perhaps better, parenetical. If we may say or imply, "The Kingdom of God *is* . . . ," then we have *metaphor*: the Kingdom of God is not being illustrated for us; rather the Kingdom confronts us through the power of metaphor to produce an impact upon the imagination, to be the bearer of reality, to induce vision. If we can hear Jesus say, "If I by the finger of God cast out demons, then the Kingdom of God *has come*," then we have symbolic language: in some way the exorcisms *represent* the Kingdom of God. This is a point to which we shall return in our concluding discussion.

At the moment we remain with the distinction between the parable as simile and the parable as metaphor. It is a most important distinction, and it is one not affected by verbal extension. A simile extended to a picture or a narrative is still governed by the *as* or *like,* and it remains essentially illustrative. A metaphor extended to a picture or narrative is still governed by the *is,* and it confronts the hearer with a new vision of reality by its power as metaphor. We shall see that Dominic Crossan particularly emphasizes and explores this aspect of the parables.

We should perhaps stress that these are modern literary distinctions, as was the distinction we made in our first study between "steno-" and "tensive" symbols. But this does not matter, any more than it matters whether Jesus actually began his parables characteristically with an actual or implied Aramaic equivalent of "The Kingdom of God is *as* . . ." or "is *like* . . ." or simply "*is.* . . ." The question is whether the parables can be shown to function as literary objects in a way characteristic of what we have defined as a simile, or in a way characteristic of what we have defined as a metaphor, or—as is most probably the case—in both ways, the function varying from parable to parable. Whichever is the case, we are on the way to a clearer and better understanding of the parables.

Let us return to Funk's discussion of the parable as metaphor. Having made the distinction between the simile as "illustrative" and the metaphor as "creative of meaning," he goes on to explore further the creative function of metaphor. "Metaphor," he asserts, "raises the potential for new meaning." It "redirects attention, not to this or that attribute but, by means of imaginative shock, to a circumspective whole that presents itself as focalized in this or that thing or event." Metaphor has always been a particular predilection of poets.

If A stands for the fresh insight that beckons the poet mutely, and B stands for the available language fund, a fund that has acquired conventions and is presided over by tradition, the poet must allow A to come to expression *through* and *out of* B. A is not "there" except as it enters language, but it cannot, because it is a fresh insight, be merely accommodated in conventional language. . . . The metaphor is a means of modifying the tradition . . . and as such it is not expendable in the apprehension of A.

In this connection Funk quotes Barfield with approval. " 'It is not surprising,' Barfield muses, 'that philologists should have had such a

vivid hallucination of metaphor bending over the cradle of meaning.' "[142] Funk echoes this language himself: "The poet summons and
is summoned by metaphor in the travail of the birth of meaning."[143]
Further, the metaphor "is open-ended temporally . . . it opens onto a
plurality of situations, a diversity of audiences, and the future." So far
as the future is concerned, "it does not foreclose but discloses the
future; it invites but does not come to rest in eventful actualization."
The metaphor therefore may be said to have a "temporal horizon," and
closely connected with this is an "existential tenor." "Imagination and
its metaphorical vehicle give themselves to being in process, to unfinished reality, so to speak, which they do not merely report but actually
participate in." So we return to the element of participation so important to Funk. "The metaphor, like the parable, is incomplete until the
hearer is drawn into it as participant."[144]

Funk next turns to the question of the *point* of a parable. He reviews
the discussion of the interpretation of the parables, showing that
Jülicher had argued that each parable had one single point, as against
the many points of an allegory, and that point was a single idea of the
widest possible generality. In the work of Dodd and Jeremias "Jülicher's moral *point* of broadest possible application has become the eschatological *point* of particular historical application . . . [but] the ideational point of Jülicher remains ideational."[145] Funk then argues that
the parable as metaphor is not "amenable to ideational reduction." In a
concrete situation it may be said to have a particular "point," in that it
comes to have a particular meaning in that situation. But the parable
can be spoken into many different situations, in which case it is possible that it may have "many points, as many points as there are situations into which it may be spoken."[146] So the parable has both an
original meaning, that it had when it was spoken into its original
historical situation, and then a series of further possible meanings,
those it comes to have as it is spoken into a series of new and different
situations. However, the original meaning, determined by historical
criticism, is not to be forgotten as the new and different meanings are
pursued. The historical-critical method determines "the original import
of the parable" and thus provides "a control over reinterpretation."[147]
But the interpreter of the parables must always be aware of the potentiality for new meaning; reduction of the meaning of the parable to
a single idea, moral, eschatological, or christological is therefore wrong.

Such reduction is in fact an attempt to control the metaphor, and "the metaphor must be left intact if it is to retain its interpretive power."[148]

Thus far Funk had taken his point of departure from the first and fourth elements of Dodd's definition of the parable. He now turns to the second, that the metaphor is drawn from nature or the common life, and the third, that it arrests the hearer by its vividness or strangeness. Funk reflects on these two elements together, claiming that the realism of the parables shows that man's destiny is at stake in his ordinary creaturely existence, that is to say, "the everydayness of the parables is translucent to the grounds of man's existence."[149] The "world" of the parable is the everyday world of man's ordinary creaturely existence, but the parable unfolds in such a way as to turn that everydayness "inside out or upside down: it is simply not cricket for the employer to pay those who worked only one hour the same wage as those who worked the full day."[150] But such unexpected "turns" are characteristic of the parables of Jesus: "In sum, the parables as pieces of everydayness have an unexpected 'turn' in them which looks through the commonplace to a new view of reality." This characteristic of the parables also explains their argumentative or provocative character, why they demand a decision.

> They present a world the listener recognizes, acknowledges. Then he is caught up in the dilemma of the metaphor: it is not his world after all! . . . He must choose to unfold with the story, be illuminated by the metaphor, or reject the call and abide with the conventional. . . . They [the parables] are language events in which the hearer has to choose between worlds. If he elects the parabolic world, he is invited to dispose himself to concrete reality as it is ordered in the parable, and venture, without benefit of landmark but on the parable's authority, into the future.[151]

With these words Funk concludes his chapter on "the parable as metaphor," having advanced the discussion very considerably in the direction that was essential to real progress, the direction it was destined to take in America. He then turns to a discussion of two of the parables, The Great Supper[152] and The Good Samaritan.[153] Since we are following the discussion of the latter parable wherever possible, we will concentrate on Funk's interpretation of that parable, beginning at the point at which he asks whether or not it is an exemplary story. In Funk's terms, as we have seen, this question is one as to whether or not the story demands a transference of judgment, as do the parables proper. To answer this Funk turns to the story itself and here he does full justice to his insight that the parable draws the hearer into it as participant. "Initially at least, the account compels the hearer to put himself in the place of that nameless fellow jogging along the wild and dangerous road. Straightway he finds himself the object of a murderous attack which leaves him stripped, beaten and half-dead. While lying helpless in the ditch. . . ."[154] Funk goes on to retell the whole story in this way, with the hearer as participant, and in doing so he does full justice to the historical details Jeremias and others had established. Every listener "as Jew" is chagrined that the "hated half-breed" ministers to the helpless victim. Funk also does justice to the insight he had developed that the parable begins with everydayness and then shatters it. The Samaritan is "the primary shock"; he is "brought into a constellation in which he cannot be anticipated," and this is the "surprising, odd turn which shatters the realism, the everydayness of the story."[155]

Thus far we have the literal meaning of the story, and we have also the hearer caught up into the story as participant, and all of this I find wholly convincing and a great advance on any previous interpretation of the parable. But now we come to the transference of judgment, to the moment of decision for the hearer-participant.

Since the metaphor gives itself existentially to unfinished reality, so that the narrative is not complete until the hearer is drawn into it as participant, the hearer is confronted with a situation in relation to which he must decide how to comport himself: is he willing to allow himself to be victim, to smile at the affront to the priest and Levite, to be served by an enemy? The parable invites, nay, compels him to make some response. And it is this response that is decisive for him. Furthermore, since the parable is temporally open-ended, it is cast onto a plurality of situations, a diversity of audiences, with the consequence that it refuses ideational crystallization. Every hearer has to hear it in *his* own way. The future which the parable discloses is the future of every hearer who grasps and is grasped by his position in the ditch.[156]

I have quoted and discussed this passage before, and on that occasion I claimed that "a passage such as this is the dawn of a new day in the interpretation of the narrative parables."[157] It is certainly that. Here for the first time the function of metaphor is being appreciated, as is the role of the hearer as participant. It would be difficult to imagine a more dramatic or effective way of presenting the dialogue between parable and hearer than that last sentence. I am the more appreciative of it because, as I pointed out earlier, Funk's point about the metaphor drawing the hearer into itself as participant can be reinforced by observing that the function of realistic narrative is to do the same thing. As realistic narrative the story of the man who went down from Jerusalem to Jericho also intends to leave the hearer in the ditch beside the Jericho road. Whatever impact the story is intended to have, it is intended to place the hearer in that situation.

Funk continues his interpretation from this perspective. "The victim is faceless and nameless, because he becomes one with the listener," since every listener finds himself in the ditch. The victim finds his true identity "in relation to the three figures who come along the road. *How* he views them determines who he is!" This is a further development of Funk's brilliant insight. The parable makes its impact upon the listener as he lies helpless in the ditch, crying mutely for aid, and hence responding viscerally to the priest and Levite passing by, and to the Samaritan coming toward him. It is at this point that the identification of the figures becomes important, and they become important because the story is what I am calling an "occasional" story; it was specifically geared to the situation between Jesus and his hearers and it depended for its impact upon the fact that it was specifically related to the world of men and ideas Jesus and his hearers shared in common. So it is important to recognize that the man in the ditch may be deliberately faceless and nameless but he is nonetheless a Jew. The story is addressed by a Jewish Jesus to his fellow Jews, to plagiarize Crossan,[158] and hence the man in the ditch, and the listener who identifies with him, is a Jew. As a Jew he had the right to expect help from particular representatives of his race and faith[159] but such help is denied him. As a Jew he had no right to expect any such help from a Samaritan, and, even more, if such help were offered him then, according to some rabbis, he should reject it because to accept it would be to delay the redemption of Israel. The function of the story as Jesus told it is to put his hearers in that position and, to use a modern idiom, let them take it from there.

I intend to develop this theme further, but in this matter I am indebted to Crossan as well as to Funk, so I will leave it until we have reviewed Crossan's initial contribution to the discussion. For the moment we will return to Funk and note that this is his initial contribution also, since he, as a key figure, returns to the discussion in the SBL

Parables Seminar.[160] So we will have occasion to come back to his enormously provocative insights as we discuss the work of that seminar below. For the moment we are content to note that his analysis of "the parable as metaphor" moves the discussion a most significant step forward at the level of *literary criticism*; his concern for the listener in the ditch as the half-dead traveler is a most significant contribution to the discussion of *hermeneutics* as the ultimate dialogue between the text and the interpreter.

E. DAN OTTO VIA, JR.:
THE PARABLE AS AESTHETIC OBJECT

We now reach the first of the two leading American interpreters of the parables of Jesus, Dan Via. Together with Dominic Crossan, he is doing the most important work on the parables today. It has fascinated me ever since I was asked to review his first book for *Interpretation*, and I have returned to it frequently.[161] Since his work is continuing, and since he is a major member of the SBL Parables Seminar, I must make it clear that I am at the moment only concerned with his book, *The Parables: Their Literary and Existential Dimension* (Philadelphia: Fortress Press, 1967). His contribution to the SBL Seminar will concern us in our Section G below. His latest book, *Kerygma and Comedy in the New Testament* (Philadelphia: Fortress Press, 1975), is not concerned with the parables.

Via begins his approach to the parables at the *literary level*, rehearsing the by now familiar distinction among *similitude* ("a typical familiar, recurring, everyday scene," e.g., The Lost Coin which "gets its force from its appeal to what is universally acknowledged"), *parable* ("a freely invented story" which "achieves its power by making the particular credible and probable," a *story* "which is analogous to, which points to but is not identical with, a situation or world of thought outside the story"), and *example story* (which is also a freely invented story but now "the meaning or thought or reality with which the story is concerned is not pointed to but is present in the story. . . . The story is an example of it directly and only needs to be generalized").[162] He then moves to the level of *historical understanding*, acknowledging that Jeremias and others had made real progress in their attempts to understand the parables in their setting in the life of Jesus, and recognizing the importance of understanding the references

4 parts to Via

1.

and allusions in the parables. But he develops four criticisms of "the severely historical approach" to the parables. (1) The non-biographical nature of the gospels makes it difficult to pinpoint a *Sitz im Leben Jesu* for the parables. But in any case we must not impose elements from Jesus' ministry and teaching upon the parable. "We must rather begin with the parable itself." (2) The severely historical approach ignores the broad element of basic humanity in the parables. (3) The historical approach threatens to leave the parables speaking to their past historical situation but with nothing to say to the present. "What is needed is a hermeneutical and literary methodology which can identify the permanently significant element *in* the parables and can elaborate a means of translating that element without distorting the original intention." (4) The severely historical approach ignores the *aesthetic nature* and the *aesthetic function* of the parables. The goal of historical and literary criticism is "to be able to take any text on its own terms," but the tendency has been to ignore the aesthetic nature of the parables by deriving their meaning from the historical context or by making them illustrations of ideas.[163]

These four criticisms of the severely historical approach to the interpretation of the parables are extremely important. They came at a time when the methods and achievements of the historical approach were fully recognized; they raised serious questions about the limitations of that approach; and they attempted to point the way forward to a possible means of overcoming those limitations. We will discuss each of the criticisms in some detail.

critique by Perrin

(1) The difficulty of adequately carrying out a severely historical approach is caused by the limitations of our historical knowledge of Jesus and his ministry. This is the weakest of the criticisms because it is not a criticism at the level of methodology. The limitations of our historical knowledge of Jesus are not an objection in terms of *hermeneutical theory* to the *hermeneutical principle* of interpreting the parables in their historical context; it is only a reminder that the task may be very difficult. But when Via goes on to say, as he does, that elements from the ministry or teaching of Jesus may not be imposed upon the parable but that "we must rather begin with the parable itself," then he is raising a most important point *at* the level of hermeneutical theory. It is not the comparative difficulty of achieving historical information about Jesus and his ministry that is the point at issue, but the funda-

mental theoretical question of the proper hermeneutical starting point. In practice earlier interpreters had started with historical knowledge of Jesus and his ministry. Dodd had started with the eschatology of Jesus; Jeremias with that and with the contours of the message of Jesus as a whole; Fuchs with the historical supposition that the parables of Jesus were "language events" in their original context in the ministry of Jesus. Each of them had then moved on to a consideration of the parables in light of these previous historical considerations. Via challenges this whole procedure on the grounds that the act of interpretation should start with the text itself, with the necessary implication that the historical factors should be taken into account insofar as, but *only* insofar as, this is demanded by the text itself. This is a point of very real importance, and we have already seen that in fact Jeremias (with, by implication, Dodd) and Fuchs did not reach a satisfactory interpretation of the parables. We ascribed this, in effect, to Jeremias's undue concern for the message of Jesus as a whole and to Fuchs's use of the sermon as the ubiquitous hermeneutical model. But those are only more particularized ways of saying that they did not begin with the text of the parable itself and move beyond the text only insofar as this might be demanded by the nature of the text itself.

(2) The severely historical approach ignores the broad element of basic humanity in the parables. This is a very important point, and one that will grow in significance as we come later to assess the relevance of narrative structuralist criticism to the interpretation of the parables. I have claimed repeatedly during the course of this discussion that the parables are "occasional" in nature, that they were directed specifically to concrete elements in the situation between Jesus and his hearers, and that they make frequent references and allusions to particular elements in the cultural-historical situation common to Jesus and his hearers. They are not folk tales appealing to the total experience and consciousness of a whole people as a people, nor are they universal stories appealing to the common experience of man as man. At the same time there are clearly universal elements in the parables of Jesus. The Prodigal Son speaks to any group of humans who have lived in families; The Good Samaritan addresses itself to any community with unsafe streets; The Lost Sheep to any people who have practiced animal husbandry; The Sower to any who have practiced a primitive form of agriculture; and so on. It therefore becomes a question of how

important the universal element is over against the particular or occasional, and vice versa. I have no answer to this question, except that I suspect that we shall find, "it varies. . . ." So I would accept Via's criticism as valid against an approach that was too narrow or particularistic, while, at the same time, I would want to utter a similar warning in the opposite direction. Too broadly humanistic an approach may ignore the strongly particularistic or "occasional" element in the parables.

(3) The severely historical approach threatens to leave the parables speaking to their past historical situation but with nothing to say to the present. This is the most important point because it emphasizes the fact that however important historical criticism may be it is not in and of itself hermeneutics. Even after one has achieved an adequate historical understanding of the parables there still remains the essential hermeneutical step of relating the historically understood text to the present of the interpreter. Having determined what it *said*, we have still to determine what it *says*; insofar, of course, as it *says* anything. We may determine that a text has only a purely historical interest for us, but most interpreters of the parables would strenuously resist that conclusion.

Our review of the discussion has shown that this is a point with which previous interpreters wrestled, but without reaching a satisfactory conclusion. Jülicher had arrived at a set of general moral principles which he held to be as relevant today as when they were first taught. Jeremias had arrived at a general message of Jesus relevant for all men everywhere. Fuchs had Jesus preaching sermons in the past and the language-event character of those past sermons being repeated in sermons in the present. In my view these attempts to solve the problem were all alike unsatisfactory, both because they failed to do justice to the nature of the parables as texts, and also because the bridge from the past to the present—the set of general moral principles, the overall message of Jesus, the ubiquitous model of the sermon—was of questionable value. A much more promising attempt to solve the problem was Bultmann's hermeneutics, not developed in connection with the parables but certainly applicable to them. According to Bultmann, as we have seen,[164] a text from the past that was an "expression of life," and the parables certainly were this, could be questioned with regard to its "understanding of existence." The understanding of existence represented in the text could then speak directly to, and challenge, that of the reader or interpreter.

Via had been enormously influenced by Bultmann; indeed there is a real sense in which his interpretation of the parables is a direct and sophisticated attempt to apply a Bultmannian hermeneutic to them, as we shall see. When he claims that "what is needed is a hermeneutical and literary methodology which can identify the permanently significant element *in* the parables," he is talking about identifying what he goes on to call "the translatable content of the parables."[165] This "translatable content" is the parables' "understanding of the possibilities of human existence," and to seek to arrive at it is an application of "Bultmann's basic hermeneutical principle."[166]

(4) Via's fourth and last criticism of the severely historical approach is that it ignores the aesthetic nature and the aesthetic function of the parables. Here he moves beyond anything that had been done before, by Bultmann or by any of the previous interpreters of the parables, in that he is insisting that in the act of interpretation the text must be taken seriously "on its own terms." In the case of the parables that means beginning with the fact that they are aesthetic objects. All the elements in a parable relate to each other within the parable, and the structure of their connections and relationships is determined "by the author's creative composition." Even if the parables make allusions to elements outside of themselves, or if they "contain images which have inescapable symbolic significance which they bring from another world of thought, this is made secondary to their fusion into the internal coherence of the parabolic story." As aesthetic objects the parables are self-contained literary objects within which various elements are carefully integrated into a patterned whole. It is within "their pattern of connections" that their meaning is to be found, and interpretation must begin by observing this internally coherent pattern, rather than by immediately looking to something outside of it. The goal of the interpretation of the parables "is better served by recognizing their aesthetic nature than by first of all deriving their meaning from the historical context or by making them illustrations of ideas."[167]

Within this point Via challenges his fellow interpreters of the parables to recognize the parables for what they are: aesthetic objects, that is, carefully organized, self-contained, coherent literary compositions.[168] As such they demand interpretation in a manner which does justice to this aspect of their essential nature. The severely historical approach had fallen short in this regard, as indeed, we may add, had all previous interpretations of the parables. As he observes and pursues this point Via becomes a true pioneer, breaking new ground in the interpretation of the parables.

Before breaking the new ground, however, Via carefully remaps some of the old. In particular he remaps the understanding of the parable as "language event." He argues that "Jesus' parables were a language event in that they introduced a new possibility into the situation of his hearers." The hearers "were offered a new way of understanding their situation in history," i.e., a new way of understanding their situation in all its concrete historicity.[169] Further, the parables "were a language event because they called for a judgment from the hearers." The hearers were challenged "not merely to see the understanding of existence in a parable but to assent to it." It is their pre-understanding that is challenged; "they must decide between their old understanding and the new one that confronts them in the parable." The parable is a language event "because it conducts man to a place— the place of decision." All this is not quite so new, however, as Fuchs and his friends seem to think, nor is it dependent upon an understanding of language derived from the later Heidegger. "We might also remind ourselves that literary critics speak of language becoming an event and of a poem, novel, or story testing a reader and having the power to move him into a new state of being or into the experience of a new horizon." Thus it may well be said that "the goal of the hermeneutical effort is the language event," but in order for this to be the case we must consider "how the parables' peculiarly aesthetic function enhances their character as events," something Fuchs and the practitioners of the "new hermeneutic" had not done.[170]

Via now begins to plot the ground he intends to cover with a chapter, "The Parables, Aesthetics, and Literary Criticism."[171] Among other things, he stresses the fact that an aesthetic object is non-referential, that is, it does not point beyond itself to something else. It creates an aesthetic experience in which "the attention is totally engaged by and riveted on the object itself"; at least it does this if it is successful. "During the successful aesthetic experience the play, painting, music, or whatever is the beholder's whole world, and his attention is not referred beyond it."[172] A further point is that as a fictitious, inwardly organized structure capable of attracting non-referential attention, a literary work is "autonomous." It is "independent of its author," and the interpreter should not commit the "intentional fallacy" of seeking the meaning of the work in the author's intention, neither should he commit the "affective fallacy" of confusing the work with its psychological effects on the reader.[173] In making this point Via is pledging his allegiance to the so-called new criticism, and he constantly quotes such representatives of that movement as Elisco Vivas, Murray Krieger, William K. Wimsatt, Monroe C. Beardsley, and others. This movement has been strongly criticized, and Via is well aware of this. So he carefully states the conclusion he is drawing from it, a conclusion he believes can stand despite the criticisms.

The peculiar function of language used aesthetically is that through its centripetal interlocking of content into form it grasps the attention of the beholder as a total psychosomatic unity—including conscious and unconscious aspects—in an intransitive or non-referential way.[174]

The literary work is autonomous, having meaning in itself, but it also points beyond itself. "The aesthetically organized form or pattern of connections itself contains implicitly a perspective on life or understanding of existence. . . . The reader of a novel will inevitably, at some level of consciousness, relate the implicit understanding of existence in the story to the understanding which he already has. In aesthetic experience, then, our attention moves both *within* the pattern of connections of the aesthetic object itself and also to the *outside* as we notice the connection between . . . the implied existential understanding in the form of the novel and our own view of things."[175] Via adopts imagery used by Murray Krieger and speaks of the successful literary work operating sequentially as window, mirror, and window. First it operates as a set of windows through which we see a world we know and can recognize. Then it becomes a series of reflecting mirrors which reorganize the familiar so that it becomes a new pattern in which there is an implicit understanding of existence. Finally, the mirrors become windows again, giving us a new vision of the world.[176]

The natural approach to the parables of Jesus as aesthetic objects is then an approach in which "focal attention" is on "the whole narrative pattern," with "attention somewhat less focal on the implied understanding of existence," because "in aesthetic experience focal attention is on the pattern of happening existence while subsidiary attention is on the implied understanding of existence." As aesthetic objects Jesus' parables are "new configurations of happening existence containing an implied understanding of existence," but they are also more than that because "as biblical texts they communicate to us the nature of faith and unfaith . . . the understanding of existence implied in the plots—in the human encounters and their outcomes—is an understanding of existence in faith and unfaith."[177] This is a very interesting way of attempting to maintain a special status for the parables. As aesthetic objects they imply an understanding of existence; as biblical texts they communicate the nature of faith and unfaith, or, as Bultmann would have put it, the understanding of existence in faith and outside of it. This is legitimate, claims Via, because the parables are part of Jesus' proclamation of the Kingdom of God, and because the element of the surprising and the extraordinary within them "suggests the divine dimension."[178]

Via is now beginning to make the distinctions which dominate his interpretation of the parables. In the paragraph following the one quoted immediately above he speaks of "literary criticism" and "theological-existential exegesis." As these rubrics are developed in the interpretation of the parables they become three: "Historico-literary criticism," "Literary-existential analysis," and "Existential-theological interpretation." Unfortunately, Via himself does not define or explain these categories for us; he leaves his reader to work them out for himself or herself. He, therefore, puts himself at the reader's mercy, or at the mercy of a possible superficiality of understanding on the part of the reader. At the risk of exposing such a possible superficiality of understanding I may say that by "historico-literary criticism" I take him to mean the effort to establish the text to be interpreted, i.e., what I have been calling "textual criticism," and, furthermore, all that is involved in reaching a historical understanding of the text, including the literary factors involved in a historical understanding, the denial of allegory, the identification of references and allusions, and so on. By "literary-existential analysis" I take Via to be referring to the total effort to see the parable as an aesthetic, literary object, with its inter-relatedness of plot movement, activity of the characters involved, the human encounters and their outcomes, etc., together with the understanding of existence which these things imply. I take, lastly, "existential-theological interpretation" to refer to the act of seeing "the parable's understanding of existence as a pointer to the divine-human relationship," an explanation Via himself does offer in the course of his interpretation of The Talents.[179]

The validity of my understanding of these categories will have to be tested against a reading of Via's interpretations of the various parables he discusses. What is, I think, evident is that Via's major interest lies at the second level, that of "literary-existential analysis", and it is certainly at this level that he has done his own most interesting work. His starting point is his concern for the parables' understanding of existence and his conviction that this is to be found "implied in the plots— in the human encounters and their outcome"—of the parables. He, therefore, sets out to analyze critically "the plots" of the parables, to investigate with literary-critical tools "the human encounters and their outcomes" in the parables. He distinguishes two basic plot movements in the parables, the comic and the tragic. "In comedy we have an upward movement toward well-being and the inclusion of the protagonist in a new or renewed society, while in tragedy we have a plot falling toward catastrophe and the isolation of the protagonist from society."[180] An important element in the plot is the encounter, often confrontation, between two characters, with attendant dialogue, and this is a feature of many of the parables of Jesus.[181] Fictions may be classified in various ways according to the protagonist's power of action. The protagonist may be superior in kind to man, a god, and this gives us the category of myth. He may be superior in degree, the hero of legend, folk tale, or fairy story. He may be superior to ordinary men but nonetheless limited by human factors and subject to criticism; this gives us the high mimetic mode of epic and classical tragedy. The protagonist may be a man among men, engaged in activity we recognize as realistic, in which case we have the low mimetic mode to which realism belongs. Finally, the protagonist may be inferior, so that we look down on bondage, frustration, and absurdity, which are characteristics of the ironic mode.[182]

If we look at the parables of Jesus in light of these distinctions, they fall with remarkable consistency into the category of the low, mimetic mode. The characters in them are "people like us who can do about what we can do." The plot movement can be either tragic or comic, so that we find either "low mimetic, realistic tragedy" in which "we see

realistic imagery and ordinary people in dramatic encounters and con-
flicts moving downward toward catastrophe," or "low mimetic, realistic
comedy" in which "we view realistic imagery and ordinary people in
dramatic, face-to-face confrontations moving upward toward well-
being." Of the parables of Jesus, eight can be identified as falling
clearly into one or other of these classes. There are the tragic parables:
The Talents (Matt. 25:14–30), The Ten Maidens (Matt. 25:1–13),
The Wedding Garment (Matt. 22:11–14), The Wicked Tenants
(Mark 12:1–9), The Unforgiving Servant (Matt. 18:23–35); and the
comic parables: The Workers in the Vineyard (Matt. 20:1–16), The
Unjust Steward (Luke 16:1–9), The Prodigal Son (Luke 15:11–32).
In the central section of his book Via then offers an interpretation of
each of these parables organized into the two groups, "The Tragic
Parables" and "The Comic Parables."[183]

Via does not discuss The Good Samaritan[184] so we will take the first
example from each of his categories to illustrate his method, the tragic
parable, The Talents, and the comic, The Workers in the Vineyard.

The Talents (Matt. 25:14–30):[185] Under the rubric "historico-literary criticism" Via discusses the allegorizing touches in, and the extent
of, the parable as Jesus taught it. He decides, in standard "historico-
literary" fashion, that the original was a non-allegorizing version of
Matt. 25:14–28. Turning to "literary-existential analysis," he observes
that the plot of the parable derives from the experience of the one-
talent man. He made a free decision to bury his talent in the ground,
but this decision leads to the tragic catastrophe of his losing his existence. "The very movement of the plot to catastrophe means that one
cannot think and act as he did without losing his existence, without
becoming existentially dead." Central to the development of the plot is
"the recognition scene" in the middle part of the parable, the scene
between the master and the servants. In tragedy in general there are
three possibilities with regard to the relationship between the recognition scene and the plot as a whole. Either, the protagonist may know
what to expect and is not surprised by his misery, or, he may have hope
of success and not be aware of the disaster his purpose entails, or, he
may proceed and suffer in ignorance. In the parables of Jesus the
recognition scene is normally of the second type, and here is "true
recognition tragedy, for here the protagonist recognizes the painful
truth only when it is too late." In the recognition scene in The Talents

we have "face to face confrontation, direct discourse, and conflict" between the master and the one talent man. By means of this scene we are led to see that the servant's breach of trust in failing to do business with his master's goods is grounded in an existential flaw. "He started as a free man, but he refused to be responsible. . . . In refusing to hold himself accountable he understood himself as a victim, and in understanding himself as a victim he *was* a victim, unable to act significantly." As we follow the plot of the parable we see "the following connected movement: *from* the refusal to take a risk, *through* repressed guilt which is projected onto someone else, *to* the loss of opportunity for meaningful existence."

The "existential-theological interpretation" of the parable involves seeing "the parable's understanding of existence as a pointer to the divine-human relationship," and then "the refusal to risk and the concomitant inability to hold oneself responsible become unfaith." Via concludes: "When we look at the world through the window of the understanding of existence in The Talents, we will have to say that the man who so understands himself that he seeks to avoid risky action rather than trusting God for the well-being of his existence, though he may live chronologically, will have no present. His time will be evacuated of content."

The Workers in the Vineyard (Matt. 20:1–16):[186] "Historico-literary criticism" reveals this to be a complete story owing its present context, and hence its present application to the disciples, to the evangelist Matthew. It probably was originally told with reference to Jesus' opponents in order to defend his association with the sinners and to attack any doctrine of legalistic merit. The vineyard imagery allusively associates the parable with the story of Israel (cf. Isaiah 5).

"Literary-existential analysis" begins by concentrating on the protagonist whose destiny gives the plot its formal shape, and who is involved in the recognition scene. There considerations show that the parable is essentially "the story of the grumbling, full-day workers." It is they who are "allowed a recognition scene," and it is "their changing fortune which gives the plot its formal shape." Actually, from the shape of its plot the parable is tragic, since the full-day workers are finally excluded from the presence of a good man. But there are comic characters in the parable—the workers hired at the end of the day—and there is the fact that the downfall of the full-day workers results from the

rejection of a comic-redemptive possibility. One gets the impression
that Via is too concerned with the classification, tragic or comic—he
finally suggests "ironic tragedy"!—but he has made an important point
in insisting that the combination plot-recognition scene shows that this
parable is the story of the full-day workers, and it must be interpreted
as such.

The recognition scene (20:12) shows the grumbling workers insisting on the strict application of a merit system of reward proportionate
to achievement. They are confident in their ability to maintain their
position in the world on such a basis. But if someone is rewarded, not
on the basis of his achievement but of another's generosity, "then there
is an incalculable element" in the situation and the full-day workers
find that their sense of being able to provide their own security is being
seriously challenged. "Their desire to have their security within their
own grasp caused them to see the incalculable, not as graciousness, but
as injustice." So they initiate the conflict with their employer "as a
result of the interpretation of their actions in relation to other realities,
and in so doing revealed their flawed self-understanding." Because
they "did not recognize the true nature of the incalculable and insisted
on strict justice where graciousness was actually to be found, in the end
they were estranged from the source of graciousness." So what the
parable teaches is that the workers "exclude themselves from the
source of grace" because of "their impenetrable legalistic understanding of existence."

The "existentialist-theological interpretation" of the parable is that
the story suggests to us "that the divine dimension may cross our
everyday reality to produce a crisis of ultimate importance in the midst
of the ordinary." Further, the formal tension in the story between the
graciousness of the employer and the tragic fate of the workers is also
important because "it embodies the existential tension that while the
ultimate meaning in life is God's gracious dealing, man may yet bring
about the tragic loss of his existence."

We are fortunate that the second of the two leading American interpreters of the parables, Dominic Crossan, has also offered a detailed
interpretation of The Workers in the Vineyard which will give us a
chance to compare the two interpretations, and to say something further about Via in comparison to Crossan.[187] For the moment we will

limit ourselves to a general evaluation of Via's work, proceeding as always under our four rubrics.

At the levels of *textual* and of *historical criticism* Via simply utilizes the insights and material offered him by the previous discussion. He neither makes nor claims to make any new contribution at these levels. Indeed the brevity of his usual discussion under the rubric "historico-literary criticism" is such as to indicate that he simply wants to establish what is necessary before going on to what is to him more important: his "literary-existentialist analysis."

Via's "literary-existentialist analysis" covers the ground that we have been covering under the rubric of *literary criticism,* and Via's studies here are certainly his major contribution to the discussion, and his major challenge to his fellow interpreters of the parables. As my previous discussions of his work indicate,[188] I have always been enormously impressed by this aspect of Via's work, and I am still enormously impressed by it. Via finally puts the discussion on firm ground so far as understanding the stories themselves is concerned. The careful analysis of the plot of the story, the identification of the protagonist, the observation of the recognition scene and its function, all of this gives us a much firmer grasp on the story and its meaning *as a story* than we have ever had before. Insofar as the parables of Jesus are stories, Via has taught us to analyze them in such a way as to be reasonably sure of their internal dynamics and hence of their formal meaning.

To anticipate something I will discuss later, I am not surprised that Via's unquestionable success in the formal analysis of the eight narrative parables he discusses should have led him on to a concern for structuralist analysis as a further means of reaching an in-depth understanding of the narrative parables *as narratives.* I can only applaud Via's continuing contribution to the discussion at this level. Many of the parables of Jesus are in fact *narratives*; they are carefully composed *stories,* and we must therefore follow Via in his attempt to understand them in depth *as* narratives, *as* stories. After Via no interpretation of the parables could be valid which failed to take into account, and to do full justice to, this kind of careful and systematic analysis of the parables as narratives, as stories. The parables of Jesus are metaphor, and they are metaphor extended to narrative; Via's contribution to the discussion comes at the level of their *extension to narrative.* I say this to prepare for a contrast with the work of Dominic Crossan, whose contribution comes, in my view, at the level of the parable as *metaphor* and as *metaphor* extended to narrative.

My problem with Via's work comes not with the *literary* aspects of his "literary-existentialist analysis" but with the *existentialist* aspects of that analysis. This problem then spills over into his "existential-theological interpretation." I have now read Via's book with some care three separate times, and I have had the same problem each time. The first time I was struck by the fact that for all Via's methodological sophistication he sometimes sounds surprisingly like Jülicher, and I compared the conclusion Via draws from The Talents, "that the man who so understands himself that he seeks to avoid risky action rather than trusting God for the well-being of his existence, though he may live long chronologically, will have no present," with Jülicher's, "only he who makes good use of God's gifts can expect to receive the last and highest gifts. . . . To do nothing is to be excluded from the Kingdom of God."[189] The second time around I was struck by the commonplace nature of many of Via's interpretations.

The Ten Maidens shows us that "The present, then, as time and room to live, is a gift; but it is also a demand. . . . Gift and demand are held paradoxically together." The Workers in the Vineyard "suggests to us . . . that the divine dimension may cross our everyday reality to produce a crisis of ultimate importance in the midst of the ordinary." There are similar lessons drawn from each of the eight parables Via discusses.[190]

I found then, as I find now, that Via's literary-critical discussion of the parables is of real interest and of obvious importance, but there is a surprising element of banality about his conclusions. There is something very incongruous about beginning with texts as powerful as the parables obviously are, going on to analyze them with critical tools as keen as those which Via uses, and then ending up with neat little existentialist insights. There has to be more to the parables than that!

As I now see the matter, the problem lies in the fact that Via has paid too little attention to the final element in the hermeneutical process, the dynamic interaction between text and interpreter. There is nothing dynamic about the interaction between the parable and the interpreter in Via's exegesis, and I think it is important to recognize the reason for this. The reason is that he has too quickly adopted Bultmann's existentialist hermeneutics. As we saw in the previous study of the interpretation of Kingdom of God, Bultmann developed his hermeneutics in connection with what he regarded as the dead language of defunct myths. Mythological language is dead; long live, therefore, the existentialist translation of what that language was trying to say! But the metaphorical language of the parables is not necessarily dead, and the task of the interpreter, therefore, is not necessarily to dissect it for the sake of its translatable content.

Another way of making the same point is to return to the very important hermeneutical insight developed by Paul Ricoeur, namely, that of the necessity for a post-critical or "second" naiveté. There is a sense in which after we have learned all that we can about a text with the aid of our critical tools we have to allow that text to address us once more as a text.[191] Via does not do this. Having learned what he can about the text by the aid of his critical tools, he then discards that text and concerns himself with things that can be learned from it. In the last resort this does not seem to be a hermeneutical procedure adequate to the parables.

With the appearance of Via's book in 1967 the interpretation of the parables took on a new dimension. It was obviously the most important book on the parables since Jeremias's, the first edition of which had appeared twenty years before, and, like Jeremias, Via clearly ushered in a new day in parable interpretation. Where Jeremias had taught us the value of a historical approach to the parables, Via taught us to recognize that that approach had limitations, and he challenged us to recognize further that a literary-critical approach was equally important. The interpreter of the parables was going to need to become both eclectic and sophisticated with regard to methodology.

F. JOHN DOMINIC CROSSAN:
THE PARABLE AS POETIC METAPHOR

We have seen that the parables of Jesus may be described as metaphor and as metaphor extended to narrative. Via concerned himself with the "extended to narrative" aspect of the parables; Crossan concerned himself with the parable as metaphor. He is a New Testament scholar who has soaked himself in poetry and in poetic criticism, and he approaches the parables from the two perspectives of, on the one hand, traditional New Testament scholarship, and, on the other hand, of poetry and poetic criticism. He is the second of the two leading

American interpreters of the parables and, like Via, he is continually engaged in parable interpretation. The respect in which his colleagues hold his work can be seen from the fact that he was invited to be chairman of the SBL Parables Seminar, in which capacity he is currently serving (1975). Since his work is in progress I will at this point arbitrarily limit myself to a consideration of his book, *In Parables: The Challenge of the Historical Jesus,* [192] leaving his further work, to be found in *Semeia* 1 and 2, to be considered in our next section.

Crossan has made important contributions to parable interpretation at several different levels, but all his contributions draw their strength from the same source, his intimate knowledge of poetry and the critical study of poetry. He has all the traditional skills of the New Testament scholar, and this is important since it means that fundamentally he relates to the texts all the New Testament scholar's awareness of the problems of the discussion of the interpretation of the parables, of the issues at stake in that discussion, and of the progress thus far made in it. In this respect he is like Via, and I call attention to this aspect of the work of Via and Crossan because it is important to recognize their competence in both New Testament and literary scholarship. Their competence in literary scholarship makes it possible for them to bring new insights and skills to the discussion of the parables, while their competence as New Testament scholars means that they are contributing to that ongoing discussion, and not to some other and quite different one.

The first contribution which Crossan makes to the discussion is in connection with the distinction between parable and allegory. This has been a point at issue in the discussion ever since 1888, when Jülicher recognized such a distinction and showed that the parables of Jesus were parables and not allegories. But between 1888 and 1973 the distinction Jülicher had drawn had worn somewhat thin. Crossan took up the matter in light of a distinction made by poets between symbol and allegory, quoting four very important poets indeed: Goethe, Coleridge, Yeats, and Eliot. Goethe saw the distinction in terms of a distinction between the expressible and the inexpressible. Allegory transforms the phenomenon into an abstract concept, the concept into an image, but in such a way that the concept can still be "expressed and be held in the image." Symbolism, on the other hand transforms the phenomenon into an idea, the idea into an image, "in such a way that the idea remains forever infinitely active and unreachable in the image, and, even if expressed in all languages, still inexpressible." Similarly Yeats distinguishes between symbolism, which says "things which could not be said so perfectly in any other way," and allegory, which says "things which could be said as well, or better, in another way." The former needs "a right instinct" for its understanding, the latter "a right knowledge." Coleridge emphasized participation in the referent as the heart of the distinction. "An allegory is but a translation of abstract notions into a picture-language which is itself but an abstraction from objects of the senses. . . ." A symbol, however, "always partakes of the reality it renders intelligible. . . ." Eliot contrasts Chesterton and Charles Williams: "Chesterton's *The Man Who Was Thursday* is an allegory; it . . . is intended to convey a definite moral and religious point expressible in intellectuals terms." But Williams has no such "palpable design" upon his reader. "His aim is to make you partake of a kind of experience that he has had, rather than make you accept some dogmatic belief."[193]

This distinction between symbol and allegory is not yet a distinction between parable and allegory, but Crossan's point is that any simple distinction between parable and allegory is inadequate to an understanding of the nature of parable. What he wants to do is to explore the nature of parable in contrast to that of allegory, so he turns to a distinction made by Paul Ricoeur between allegory and myth. "An allegory can always be *translated* into a text that can be understood by itself; once this better text has been made out, the allegory falls away like a useless garment; what the allegory showed, while concealing it, can be said in a direct discourse that replaces the allegory." But the myth "has a way of *revealing* things that is not reducible from a language in cipher to a clear language."[194]

Crossan is developing an argument to the effect that the parables of Jesus contrast with allegory as symbol contrasts with allegory in the eyes of the poets, and as myth contrasts with allegory in the eyes of Paul Ricoeur. Parable, like symbol, expresses what cannot be expressed in any other way, demands "a right instinct" for understanding, partakes of the reality it renders intelligible, and invites participation in its referent. Parable, like myth, reveals something not reducible to a clear language. Allegory, by contrast, expresses what can and should be expressed in another way; it demands "a right knowledge" for understanding; it is an abstraction from reality; it intends to convey a point in intellectual terms; it can be abandoned when its message has been grasped. Crossan now turns to metaphor, since recent works on the parables of Jesus have placed "special emphasis on their relationship to the world of poetic metaphor," and makes a similar distinction with regard to metaphor. Metaphor can be used as illustration, illustrating information a teacher wishes to impart to a student. In this case the metaphor is a pedagogical device, and "in any final analysis such metaphors are expendable." In contrast to this Crossan argues that "metaphor can also articulate a referent so new or so alien to consciousness that this referent can only be grasped within the metaphor itself." Such a metaphor "contains a new possibility of world and of language so that any information one might obtain from it can only be received *after* one has participated through the metaphor in its new and alien referential world." In other words, "there are metaphors in which information precedes participation so that the function of metaphor is to illustrate information about the metaphors referent; but there are also metaphors in which participation precedes information so that the function of metaphor is to create participation in the metaphor's referent."[195]

In light of these distinctions Crossan goes on to define the terms he intends to use. He understands figurative language as having two quite different functions, to illustrate information so that information precedes participation, and to create participation so that participation precedes information. "The former function produces allegories and examples, pedagogic devices which are intrinsically expendable. The latter produces *metaphor* on the verbal level and *symbol* on the nonverbal level. At their best they are absolutely inexpendable and even at their worst they are dormant rather than dead." Crossan is interested in "the verbal phenomenon of metaphor," and in this connection he makes a further distinction: "Metaphor can appear as either parable or myth." To illustrate this distinction he borrows "a famous line from Marianne Moore," and claims that "a *parable* gives us 'imaginary gardens with real toads in them,'" whereas "a myth gives us imaginary gardens with imaginary toads in them." So "a parable tells a story which, on its surface level, is absolutely possible or even factual within the normalcy of life," while "a myth tells one which is neither of these on its surface level."[196]

These are most important distinctions, and what is particularly interesting is the link developed between metaphor and symbol. Clearly
this has consequences both for the interpretation of the parables and
for the interpretation of the Kingdom proclamation of Jesus, and we
shall return to it in a concluding discussion. At the moment we are
concerned with Crossan's contribution to the discussion of the interpretation of the parables, and we continue our consideration of that by
calling attention to the subtitle of his book, *The Challenge of the
Historical Jesus*. Crossan is concerned with the Jesus of the parables,
and in this respect he contrasts most sharply with Via. Via has no
interest in Jesus as the author of the parables, only in the parables as
texts to be interpreted. Crossan is enormously interested in Jesus as the
author of the parables, and in the parables as a paradigm of the message of Jesus; he claims that the parables are crucial to an understanding of Jesus. The parables are such that "they express and they contain
the temporality of Jesus' experience of God; they proclaim and they
establish the historicity of Jesus' response to the Kingdom." They are
not timeless truths or metahistorical models; rather they are the "ontological ground" of the life of Jesus; they are a fundamental expression of his experience of God, the cause and not the effect of his other
words and of his deeds. Jesus "was not crucified for parables but for
ways of acting which resulted from the experience of God presented in
the parables." The parables are, therefore, not only paradigmatic of the
message of Jesus, they are also constitutive of Jesus as a historical
phenomenon. "Jesus' parables are radically constitutive of his own distinctive historicity and all else is located in them." Because of this,
"parable is the house of God."[197]

Crossan now turns to the interpretation of the parables, and he
begins by identifying three parables which he understands as being the
key to the other parables, and hence to the message of Jesus as a
whole. They are "key" parables, "paradigmatic, reference" parables,
just as for Lévi-Strauss the myth of the Bororo Indians of Central
Brazil is the "key myth; his paradigmatic, reference myth." They are
three parables "which show most clearly the deep structure of the
Kingdom's temporality and which contain in themselves the entire
parabolic melody: they are key, overture, paradigm; they are above all
what Maurice Merleau-Ponty called *"la parole originaire."*[198] These

three parables are The Hid Treasure and The Pearl of Great Price (Matt. 13:44–45), and The Great Fish (Gospel of Thomas 81:28–82:3).[199]

In these three parables Crossan finds a structural sequence which is paradigmatic of man's experience of the Kingdom of God. In The Treasure and The Pearl the sequence is found in the verbs "finds-sells-buys," and in The Fish, "found-threw-chose." In these parables "we are confronted with a man whose normalcy of past-present-future is rudely but happily shattered" by the "*advent*" of the treasure, pearl, or fish. In each case "the future he had presumably planned and projected for himself is totally invalidated by the *advent* (which) opens up new world and unforeseen possibilities." In the force of this advent "he willingly *reverses* his entire past, quite rightly and wisely he sells 'all that he has'"; he throws "all the small fish down into the sea." The key is therefore the combination of *advent* and *reversal*; from these the man obtains that which "gives him a new world of life and *action* he did not have before and he could not have programmed for himself."[200]

In these parables Crossan finds the key to understanding the parables and indeed the whole message of Jesus, and he constantly expresses that key in terms of the three words: *advent* (of new world and unforeseen possibilities), *reversal* (of man's entire past), and *action* (the expression of the new world and the new possibilities).[201] For Crossan the key to the challenge of Jesus as a whole is to be found in the three words advent-reversal-action. This conclusion Crossan has drawn from his consideration of the "key, paradigmatic, reference" parables. He now proceeds to an interpretation of the parables organized under these three rubrics, listing all of the parables and investigating some in detail. The lists are as follows:

Parables of Advent
  The Fig Tree (Mark 13:28)[202]
  The Leaven (Matt. 13:33)
  The Sower (Mark 4:3–8, discussed in detail)
  The Mustard Seed (Mark 4:30–32, discussed in detail)
  The Lost Sheep (Matt. 18:12–13)
  The Lost Coin (Luke 15:8–9)
Parables of Reversal[203]
  The Good Samaritan (Luke 10:30–37, discussed in detail)
  The Rich Man and Lazarus (Luke 16:19–31)
  The Pharisee and the Publican (Luke 18:10–14)

The Wedding Guest (Luke 14:7–11)
The Proper Guests (Luke 14:12–14)
The Great Supper (Matt. 22:1–10)
The Prodigal Son (Luke 15:11–32)
Parables of Action
The Wicked Husbandmen (Mark 12:1–12, discussed in detail)
The Servant Parables (discussed as a group)[204]
The Doorkeeper (Mark 13:37)
The Overseer (Luke 12:42–46)
The Talents (Matt. 25:14–30)
The Throne Claimant (Luke 19:12b, 14–15a, 27)
The Unmerciful Servant (Matt. 18:23–28)
The Servant's Reward (Luke 17:7–10)
The Unjust Steward (Luke 16:1–7)
The Workers in the Vineyard (Matt. 20:1–13)

This arrangement of the parables is reminiscent of Jeremias, who also arranged the parables under rubrics. But there is an important difference between Jeremias and Crossan. Jeremias had derived his rubrics from a consideration of the message of Jesus as a whole, whereas Crossan derives his from a consideration of the three parables he regards as "key" parables. Jeremias's rubrics were illegitimate, because they were not derived from an exegesis of the parables themselves, or even from an analysis of the various literary forms characteristic of the message of Jesus. They were derived in fact from an overall understanding of the message of Jesus which owed a good deal to the assumption that the message of Jesus was the foundation of later Christian preaching. Crossan's rubrics are legitimate to the extent that he is justified in his claim that the three parables are "key" parables. Is it the case that The Treasure, The Pearl, and The Great Fish are paradigmatic of the parables as a whole, so that they may be understood as the key to all the parables? There are at least two arguments that could be advanced in support of Crossan's claim that they are. In the first place, the parables have been used in that way, unreflectively, by previous exegetes.[205] They function naturally as key parables. Then, secondly, Crossan's categories of advent, reversal, and action do in practice make sense in the context of the message of Jesus as a whole; they can be supported from other literary forms used in that message. We saw in the study of the use of Kingdom of God earlier in this volume that the proclamation of the "coming" of the Kingdom is the central aspect of the message of Jesus; that the proverbial sayings make characteristic use of the "reversal" theme; and that all aspects of the message contain an element of parenesis, a challenge to "action" in the form of an appropriate response. I regard this argument as strong enough to accept Crossan's categories—though not necessarily his terminology.

We will now indicate something of Crossan's interpretation of the parables, beginning with his interpretation of The Sower and The Mustard Seed, which he includes under the rubric "parables of advent."

The Sower is now found in four versions: Mark 4:3–8; Matt. 13:3–8; Luke 8:5–8; Thom. 82:3–13.[206] Of these, Matthew and Luke are derived from Mark, but the version in Thomas is independent. Mark and Thomas show striking similarities in their paratactic construction and their constant use of threefold structure. Crossan argues for an original parable using paratactic construction, i.e., using short terse sentences connected by "and," and favoring a threefold construction as much as possible. It would be a version like Mark 4:3–8 "without the insertions in 4:5–6 and 4:8." It contrasted sharply "three varying degrees of wasted seed (path, rocks, thorns) with three varying degrees of fruitful seed (30, 60, 100)." The contrast "was heightened by the longer description of the former cases and the terse but triumphant announcement of the latter ones." The "threes" had no allegorical function; "they represent a contrast rendered in poetic stylization." The Sower, therefore, sharply juxtaposes "three instances of sowing losses and three instances of harvest gains." This is not a "parable of growth," because the diptych of juxtaposition does not wish to emphasize growth but miracle, not organic and biological development but the gift-like nature, the graciousness and the surprise of the ordinary. "It is like this that the Kingdom is an advent. It is surprise and it is gift."

Under the rubric "parables of reversal" Crossan offers an interpretation of The Good Samaritan, Luke 10:30–37. This is our sample parable, the interpretation of which we are discussing wherever possible, so we will now summarize Crossan's interpretation.[207] Moreover his interpretation is strong; indeed the publication of his original essay on this parable in New Testament Studies in 1971/72, established him immediately as a major interpreter of the parables. Crossan begins, as always, with the question of the text to be interpreted. Luke 10:25–37 consists of four separate units: the question concerning eternal life,

10:25–28; the question of one's neighbor, 10:29; the parable, 10:30–35; the concluding dialogue, 10:36–37. 10:25–28 has "neighbor" in the passive sense, as one to whom help is offered, and it is readily separable from the parable. It is not part of the unit to be interpreted. 10:29 continues this use of "neighbor" and has no other attestation in the tradition. It is a link between the originally independent units, 10:27–28 and 10:30–36, which it serves to connect. It is not part of the unit to be interpreted. 10:30–35 is the parable to be interpreted, and the only question here is whether it should be held to include any part of the fourth unit. 10:36–37 uses "neighbor" in the active sense of one who offers help, so verses 27, 29 pull the parable one way, the neighbor is the man in the ditch; while verses 36–37 pull it the other way, the neighbor is the Samaritan. Did the original parable include any part of the fourth unit, 10:36–37, or must verses 30–35 only be regarded as the text to be interpreted? Crossan argues that the rhetorical question in verse 36 was originally the conclusion of the parable, and that it has been expanded subsequently in the tradition. The text to be interpreted is, therefore, Luke 10:30–36.

In order to interpret the parable Crossan considers, first, the *structure* of the narrative. This he analyzes as follows.

(a)	10:30a	"a man . . . fell among robbers"
(b)	10:30b	terse description of action of robbers
(c)	10:31	"a priest . . . saw him . . . passed by on the other side"
	10:32	"a Levite . . . saw him . . . passed by on the other side"
	10:33	"a Samaritan . . . saw him . . . he had compassion"
(b¹)	10:34–35	very long description of the action of the Samaritan
(a¹)	10:36	"the man . . . fell among the robbers"

The effect of this structure is obvious. The balanced reactions of the three characters, priest, Levite, Samaritan, provide a first climax, and here the emphasis is clearly clerics versus Samaritan. Then there is a second and final climax in the rhetorical question in verse 36, where, however, the emphasis has shifted to hearer(s) versus Samaritan. "In literary sequence the robbers recede into the background, the clerics follow them into stylistic oblivion, and in 10:36 the hearer(s) has only one person left to face, and to be faced by one's own necessary decision: the Samaritan judged as good." At this point the length and detail of the description of the Samaritan's activity become important. "When the hearer is confronted with the rhetorical question in 10:36 he might negate the entire process by simply denying that *any* Samaritan would so act. So, before the question can be put, the hearer must see, feel, and hear the goodness of the Samaritan for himself. The long description of verses 34–35 "involve the hearer in the activity" of the Samaritan so that "the objection is stifled at birth."

This brings Crossan to "the importance of 'Samaritan.'" If Jesus had wanted to teach love of neighbor in distress, then it would have been sufficient to talk of one person, a second person, and a third person. If he had wanted to add a jibe against the clerical circles of Jerusalem he could have mentioned priest, Levite, and Jewish lay-person. If he had wanted to inculcate love of one's enemies, then "it would have been radical enough to have a Jewish person stop and assist a wounded Samaritan," because to the Jews at the time of Jesus a Samaritan was "a socio-religious outcast." But the story has the Samaritan help the traveler, so that "the internal structure of the story and the historical setting of Jesus' time agree that the literal point of the story challenges the hearer to put together two impossible and contradictory words for the same person: 'Samaritan' (10:33) and 'neighbor' (10:36)." As told by a Jewish Jesus to a Jewish audience, "the whole thrust of the story demands that one say what cannot be said, what is a contradiction in terms: Good + Samaritan." The story is a story of reversal, because "when good (clerics) and bad (Samaritan) become, respectively, bad and good, a world is being challenged and we are faced with polar reversal."

The tradition has treated The Good Samaritan as an exemplary story, a story which moves at the same level as that which it exemplifies. Almost all modern exegetes have treated the story in this way. The story exemplifies neighborliness, that is its metaphorical point, and it gives an example of behavior to be imitated, that is its literal point. But both the metaphorical and the literal point move at the same level, so that the natural challenge of all exemplary stories, "Go and do likewise," moves naturally and easily from one to the other. But Crossan challenges this virtually unanimous opinion of the tradition and of modern exegesis. The Good Samaritan is a parable *not* an exemplary story, and so the literal point and the metaphorical point move at different levels. In a parable there is a "leap from the literal point to the metaphorical point which is the real purpose of the literary creation." In the case of The Good Samaritan "the literal point confronted the hearers with the necessity of saying the impossible and having their world turned upside down and radically questioned in its presuppositions." The metaphorical point is "that *just* so does the Kingdom of God break abruptly into human consciousness and demand the overturn of prior values, closed options, set judgments, and established conclusions." The result is that "the hearer struggling with the contradictory dualism of Good/Samaritan is actually experiencing the inbreaking of the Kingdom." "Not only does it happen like this," Crossan continues, "it happens in this. The original parabolic point was the reversal caused by the advent of the Kingdom in and through the challenge to utter the unutterable and to admit thereby that other world which was at that very moment placing their own under radical judgment."

Among the parables considered under the rubric "parables of action" is The Vineyard Workers, Matt. 20:1–13. We will consider Crossan's interpretation of this parable,[208] and contrast with it Via's interpretation considered above.[209] As always, Crossan begins with a careful discussion of the text to be interpreted, arguing that the parable proper is to be found in verses 1–13, verses 14, 15, and 16 all being interpretive additions.[210] Verses 1–13 are then analyzed according to their structure. Crossan calls attention to the two carefully contrasted sequences, verses 1–7, beginning "early in the morning," and verses 8–13, beginning "when evening came." Within each sequence, the workers appear in order, except that in the second sequence the order is reversed, the last coming first. This reversal in order of presenting the servants "already points to the reversal of expectations which ensues in 20.9–13." Crossan finds in this reversal the theme of the parable, contrasting his conclusion with that drawn by Via.

It is reversal of expectation which is central: "they thought" in 20:10. D. O. Via summed up the parable with this: "Our very existence depends on whether we will accept God's gracious dealings, his dealings which shatter our calculations about how things ought to be ordered in the world." But God also shatters our understanding of graciousness and that is the most difficult of all to accept.

I regard Via and Crossan as the leading contemporary interpreters of the parables, and as particularly important because of their use of the insights and methods of literary criticism in their interpretation. Their different treatments of this parable are therefore both interesting and important. Via has concentrated on the all-day workers, their "recognition scene" and their role in the "plot" of the story. Crossan has concentrated on the structure of the narrative and the reversal of order in the two presentations of the workers in sequence. In this particular instance I find Via the more convincing, because his analysis grows out of the narrative itself, while Crossan's is somewhat forced upon it. Moreover, Crossan has, I suspect, been unduly impressed by the element of reversal in presentation of the sequence; he has a passion for the reversal theme!

I will now summarize my impression of Crossan's initial contribution to the discussion of the interpretation of the parables, considering his work under the usual four rubrics. So far as *textual criticism* is concerned, Crossan does the most important work since Jeremias in establishing the text to be interpreted. He always discusses carefully this aspect of any parable he sets out to interpret, and he adds to the skills that Jeremias had bequeathed to the discussion the insights of the redaction critic, an imaginative use of the material in the Gospel of Thomas, and the literary critic's understanding of the natural shape of a narrative.[211] Even if one finally comes to question some of his conclusions, and we shall see that the subsequent discussion questions his inclusion of the rhetorical question at the end of The Good Samaritan, there can be no doubt of the importance of his concern in this matter. Nor is there any doubt of the fact that the method he develops is an important advance on anything that had gone before him.

At the level of the *historical understanding* of the parables Crossan makes a most important contribution to the discussion. Indeed his contribution here goes beyond the parables in that he makes a major contribution to our historical understanding of the message of Jesus altogether.[212] His contention that The Treasure, Pearl, and Great Fish are "key" parables, his careful exegesis of them in terms of "advent-reversal-action," and his use of this as a way of approaching the historical understanding of the parables as a whole carry conviction. This is the more the case since, as I argued in this context, similar results are obtained from an approach to the Kingdom proclamation and the proverbial sayings of Jesus such as I carried out in the first study in this volume. It may be the case, as I also suggested, that Crossan sometimes allows his passion for the reversal theme to run away with him, but this does not alter the fact that his work marks a very considerable advance in our historical knowledge of the parables of Jesus, and hence of the message of Jesus as a whole.

Crossan is able to make his contribution to our historical understanding of the parables because of his advances at the level of *literary criticism.* As I have noted, he brings to the parables a deep appreciation of poetry and poetic criticism, and he is able, therefore, to deepen our appreciation of the parables as poetic metaphor and as developed narratives. In this respect his work matches Via's, and the fact that the two tend to use a different set of literary-critical tools gives us the opportunity to appreciate some of the possibilities of a literary-critical approach to the parables. Another important aspect of the contrast between Crossan and Via is that Crossan is concerned with the parables as parables of Jesus, so that his use of literary criticism is ultimately still in the aid of an essentially historical understanding of the parable. Via, on the other hand, is only interested in the parables as literary objects divorced from their original historical context, so that his use of literary criticism is ultimately concerned with a contemporary understanding of the parables. In the last analysis both of these approaches are going to be necessary to the discussion as a whole so that, again, Via and Crossan tend to complement one another.

The fact that Via and Crossan tend to complement one another's interests and concerns should not hide from us the fact that they can disagree with regard to the analysis and interpretation of a parable. Such disagreement should not be hidden behind the claim that Crossan has a predominantly historical interest and Via a quite different one. The fact is that both are concerned to analyze and interpret the parables as parables, and differences between them can be important and instructive. We noted one such disagreement in the case of the interpretation of The Workers in the Vineyard, and in that instance I am inclined to follow Via, on the grounds that his analysis seems to make more sense of the text of that particular parable. There would no doubt be instances where the opposite would be the case. But the test would always be that the analysis made sense of the particular text concerned, and in this regard Crossan's analysis and interpretation of The Good Samaritan seems particularly strong. He has certainly convinced me that this is a parable and not an exemplary story, despite my claims to the opposite in my *Rediscovering the Teaching of Jesus*![213] We shall have occasion to test his interpretation further as we follow the discussion of the parable in the SBL Parables Seminar.

A further contrast between Via and Crossan becomes evident at the *final level of hermeneutics*, the act of interpretation of the text into the present of the interpreter. We saw that Via was deeply concerned for this, that he believed that it was achieved by means of an existential interpretation, and that this concern manifested itself at every stage of his exegesis of the text. He approached the text from the standpoint of the final act of interpretation, and everything he did served that purpose. Crossan starts, so to speak, at the other end of the hermeneutical process. His concern is for the meaning of the text on the lips of Jesus. His whole endeavor is to make possible a sophisticated understanding of the parable as Jesus taught it; everything he does serves that purpose. If he ever self-consciously addresses the problem of the final act of interpretation of the text into the present of a contemporary reader, then, in several readings of his book, I have missed the place where he does so. His solution to the problem is the assumption that, as he puts it, poetic metaphor does not die, at its worst it lies dormant.[214] His concern is to help us to see the parables of Jesus as poetic metaphor, so that the metaphor may come alive for us. He is convinced that the parable as poetic metaphor contains *for us* "a new possibility of world and of language," a possibility which opens up for us only *after* we have "participated through the metaphor in its new and alien referential world," the world that is God and Kingdom of God.[215]

The student of the discussion is in the position of finding that, on the one hand, Via claims that the final act of interpretation requires a self-conscious and complex existentialist approach to the parables, while, on the other hand, Crossan claims that once we can appreciate the parables as poetic metaphor they address us as they addressed their first hearers. They convey to us, as they did to them, "the challenge of the historical Jesus." As a student of the discussion I find elements of importance in both claims, but I remain wholly convinced by neither.

G.   THE SBL PARABLES SEMINAR

The Society of Biblical Literature formed its Seminar on the Parables in 1972, with its first meeting to be held in 1973 and an anticipated five-year life span. The leading interpreters of the parables in

America were invited to participate, Wilder, Funk, Via, and Crossan, together with other scholars who had a special interest in the parables, or in the use of literary skills in biblical interpretation. The seminar worked for the first year on "A Structuralist Approach to the Parables," publishing the results of that year's work in *Semeia* 1 (1974). In the second year it took up the interpretation of The Good Samaritan, publishing the results of that year's work in *Semeia* 2 (also 1974). In the current year, 1974–75, it is considering The Prodigal Son, and no doubt this year's work will also be published in a future issue of *Semeia*, and, in due course, the work of subsequent years.

The seminar is a deliberate attempt to organize an advance in scholarly research.[216] It was recognized that with Jeremias the purely historical approach to the parables had reached a level at which further refinement in method might be expected, but not further major advances in method. At the same time there was growing interest in a more literary approach to the parables, and a realization that the opportunities for exploring the possibilities of such an approach were more evident in America than elsewhere. The major publications in this area had come from American scholars—Wilder, Funk, Via, and Crossan[217]—who were all still actively engaged in parable interpretation, and there were other American scholars at work in the same area. Finally, a new method in interpretation, structuralism, was hovering in the wings and obviously needed to be given serious consideration in connection with the parables. The seminar was designed to explore possibilities in parable interpretation at the level of methodology, and it was anticipated that it would be seminal with regard to future interpretations of the parables rather than immediately productive of interpretations. It is, I believe, fulfilling all expectations with regard to the course and results of its work.

Since the seminar is currently only half way through its anticipated life span it would be inappropriate for me to comment in any detail on its work, or on contributions made by individual members to its deliberations. I am a member of the seminar and any such comments I have can and should be made within the seminar itself. However, there are papers engendered by the seminar which have been published and upon which I may, therefore, quite properly comment, the more so since they continue directly the discussion I have been reviewing up to this point. In particular the seminar continued the discussion of The Good Samaritan, and it is this aspect of the seminar's work to date that I propose to review and discuss.

In the first year of the seminar Crossan contributed to its deliberations a revised and expanded version of his work on "The Servant Parables" and on "Parable and Example in the Teaching of Jesus," the latter being fundamentally a discussion of The Good Samaritan.[218] Via responded with a paper that was largely a discussion of The Good Samaritan from a structuralist standpoint,[219] and there ensued a general discussion among Crossan, Via, and Funk.[220] Then Wilder reviewed this discussion in an introductory contribution to *Semeia* 1.[221] I will review this discussion insofar as it concerns the interpretation of The Good Samaritan.

Crossan's further interpretation of the parable does not differ significantly from his earlier version, considered above.[222] He still argues that the unit to be interpreted is Luke 10:30–36, and that this unit is a parable and not an exemplary story. He repeats his contention that the literal point of the parable is the demand upon the hearer "that he say what cannot be said: Good + Samaritan," and that the metaphorical point is "that *just so* does the Kingdom of God break into a person's consciousness and demand the overturn of prior values, closed options, set judgments, and established conclusions." As Wilder puts it his concern is still for "metaphorical tension and the ontological 'clash of worlds' in Jesus' sayings."[223]

If Crossan has remained the same, Via has changed, although not in his passion for hyphenated rubrics! He has spent the years since completing his book on the parables in an intense study of structuralism, so he now responds to Crossan, not with a "literary-existential analysis" of The Good Samaritan, but with a "literary-structural approach" to the parable.[224] He begins by distinguishing between "story" and "discourse" within a narrative. Luke 10:25–37 is a distinct unit of Luke's gospel, and within that unit there is *Jesus' discourse* with the scribe (10:25b–10:37). Within that discourse there is a further unit, 10:30–35, which is "a distinct enclave of *story*." So the unit for our analysis is either the total unit of discourse with story, 10:25–37, or the story alone, 10:30–35. The unit Crossan concerns himself with, 10:30–36, the story ending with the rhetorical question, is "not a legitimate one for analysis," and insofar as Crossan's interpretation is dependent upon the rhetorical question it is illegitimate; it "ignores the autonomy of the story."

Within the story itself two levels may be identified and distinguished: *plot* (sequential analysis), a tightly cohering organic unity of three episodes which open, maintain, and close the sequence, and *actants* (*actantiel* analysis), a group of not more than six functions, roles, or structures "whose quality is to be the subject of or participant in a constant action." The *actant* is usually a personal character, but it need not necessarily be so.

The analysis of a story in terms of *actants* is a fundamental aspect of a structuralist approach to narrative. It is built upon the presupposition that all stories are variations on one fundamental pattern, a pattern in which an *object* proceeds from an *ordainer,* and a *subject* desires either to possess the object or to communicate it to a *recipient.* In this effort the subject may be aided by a *helper* or impeded by an *opponent.* The fundamental scheme may be presented in the form of a diagram or grid as follows:

$$\text{ordainer} \longrightarrow \text{object} \longrightarrow \text{recipient}$$
$$\uparrow$$
$$\text{helper} \longrightarrow \text{subject} \longleftarrow \text{opponent}$$

If we approach the *story* of the Samaritan (Luke 10:30–35) from this standpoint then we have the following diagram, or grid.

$$\text{Samaritan} \longrightarrow \text{aid and healing} \longrightarrow \text{traveler}$$
$$\uparrow$$

oil, wine, $\longrightarrow$ Samaritan $\longleftarrow$ priest and Levite
donkey, inn-
keeper, robbers

The story is understood as one in which a Samaritan desires to communicate aid and healing to a traveler. The aid and healing proceeds from his own concern so he is both ordainer and subject. The *actantiel* role of helper is filled by a variety of things and people, while that of opponent is filled by the priest and Levite, who, if they "are not in the strictest sense the Samaritan's opponents . . . are, nevertheless, his opposites."

If we approach the *discourse* with the lawyer (Luke 10:25–37) then the diagram or grid is as follows:

Jesus   ⟶   the meaning of ⟶ ? (lawyer)
              "neighbor"

                ↑

the story ⟶   Jesus   ⟵ Jewish
                               exclusivism
                               represented in
                               the scribe

Jesus wants to communicate to the lawyer his own understanding of "neighbor." He is helped by the story, and hindered by the lawyer's own Jewish exclusivism. Whether the lawyer becomes a real recipient by accepting the understanding remains uncertain.

According to this analysis, our concern is either with a story of a Samaritan communicating aid and healing to a traveler, or with a story of Jesus attempting to communicate his understanding of "neighbor" to a lawyer, depending upon whether our unit of concern is the story alone, or the discourse as a whole.

Via now turns to the question of metaphor, which he argues is composed of two elements: "a vehicle which is relatively well known and a tenor which is less well known." In the metaphor "meaning passes from the vehicle to the tenor," and the important factor is the "semantic distance or tension between vehicle and tenor" which must be overcome by "semantic motion." This semantic motion "gives a new vision of reality by evoking a sense of similarity between what are seen as dissimilars: a new vision which comes as a shock, but a shock of recognition." In the case of the parables of Jesus there are eight true narrative parables: The Talents, Ten Maidens, Wedding Garment, Wicked Tenants, Unforgiving Servant, Workers in the Vineyard, Unjust Steward, Prodigal Son. These are the parables Via had discussed in his book,[225] and he reaffirms their distinctive nature as compared with the other parables of Jesus.[226] These eight narrative parables, are "metaphors of the Kingdom of God: they give a new vision of everyday existence as transected by the surprising incursion of the transcendent." Sometimes the Kingdom is specifically mentioned, and sometimes it is not, but "it is always represented implicitly and subsidiarily in the story by the King-master-father figure who is the *actan-*

tiel ordainer." In the story this figure "is involved in a dramatic encounter with a son-servant-subordinate figure who is the *actantiel*
subject." The Kingdom of God, the tenor of the metaphor, is in this
way drawn into the narrative, which is the vehicle of the metaphor.
"Thus the tenor is drawn into and becomes a part of the vehicle, a
story suggesting a paradigm of human existence." It is because of this
"that it is legitimate to say that the parable gives a new vision of
human existence as crossed by the divine." Or, perhaps better, that "the
Kingdom is seen as a qualification of human existence." The parable is
a metaphor of the Kingdom of God "because the semantic distance and
tension between the divine and the human is supported by the distance
between ordainer (King-father) and the subject (servant-son) who are
always separate and distinct characters."

Via is, therefore, working with three separate considerations: the
distinction between story and discourse, which establishes the text to
be interpreted; the *actantiel* analysis of the story, which enables us to
understand it; and the relationship between the parts of the metaphor
and the *actants* of the story, which makes the story a metaphor of the
Kingdom of God. He rejects Crossan's interpretation of The Good
Samaritan because Crossan analyzes Luke 10:30–36, which is not the
text to be interpreted, and because, when 10:30–35 is analyzed, the
Samaritan is seen to be both *ordainer* and *subject*. So the story is not a
parable, not a metaphor of the Kingdom of God, because in that case
"the semantic tension would have to be between ordainer and subject,
but in The Good Samaritan those actants are identical." If we analyze
only 10:30–35 "in a Jewish context" there is still sufficient "semantic
distance" between "Samaritan" and "compassion" to make the story a
metaphor. The narrative "is a metaphor which gives a new meaning to
the responsibilities of neighborliness."[227]

Of the points which Via was concerned to make the first, concerning
the unit to be interpreted, seemed well taken, and Crossan accepted it
on the basis of "*structural* logic," although he was prepared to defend
his original unit on the basis of "*traditio-critical* logic."[228] But even if
10:30–35 is accepted as a "discrete enclave as *story*," this still is to be
interpreted as he had interpreted 10:30–36. As story it is still "a parable and not an example, a metaphor-story of the Kingdom's advent as
a world-shattering event."

Crossan took up Via's *actantiel* analysis of the story and attacked it at three points. He argued from the internal dynamics of the text of the story itself that the receiver was to be identified as a Jew: "The narrator . . . identifies the Receiver implicitly, indirectly and topographically as a Jew." Then the "oil, wine, innkeeper" are not helpers; "they are simply instruments of the Subject's action." Neither can the robbers be considered helpers, they are part of the "initial action" of the story. The helper is the Samaritan himself who therefore functions as subject, ordainer, and helper in the story. Nor are the priest and Levite the opponents, "the *actantiel* opponent is, quite simply, prejudice or socio-religious exclusivism." These proposed changes give Crossan an *actantiel* grid from which he can argue his point about the meaning of the story.

A second point argued by Crossan concerns Via's claim that to be "a metaphor of the Kingdom" a parable had to exhibit "semantic distance" between the ordainer and the subject on the *actantiel* grid. Here he uses structuralist analysis—in analyzing the binary opposites present in the "deep structure" of Jesus' "parabolic narration"—as a basis for repeating his claim that many of the parables of Jesus reflect a concern for polar reversal, and it is this which makes them metaphors of the Kingdom.

At this point a student of the discussion begins to wonder whether the recourse to structuralist analysis in the form of the *actantiel* analysis of the narrative has helped us very much. Via can propose one form of the fundamental diagram or grid, and Crossan another. Even if one version could be shown to be clearly superior to the other, it is still not clear what this would mean in terms of our understanding of the narrative or story in Luke 10:30–35. The diagram or grid may or may not show us what this story has in common with other stories which might be subject to the same analysis, or how far and in what ways it matches some hypothetical *Ur*-story, but it is not evident what this might mean for our understanding of the story in Luke 10:30–35. Neither Via nor Crossan has demonstrated that recourse to such an analysis is necessary, or even apposite, in this particular instance. Via simply points to it as something widely practiced and proceeds to use it, and Crossan accepts it because, one suspects, he can make his points as readily in this way as in any other. But for the student of the discussion as a whole the question is whether such an analysis helps us to see something about the text under consideration that is obviously important and that we had not seen before. Neither in the hands of Via or of Crossan does the *actantiel* analysis satisfy such a criterion.

I have spoken in terms of "a student of the discussion" but I am obviously stating my own views. Because of the apparent inconclusiveness of this initial application of structural analysis to The Good Samaritan I find myself sympathetic to an aspect of Funk's contribution to this phase of the discussion.[229] Among other things, he reminds us that a narrative is "a device which invites hearers or readers to witness a series of events in a certain way." But the listener is not passive, because a narrative "calls for an act of answering imagination"; it "evokes response." The parables of Jesus "precipitate the hearer's judgment" by setting up "contrasting responses which prompt the listener to take sides in the story." They tend, deliberately, "to polarize the hearers along lines suggested by the contrasting responses" in the parables themselves. Sometimes the responses are made explicit, as in the cases of the brothers in The Prodigal Son; sometimes they are not made explicit; "how the listener works out his relationship to the options posed by the parable is left mostly to his private imagination." The Good Samaritan is "non-explicit."

This new statement by Funk is clearly in line with his previous claim that the narrative involves the hearer as participant, and with his previous concern for the hearer of The Good Samaritan being grasped by "his [the hearer's] position in the ditch."[230] For my part I find it a most welcome oasis after the desert of *actantiel* analysis, and I would reinforce it by pointing out that it is a point which does justice to the *realism* of Jesus' narratives. Obviously the listener is the more readily caught up into realistic than into non-realistic narrative.

Via's final contribution to *Semeia* 1[231] is concerned with issues at stake in the discussion in the seminar which we are deliberately omitting from this discussion, and I turn therefore to *Semeia* 2 (1974) where The Good Samaritan is discussed at length by four scholars: Daniel Patte, Georges Crespy, Funk, and Crossan.[232] From the standpoint of my discussion here only Funk's paper warrants treatment at any length. Patte is helpful in that he introduces us to structuralist method and terminology, but he uses The Good Samaritan simply to exemplify the method and terminology; he is not concerned to offer a discussion or an interpretation of the parable itself. Crespy's essay is misnamed, being called in English, "The Parable of the Good Samaritan: An Essay in Structural Research." It may be an essay in structural research, but it is not concerned with The Good Samaritan as the discussion has defined that parable, i.e., Luke 10:30–35(36), but rather with the total discourse between Jesus and the lawyer, i.e., Luke 10:25–37.[233] Crossan offers a very useful introduction to the historical development of structural analysis as a method, an introduction relating it not only to narrative but also to riddle and charm. He argues for a relationship between a parable and a charm, "a process whose final outcome is not to be found in it (as is the case in a narrative) but in the patient." So he is able to speak not only of the "parable-story" but also of the "parable-event," and to interpret The Good Samaritan as "a duel between the Speaker and the Hearer," as "an attack on the hearer at the most profound level." As a parable it is "an attack on world, a raid on the articulate," and, in light of his new discussion, Crossan can now say that it is "a story whose artistic surface structure allows its deep structure to invade one's hearing in direct contradiction to the deep structure of one's expectation."[234] It is evident that Crossan is finding ever new ways of expressing the insight that has characterized his interpretation of the parables from the beginning.

Funk's essay is also related to his initial insight with regard to the parable as metaphor, and I find in his "The Good Samaritan as Metaphor" a most important development of the insights first presented in the chapter, "The Parable as Metaphor" in his book *Language, Hermeneutic, and Word of God*.[235] He takes up the question of the language of The Good Samaritan, noting that in "the Jesus tradition" the parables were understood either as "allegories (coded theologies)" or as "example stories (models of right behavior)."[236] After "the revolutionary work of Adolf Jülicher" the parables were understood as example stories or as "illustrations of a point that could have been made, without essential loss, in discursive, non-figurative language" by, for example, Dodd and Jeremias. But if the parables originally functioned as metaphor then they had "an altogether different locus in language" from that of allegory, example story, or illustration. The knowledge communicated by the parable as metaphor is pre-conceptual knowledge, not conceptual knowledge. The parable "does not involve a transfer of information and ideas from one head to another"; rather "it opens onto an unfinished world because that world is in the course of conception." Funk claims that these ideas are derived from the concrete example of The Good Samaritan, so he offers a "reading" of the parable; that is, by the use of critical tools he offers the modern auditor a chance to hear the parable "in the appropriate key."

In effect Funk takes us through the parable, recreating the effect the story may be supposed to have had on its original hearers. As people familiar with the Jericho road and its dangers they would have identified with the traveler; as the narrative progresses they would be drawn to "the victim in the ditch at the side of the road," and they would pass judgment on the characters and incidents involved in the remainder of the narrative from that perspective. If they had clerical sympathies they would resent the fact that the narrative puts the priest and the Levite in the bad light of refusing to help; if they were anti-clerically inclined they would see the behavior of the priest and Levite as what was only to be expected. But the Samaritan would be a shock to everyone. The Samaritan was the "hated half-brother" of the Jew, and the Jew "who was excessively proud of his blood and a chauvinist about his tradition would not permit a Samaritan to touch him, much less minister to him." A Jew going from Galilee to Judea "would cross and recross the Jordan to avoid going through Samaria." So the story forces upon the hearer the question: "who among you will permit himself to be served by a Samaritan?" At this point I might add something noted earlier in the discussion, that according to some rabbinical opinion the acceptance of alms by a Jew from a Samaritan delayed the redemption of Israel.[237] The remainder of the story forces the auditor to accept the help of the Samaritan. The auditor/man in the ditch is half dead and unable to refuse—"permission to be served by the Samaritan is inability to resist"—and I might add that the story itself overwhelms the auditor with the details of the Samaritan's helpfulness. The impact of the story is to make the auditor, as a Jew, come to understand "what it means to be the victim in the ditch," and as the auditor does this, "he/she also understands what the Kingdom is all about."

I find myself extremely sympathetic to this "reading" of The Good Samaritan, because it puts the emphasis upon the function of the parable as a story, and because it does justice to the distinctive features of the story: the realism of its narrative, the force of its references and allusions in their impact upon the auditor, the fact that the story as metaphor of the Kingdom challenges the auditor to make a transference of judgment from the story as vehicle to the Kingdom as tenor of that metaphor, and the fact that it does this last thing the more effectively because it lays down no guidelines for it but leaves the auditor on his own confronted by that "clash of worlds" which itself is, to plagiarize Jüngel, the coming of the Kingdom as parable.

In the seminar a short paper was circulated by Robert C. Tannehill commenting on Funk's "The Good Samaritan," a paper not subsequently published. In this paper Tannehill challenged Funk's claim that the auditor would identify with the man in the ditch. The needs of that man are indeed the focal point of the story, but this will lead the audience to identify with the one who meets these needs, the Samaritan.

In this story the audience identifies with him before he appears, for the aborted sequence of the Priest and Levite heighten the tension and point forward to one who will do what they failed to do. Furthermore, the "law of three" leads the audience to expect that the resolution will take place when a third man comes by. The audience awaits this man as the hero of the story and the representation which has been encouraged by the story's structure of anticipation is thwarted by introduction of a Samaritan. He is clearly the hero, and yet the story makes it brutally hard for the audience to identify with him. He appears now not as the representative of their goodness but as representative of an alien goodness. He is an alien and what he does is alien, for he steps across the boundaries which men put around their love.

As a story The Good Samaritan "has the power to break open the hearer's world so long as the tension which both invites and thwarts the hearer's identification with the Samaritan is maintained."

Tannehill is offering a second possibility with regard to the "reading" of the story. Accepting the fact of audience identification as the key to interpreting the story as an event, he is arguing that the natural identification is with the Samaritan rather than with the "man in the ditch." This is a possibility to be given serious consideration, and one which probably has ultimately to be left to the individual auditor. But whether the identification is with victim or with rescuer, the fact of audience identification is still the key to understanding the impact of the parable as a story, to understanding the story as "event," or, to use the language of the "new hermeneutic," it is the key to understanding the parable as "language event." Furthermore, whether the audience identification is with victim or with rescuer, the fact that the victim is a Jew and the rescuer a Samaritan guarantees that the story will effect that "clash of worlds," or that "breaking open of the hearer's world," in which the Kingdom "comes."

I contend that, with these contributions by Funk and Tannehill to the SBL Parables Seminar, The Good Samaritan has been adequately and properly interpreted, that justice is now, finally, being done to the nature of the text itself, and that the many points made about this parable in the discussion are now being taken into account, insofar as they are valid.

I must repeat that I have only taken from the discussion of the SBL Parables Seminar such material as directly concerns the interpretation of The Good Samaritan, and that this by no means does justice to the work that the seminar is doing. But it does bring to a climax the discussion of that parable which began with Jülicher and I may, therefore, be permitted to summarize what I would regard as the conclusions to be drawn from its work.

At the level of the *text to be interpreted* The Good Samaritan is to be found in Luke 10:30–35. Form and redaction criticism had gradually taught us to recognize distinctions between parable and application, and between parable and settings given to it at various stages in the composition of the text finally represented by the Gospel of Luke. When we add to these considerations the structuralist insights mediated by Via the matter becomes incontrovertible: the interpreter of the parables is concerned with Luke 10:30–35 and not with anything from the discourse or dialogue in which those verses are now set.

So far as the *historical understanding* of the parable is concerned Crossan may be said to have carried the day with his understanding of the parable as concerned with the "clash of worlds," to use Wilder's description of Crossan's understanding. Although they may differ from Crossan in other points, all the other interpreters have come to agree on this as the point of Jesus' concern, and they tend to use this kind of language to describe the concern. So Via can say that "the narrative parables are metaphors of the Kingdom of God: they give a new vision of everyday existence as transected by the surprising incursion of the transcendent."[238] Funk, very circumspectly, suggests that the "enterprising theologian" might draw from The Good Samaritan the proposition, "In the Kingdom mercy is always a surprise,"[239] while Tannehill speaks of "the imaginative shock that can overturn worlds," and of The Good Samaritan as having "the power to break open the hearer's world."[240] That this, or something very like it, is the message of The Good Samaritan at the historical level may now be taken as established.

It is at the level of *literary criticism* that the discussion of The Good Samaritan in the SBL Parables Seminar makes its greatest impact and that, quite obviously, because of the application of the insights of *structuralist criticism* to the parable. But this impact turns out to be extremely disappointing to the interpreter of the parables. Patte helps us to understand structuralist method and terminology, in itself not an inconsiderable service(!), but he does not advance the interpretation of the parable itself.[241] Crespy, for all the title of his essay, is not in fact concerned with the parable as such, and in any case his essay presents serious problems to the biblical scholar. Crossan is finding new ways to express his original insights, in itself wholly valid but not in any way distinctively structuralist. Via is a very different matter. He is a leading biblical scholar and a major interpreter of the parables. When he programmatically advocates a structuralist interpretation of the parable he is, therefore, to be taken very seriously indeed. For this reason his "literary-structuralist approach" to the parable—with its obvious deliberate variation from his previous "literary-existentialist analysis" of the major narrative parables—demands our most careful attention. But it is at precisely this point that the non-structuralist student of the discussion becomes disappointed. Whereas Via's earlier "literary-existentialist analysis" of certain of the parables had immediately and obviously very considerably advanced our understanding of the parables concerned, his "literary-structuralist approach" to The Good Samaritan does no such thing. His *actantiel* grid is apparently suspect—since Crossan was immediately able to attack it—and, what is much more important, it did not offer the interpreter of the parable any kind of immediate help. The contrast here between his "literary-structuralist approach" and his previous "literary-existentialist analysis" is striking. For all the problems one might have with the latter, the contribution to the interpretation of the parable concerned was obvious and immediate. In the case of the former, the "literary-structuralist approach," the contribution this may make to the understanding and interpretation of this or any parable is by no means either obvious or immediate.

When one looks at the story of the modern interpretation of the parables one is struck by the sheer *impact* of the new developments in the discussion. Jülicher's demonstration that the parables were not allegories, Dodd's that they had to be set in the context of the eschatology of Jesus, Jeremias's that they had to be illuminated by an ability to set them in their original cultural-historical context, Via's original insistence on understanding them as literary-aesthetic objects, Crossan's on understanding them as poetic metaphors—all of these developments confront the interpreter and are obviously relevant to his task. At the very least it can be said that the structuralist approach makes no such immediate demand on the interpreter of the parables.

What is in many ways most interesting in the recent discussion of the interpretation of The Good Samaritan is to be found at the level of *interpretation into the present of the interpreter*. Here we have witnessed a most remarkable systematic attempt to allow the parable to speak on its own terms into the present. Whereas Jülicher had seen it as an instance of moral instruction, Jeremias as an aspect of the message of Jesus as a whole, and the "new hermeneutic" as a sermon preached by Jesus to his contemporaries, the recent American interpretation has attempted to allow the parable to speak for itself. The assumption has been that if we can understand the parable as metaphor, if we can understand the parable as a story, then the metaphor can be the bearer of reality for us, the story can speak directly to us. We are reaching quite deliberately toward what Paul Ricoeur calls a "post-critical naiveté" with regard to the text, toward a reading of the text fully appreciative of its *natural* force and potential meaning. In my view this point is reached in the case of The Good Samaritan with Funk's "reading" of the text, and Tannehill's "comments" on that reading. What this may mean in terms of the broader hermeneutical enterprise is something I propose to explore in a final study of "The Kingdom of God and the Parables of Jesus" in this volume.

NOTES

1. I should perhaps make it clear at the outset that I was a pupil of Professor Jeremias, receiving my doctorate from the University of Göttingen in 1959.

2. The concern for establishing historical information about Jesus is known as "the quest of the historical Jesus," an allusion to the title of Albert Schweitzer's famous book reviewing the nineteenth-century "quest." When the pupils of Bultmann, Ernst Käsemann, Günther Bornkamm, Ernst Fuchs, et al., renewed interest in *Die Frage nach dem historischen Jesu* ("the question of the historical Jesus") their work became known in English as "the new quest of the historical Jesus," the title of James M. Robinson's book describing the movement (see note 51 below). Both the "old quest" and the "new quest" are interested in historical information about Jesus; the distinction between them is that the former in concerned with any and all of such information while the latter is concerned with "the intentions, the stances, the understanding of existence . . . that can be established with regard to Jesus." (James M. Robinson, quoted in the Christmas, 1974, issue of *Time* magazine, p. 39).

3. A. Jülicher *Die Gleichnisreden Jesu*, published in two volumes, I (1888, 1899²), II (1899, 1910²). The work has not been translated into English.

4. Jülicher, I, pp. 203–322. We give an example of allegorical interpretation, Augustine's interpretation of The Good Samaritan, below, p. 94.

5. Jeremias, *The Parables of Jesus* (rev. ed.; New York: Scribner's, 1963), p. 18.

6. This is perhaps particularly true of the recent American discussion, which is very strong on literary factors and hence could have been expected to make a decisive contribution on a point like this, and indeed has done so. See especially Crossan, below, pp. 156–158.

7. E. Jüngel, *Paulus und Jesus* (Tübingen: J. C. B. Mohr [Paul Siebeck], 1962), pp. 91–94, has questioned the accuracy of Jülicher's appeal to Aristotle, claiming that the appeal is to Aristotle's logic rather than to his rhetoric, as Jülicher himself claims. But in any case, Jülicher's categories are drawn from Aristotle; they are not drawn from the immediate historical context of the parables, the use of parables in ancient Judaism. As one of Jülicher's critics put it, so far as Jülicher was concerned the Talmud was *terra incognita* (P. Fiebig, *Die Gleichnisreden Jesu im Lichte der rabbinischen Gleichnisse des neutestamentlichen Zeitalters* [1912], p. 121, quoted by Jüngel, p. 96, n. 1).

8. Jülicher, I, p. 83.

9. Ibid.

10. Taken from C. H. Dodd, *The Parables of the Kingdom* (rev. ed., New York: Scribner's, 1961), pp. 1–2.

11. Jülicher divided the parables of Jesus into three categories: *Gleichnisse, Parabeln,* and *Beispeilerzählungen.* These may be represented in English as similitude, parable, and exemplary story. A *similitude* is a simple comparison, e.g., The Hid Treasure, The Pearl of Great Price (Matt. 13:44–46), The Tower Builder, The King Going to War (Luke 14:28–32). A *parable* is a comparison extended into a story, e.g., The Lost Sheep, The Lost Coin, The Prodigal Son (Luke 15). An *exemplary story* is a story giving an example or illustrating a point. Jülicher counted four exemplary stories: The Good Samaritan (Luke 10:29–37), The Pharisee and Tax-Collector (Luke 18:9–14), The Rich Fool (Luke 12:16–21), The Rich Man and Lazarus (Luke 16:19–31). These distinctions have been maintained by the form critics.

Bultmann, for example, distinguishes between *similitude* ("distinguished from comparisons . . . only by the detail in which the picture is painted"), *parable* ("transposes the facts which serve for a similitude into a story, or, to put it in different terms, gives as its picture not a typical condition or a typical, recurrent event, but some interesting particular situation") and *exemplary story* ("stories offering examples or models of right behavior"), *The History of the Synoptic Tradition* (New York: Harper & Row and Oxford: Basil Blackwell, 1963; rev. ed. 1968), pp. 170, 174, 178. The English language discussion has generally not found these distinctions very helpful; as we shall see, Dodd specifically challenged them.

12. Jülicher, II, p. 585. The discussion of The Good Samaritan is pp. 585–598.

13. Ibid., p. 595.

14. Ibid., p. 596.

15. Jülicher lays great stress on the instructional nature of the parables, speaking often of them as "aids to understanding," or of the hearers' "fund of knowledge" being increased by them, e.g., I, p. 73.

16. Fiebig's challenge to Jülicher is in two books, of which this is the second. The books are *Altjüdische Gleichnisse und die Gleichnisse Jesu* (1904) and *Die Gleichnisreden Jesu im Lichte der rabbinischen Glichnisse des neutestamentlichen Zeitalters* (1912). For a review of this discussion in English see Geraint Vaughan Jones, *The Art and Truth of the Parables* (London: SPCK, 1964), pp. 22–24.

17. Jülicher, I, p. 149.

18. Ibid.

19. N. Perrin, "The Modern Interpretation of the Parables of Jesus and the Problem of Hermeneutics," *Interpretation* 25 (1971), p. 132.

20. See above, pp. 34–40.

21. See our discussion of this book and its impact on the discussion of Kingdom of God, above, pp. 37–39.

22. See above, p. 38.

23. See above, p. 39 note 39.

24. Jeremias, *Parables*, p. 230.

25. Dodd, *Parables*, p. 85.

26. Ibid., chap. IV, pp. 85–121: "The Setting in Life."

27. Ibid., p. 9.

28. Ibid., p. 10.

29. See below, pp. 133–138.

30. I am now summarizing, with occasional quotations, Dodd, *Parables*, pp. 5–7.

31. Remember Paul Ricoeur: "The symbol gives rise to thought"!

32. Dodd, *Parables*, p. 7.

33. Ibid., p. 4.

34. I may perhaps be permitted to add that he demanded that his students should also conduct such a study. The results of my own work here show in *Rediscovering the Teaching of Jesus* (New York: Harper & Row and London: SCM Press, 1967) where I regularly move from the earlier rabbinical literature to the parables of Jesus, e.g., pp. 84–87, 91–98, 110–114, 117–119.

35. For an example of this see below, pp. 170–171.
36. Jeremias, *Parables*, p. 9.
37. Ibid., p. 114.
38. Ibid., pp. 202–205.
39. Ibid., p. 206. Jeremias can include this because he interprets "parable" so widely as to include "apocalyptic revelation." Most other interpreters would not include this as a "parable." In any case it has little claim to authenticity.
40. Ibid., p. 205.
41. Ibid., p. 204.
42. Ibid.
43. The "new hermeneutic" has generated a considerable literature in English. The standard critical statement of the movement is John Cobb and James M. Robinson (eds.), *The New Hermeneutic* (New York: Harper & Row, 1964), and a good introduction to it is Paul Achtemeier, *An Introduction to the New Hermeneutic* (Philadelphia: Westminster Press, 1969). Fuchs has published a book in German, not translated, *Hermeneutik*, but that is little more than a set of lecture notes for a course that he used to give (and which, incidentally, I once audited). He tends to have done his most important work in essays, the most relevant of which have been translated in Ernst Fuchs, *Studies of the Historical Jesus* (SBT 42; London: SCM Press, 1964). One of his pupils, Ms. Eta Linnemann, has written a book on the parables, *Jesus of the Parables* (New York: Harper & Row and London: SPCK, 1966). For further literature see Achtemeier, *Introduction*.
44. The other is in a willingness to concern himself with the historical Jesus in matters of faith. See immediately below.
45. See above, pp. 10–12, 71–80.
46. For what follows see especially Bultmann, "The Primitive Christian Kerygma and the Historical Jesus," (above, p. 10 note 11), and N. Perrin, *The Promise of Bultmann* (Philadelphia: Lippincott, 1969), *passim*.
47. For more details on what follows see Perrin, *Promise* pp. 22–36.
48. Bultmann, as quoted in Perrin, *Promise*, p. 35. The quotation is from *Existence and Faith* (New York: Meridian Books, 1960 and London: Fontana Books, 1964), p. 107.
49. One should note that for Bultmann "self-understanding" and "understanding of [the self's] existence in the world" are co-terminous.
50. Bultmann, as quoted in Perrin, *Promise*, p. 62. The quotation is from R. Bultmann, *Theology of the New Testament* II (New York: Scribner's, and London: SCM Press, 1955), p. 239. Bultmann's italics.
51. I discussed the "new quest" briefly above, note 2, pointing out that it is a movement which takes its name from the title of a book by James M. Robinson describing its origins, *A New Quest of the Historical Jesus* (SBT 25; London: SCM Press, 1959). I chronicled the movement down to 1964 in *Rediscovering the Teaching of Jesus*, pp. 207–248 and 262–265 (annotated bibliography). Since 1964 the movement has lost both its momentum and its unity. Today it is the "question" of the historical Jesus and his significance for Christian faith (as it always was in German). The most recent discussion of that question in English is Leander E. Keck, *A Future for the*

Historical Jesus (New York and Nashville: Abingdon Press and London: SCM Press, 1972).

52. J. L. Austin, "Performative Utterances," in his *Philosophical Papers* (Oxford: Clarendon Press, 1961), pp. 220–239. Like so many other New Testament scholars, I owe my knowledge of Austin's work to R. W. Funk, *Language, Hermeneutic, and Word of God* (New York: Harper & Row, 1966), a book I shall discuss in some detail below. Funk's summary (pp. 26–27) of Austin's insight is as follows:

> In this order of discourse, a person is not merely *saying* something, he is doing something. The language itself is act. The vows exchanged in a wedding ceremony are good examples: one is not there reporting on marriage—which means that the vows are not subject to verification—but indulging in marriage. Other examples would be the sentence pronounced by a judge, the christening of a ship, the knighting of a hero, a provision in a will, an apology, a Presidential proclamation. This type of utterance cannot be adjudged either true or false.

53. Fuchs, "The Essence of 'Language Event' and Christology," in *Studies*, pp. 213–228, esp. 220.

54. Ibid., pp. 220–221.

55. It is a moot point among interpreters of Bultmann whether or not he could be pushed into acknowledging that the message of Jesus mediated the possibility of authentic existence for the hearer of Jesus. A typical statement is in his reply to his students on the "question of the historical Jesus": "We can say, however, that Jesus' appearance and his preaching imply a christology insofar as he called for a decision over against his person as the bearer of the word of God, a decision determining salvation or destruction." (Bultmann, "The Primitive Christian Kerygma and the Historical Jesus," in *The Historical Jesus and the Kerygmatic Christ*, ed. Braaten and Harrisville [New York and Nashville: Abingdon Press, 1964], p. 28). Whether such a statement means that Bultmann would have acknowledged that the message of Jesus mediated the possibility of authentic existence at the time of the hearing of the message, or only at the future coming of the Kingdom, is for the reader to decide. Bultmann himself would probably have refused to answer such a question, on the grounds that the temporal terms in which it is couched—the antithesis between present and future—are inappropriate to an existentialist understanding of the message of Jesus. But, in any case, Bultmann always insisted that only the kerygma of the church mediates the possibility of authentic existence now, and Fuchs is self-consciously varying from Bultmann in claiming that "Jesus' proclamation bestows on these people freedom for the word," so my sharply antithetical formulation of the matter is justifiable in the immediate context of a delineation of the differences between Bultmann and Fuchs. In the context of a careful presentation of the Bultmannian theology, however, one would probably want to be more circumspect.

56. Bultmann would have no problem with the parable mediating the possibility of authentic existence to the subsequent interpreter, *providing it was presented to the interpreter as part of the kerygma of the church*. But he would strenuously resist the idea of this being a sharing of Jesus' under-

standing of existence, because we do not know what Jesus' understanding of existence was. Jesus could only be said to have experienced authentic existence if we could know how he understood his own death, because authentic existence by definition includes the overcoming of the fear of death. But how Jesus understood his own death is precisely what we do not know about him. See Bultmann, "Primitive Christian Kerygma," p. 23.

57. ". . . an improbable psychological construction." Bultmann, "Primitive Christian Kerygma," p. 23, in specific reference to Fuchs's views.

58. Fuchs, *Studies*, p. 23, from an essay "The Quest of the Historical Jesus." It was this which Bultmann dismissed as "an improbable psychological construction."

59. Ibid., pp. 93–94, from an essay "What is Interpreted in the Exegesis of the New Testament?"

60. E. Linnemann, *Jesus of the Parables: Introduction and Exposition* (New York: Harper & Row and London: SPCK, 1966). German original *Gleichnisse Jesu, Einführung und Auslegung* (1961, 1964³). "The Parables as 'Language Events' " is pp. 30–33 of the English translation.

61. Ibid., p. 31.

62. Ibid., p. 32.

63. Ibid., p. 33.

64. Ibid.

65. Ibid., pp. 51–58.

66. Ibid., pp. 55–56.

67. Linnemann's translation of Luke 18:14, ibid., p. 62.

68. The quotations are from *Jesus of the Parables*, pp. 63, 72–73, 80, 86–87, 90–91, 102.

69. Jüngel, *Paulus und Jesus*. The book was originally a doctoral dissertation examining "the relationship between the Pauline doctrine of justification by faith and the proclamation of Jesus."

70. I did not judge Lohmeyer important enough in this discussion to warrant attention in this review. He wrote an essay *"Vom Sinn der Gleichnisse Jesu"* ("On the Meaning of the Parables of Jesus") which, as Jüngel says (p. 121), "exercised no influence on the progress of New Testament research."

71. See note 7 above.

72. Jüngel, *Paulus und Jesus*, pp. 135–139.

73. I think this point is very well taken. To distinguish between an outer dispensable form and an inner indispensable intent is a very dubious procedure in the case of so dynamic a literary form as the parable. This was the fundamental element in my criticism of Jeremias for drawing a "message" from the parables above.

74. Again, a point very well taken. I would make the same point by saying that the parables do not expound a conception of the Kingdom of God; they mediate an experience of God as king as existential reality.

75. Jüngel's *italics*. At this point Jüngel becomes the victim of a passion for enigmatic expression. I will attempt to establish what he means by this enigmatic italicized statement below.

76. Again, a point well taken.

77. Jüngel, pp. 136–137.

78. (6) distinguishes between parable and allegory in terms of the parable's constant reference toward the one point of all the parables. (7) distinguishes between the parable as *revealing* in that it directs attention to the one ultimate point of all the parables, and as *concealing* in that one point is evident only from the totality of the parables. (8) concerns the fact that the parables are self-contained literary units: as "language events" they do not need completion by reference to something outside themselves. (9) makes a very obscure point about the alleged fact that, since the parables manifest the Kingdom of God as parable, they preserve the distinction between God and the world. (10) claims that since the Kingdom of God comes *zur Sprache* in the parables *of Jesus* then there is a necessary relationship between this and Jesus himself. (11) reiterates a claim of Fuchs that Jesus himself in his life and attitude (*Verhalten*) was a commentary on the parables. With the transmission of parables in the tradition of the church this commentary was necessarily lost, and other interpretations were supplied. (12) claims that now this original commentary can be recovered as we recognize the eschatological nature of Jesus' *Verhalten*.

79. Jüngel, *Paulus und Jesus*, pp. 139–174.

80. Ibid., p. 145, with a quotation from Fuchs, "Jesus' Understanding of Time," *Studies*, p. 130.

81. Ibid., p. 147 Jüngel's *italics*.

82. Ibid., p. 151.

83. Cf. Fuchs, *Studies*, p. 140 "Jesus . . . is not just illustrating something huge; he is issuing a *summons* for the *Basileia*."

84. Jüngel, *Jesus und Paulus*, pp. 153–154.

85. Ibid., pp. 155–169.

86. Ibid., pp. 169–173. What follows is a summary of these pages with occasional quotations.

87. In his review of Jülicher, Jungel had found Jülicher's division of the parables into the various classes of similitude, parable, and exemplary story to be very useful, ibid., p. 95.

88. The context slips back into the interpretation!

89. Fuchs, *Studies*, p. 84, from an essay "What is Interpreted in the Exegesis of the New Testament?" How far Fuchs follows the principles he states so well is a good question!

90. Jüngel tends not to speak of Jesus' decisions although he does echo Fuchs in other uses of highly personal language in connection with Jesus: Jesus "gathers," "guarantees," "wagers," etc.

91. Gerhard Ebeling, co-leader with Fuchs of the "new hermeneutic" as a theological movement, did in fact make precisely this response to Bultmann. See Perrin, *Rediscovering the Teaching of Jesus*, p. 229, with references.

92. See below, pp. 130–131.

93. James M. Robinson, "Jesus' Parables as God Happening" in *Jesus and the Historian*, ed. F. Thomas Trotter (Philadelphia: Westminster Press, 1968), pp. 134–150. Robinson is the leading American representative of the movement, and perhaps its most important theoretician. He has published a brilliant survey of the recent developments in hermeneutical theory, from the standpoint of one to whom the "new hermeneutic" is the natural climax of those developments: "Hermeneutic since Barth," *The New Hermeneutic*,

ed. John B. Cobb and James M. Robinson (New York: Harper & Row, 1964), pp. 1–77.

94. Robinson, "Jesus' Parables," p. 141.

95. See our discussion above, especially pp. 117–118.

96. In what follows I am greatly indebted to R. W. Funk, *Language, Hermeneutic, and Word of God*, pp. 20–46 ("Language as Event: Bultmann and Heidegger") and 47–71 ("Language as Event: Fuchs and Ebeling"). This is a most sympathetic and helpful presentation of the insights with which the "new hermeneutic" is working. Funk himself goes on to discuss the parables at length in part II of the book, pp. 124–222 ("Language as It Occurs in the New Testament: Parable"), and it is both interesting and important to note that he begins that discussion with a chapter on "The Parable as Metaphor" (pp. 133–162), thereby recognizing the necessity to go beyond "language as event" before one can interpret the parables. Funk's discussion of metaphor and his interpretation of the parables will concern us in detail below, pp. 132–141.

97. Funk, *Language, Hermeneutic, and Word of God*, p. 39, with quotations from an essay by Heidegger, "Hölderlin and the Essence of Poetry."

98. Funk, ibid., p. 40.

99. Funk, ibid.

100. A quotation from Heidegger, *Über der Humanismus*, Funk, ibid.

101. Funk, ibid., p. 45.

102. Funk notes this: ". . . what Heidegger is about is being carried on elsewhere by littérateurs and artists." Ibid., p. 45.

103. Robinson, "Jesus' Parables," p. 145.

104. Fuchs, *Studies*, p. 220, from an essay "The Essence of the 'Language-event' and Christology." We quoted part of this passage above, note 52.

105. Ibid., p. 20, from an essay "The Quest of the Historical Jesus."

106. Robinson, "Jesus' Parables," p. 140.

107. Fuchs, *Studies*, p. 211, from an essay "What is a 'Language-event'?"

108. Funk, *Language, Hermeneutic, and Word of God*, p. 50.

109. Fuchs, *Studies*, p. 8.

110. See above, note 58.

111. Amos Wilder, *Early Christian Rhetoric: The Language of the Gospel* (New York: Harper & Row, 1964, rev. ed., Cambridge, Mass.: Harvard University Press, 1971). I quote the revised edition.

112. Eighteen pages, ibid., pp. 71–88.

113. Ibid., p. 72. This is, of course, a variation of the division with which we have become familiar: similitude, parable, exemplary story. Wilder is distinguishing between exemplary stories as narratives which serve to exemplify models to be imitated or warnings to be observed and revelatory images, either simple, the similitude, or extended, the parable.

114. Ibid., p. 72 and note 1.

115. Ibid.

116. Ibid., pp. 72–73.

117. Ibid., p. 73.

118. Ibid., p. 75.

119. Ibid., p. 77.

120. Ibid., pp. 82–86.

121. Ibid., p. 82.

122. Ibid., p. 84.

123. Ibid., pp. 84, 85.

124. Ibid., p. 85.

125. Ibid.

126. Ibid. The quotation is from Fuchs, *Hermeneutik*, p. 228.

127. The Coptic text had been edited and published, with an English translation, by A. Guillament et al, as *The Gospel According to Thomas* (Leiden: E. J. Brill, 1959).

128. A major feature of the parables in Thomas is that they seem in many cases to have escaped the process of allegorization which has so strongly affected the text of the parables in the canonical gospels. Two striking instances of this are The Great Supper (Matt. 22:1–14; Luke 14:16–24; Thom. 92:10–35) and The Wicked Husbandman (Mark 12:1–12; Thom. 93:1–18).

129. In the sixth German edition of his book on the parables, and hence in the revised English translation, Jeremias made use of the Gospel of Thomas in this way, as I did in my *Rediscovering the Teaching of Jesus*. It is now standard practice among interpreters who are particularly concerned with the parables as parables *of Jesus*, e.g., Dominic Crossan.

130. Of the pioneer redaction critical works, Bornkamm's two articles on Matthew appeared in 1947 and 1954, Conzelmann's book on the theology of Luke in 1954 and Marxsen's study of the evangelist Mark in 1956. See N. Perrin, *What is Redaction Criticism?* (Philadelphia: Fortress Press, 1969 and London: SPCK, 1970), pp. 25, 39.

131. The most comprehensive and perhaps the best work to come out of this period is Günther Bornkamm's *Jesus of Nazareth*. The third German edition appeared in 1959 and was translated into English in 1960. The format of Bornkamm's original publication forbade detailed treatment of technical issues, a situation I tried to remedy in *Rediscovering the Teaching of Jesus* in 1967 (a German translation of a slightly revised version appeared in 1974 as *Was Lehrt Jesu Wirklich?*). Bornkamm has updated his work in the article "Jesus Christ" in the third edition of the *Encylopedia Britannica* (1974) and I mine in *The New Testament: An Introduction* (1974), and also in the studies in this volume.

132. See above, pp. 99–100.

133. R. W. Funk, *Language, Hermeneutic, and Word of God* pp. 133–162.

134. Ibid., p. 133.

135. Ibid.

136. Ibid., pp. 133, 134.

137. Ibid., p. 135.

138. This is my comparison, not Funk's, but I think it is a legitimate comparison.

139. Funk, ibid., p. 137.

140. Funk does not use the last equation, but I believe it represents his insight.

141. Funk, ibid., p. 137.

142. Ibid., p. 139.

143. Ibid., p. 140.

144. Ibid., p. 144.
145. Ibid., pp. 148–149.
146. Ibid., p. 151.
147. Ibid.
148. Ibid., p. 152.
149. Ibid., p. 155.
150. Ibid., p. 161.
151. Ibid., pp. 161–162.
152. Ibid., pp. 163–198.
153. Ibid., pp. 199–222.
154. Ibid., p. 212.
155. Ibid., pp. 212–213.
156. Ibid., p. 214.
157. Perrin, "Modern Interpretation," p. 141.
158. See below, pp. 162–165.
159. I share the view of Jeremias who does not see in the story any reference to the possible excuse of the priest or Levite that touching a dead man might defile them and hence make it impossible for them to carry out their duties. As Jeremias points out, this would only be true under certain special conditions, and there is no hint in the story of any such consideration. See above, p. 107 and Jeremias, *Parables*, pp. 203–204.
160. I should also point out that I am deliberately omitting any reference to the last phases of Funk's discussion of The Good Samaritan, pp. 215–222, phases in which he takes up the question of a possible christological interpretation of the parable, and the further question of the significance of the parable as an interpretation of the Old Testament. He himself tends to abandon these as not essential to the immediate "reading" of the parable when he returns to the parable in the SBL Parables Seminar. See below, pp. 176–178.
161. Perrin, "Biblical Scholarship in a New Vein," *Interpretation* 21 (1967), pp. 465–469; "The Parables of Jesus as Parables, as Metaphors and as Aesthetic Objects," *JR* 50 (1970), pp. 340–346; "Modern Interpretation," *Interpretation* 25 (1971), pp. 142–143. I should perhaps make it clear, however, that I am not now repeating anything I have said earlier, but rather I am attempting a new assessment of Via and his work.
162. Dan O. Via, Jr., *The Parables: Their Literary and Existential Dimension* (Philadelphia: Fortress Press, 1967), pp. 11–12.
163. Ibid., pp. 21–24.
164. See the previous discussion of Bultmann's hermeneutics, above, pp. 10–12, 71–80, 108–110.
165. Via, *Parables*, pp. 37–43.
166. Ibid., p. 39.
167. Ibid., pp. 24–25.
168. The fact that they were originally oral compositions does not change this point. Even as oral compositions they were carefully organized, self-contained coherent wholes, and in any case they confront us as literary compositions.
169. Via, ibid., p. 53.

170. Ibid., pp. 53–57.
171. Ibid., pp. 70–107.
172. Ibid., p. 74.
173. Ibid., p. 77.
174. Ibid., p. 79.
175. Ibid., pp. 82–83.
176. Ibid., p. 84. Via returns to this imagery again and again in his interpretation of the parables.
177. Ibid., pp. 88, 93–95.
178. Ibid., p. 95.
179. Ibid., p. 120.
180. Ibid., p. 96.
181. Ibid., p. 97.
182. Ibid., pp. 97–98.
183. Ibid., pp. 110–144 and 145–176. At this stage of his work Via does not explain why he limits his interpretation to these eight parables. Later he was to explain that only in these eight parables do we find "organically united" plots with the same figure present in all the episodes giving the plot its shape. Via, "Parable and Example Story," *Semeia* 1 (1974), p. 115.
184. He was later to claim that it was not a parable with an organically united plot, *Semeia* 1 (1974), pp. 115–116.
185. What follows is a summary, with occasional quotations, of Via, *Parables*, pp. 113–122.
186. What follows is a summary, with occasional quotations, of Via, *Parables*, pp. 147–155.
187. See below, pp. 165–166.
188. See note 161 above.
189. *Interpretation* 21 (1967), p. 408.
190. *Interpretation* 25 (1974), p. 142.
191. See Paul Ricoeur, *The Symbolism of Evil* (Boston: Beacon Press, 1969), *passim*.
192. John Dominic Crossan, *In Parables: The Challenge of the Historical Jesus* (New York: Harper & Row, 1973). The material in the book itself had a previous publication history. Chapter 1, "Parables and the Temporality of the Kingdom," is an expansion and revision of "Parable as Poetic and Religious Experience," *JR* 53 (1973), pp. 330–358. Chapter 2, "Parables of Advent," was originally part of an article, "The Seed Parables of Jesus," *JBL* 92 (1973), pp. 244–266. Chapter 3, "Parables of Reversal," appeared earlier as, "Parable and Example in the Teaching of Jesus," *NTS* 18 (1971–72), pp. 285–307. Chapter 4, "Parables of Action," includes material published earlier as, "The Parable of the Wicked Husbandmen," *JBL* 90 (1971), pp. 451–465. Further, one section of the book itself was reworked for publication in *Semeia* 1; "The Servant Parables," *In Parables*, pp. 96–120, became "The Servant Parables of Jesus," *Semeia* 1, pp. 17–62.
193. Crossan, *In Parables*, pp. 9–10.
194. Ibid., p. 11, quoting Ricoeur, *Symbolism of Evil*, pp. 163–164.
195. Ibid., pp. 12–14.
196. Ibid., p. 15.
197. Ibid., pp. 32–33. The concluding aphorism is obviously an allusion

to the one used so often in connection with Heidegger, "language is the house of Being."

198. Ibid., p. 33.

199. "And He said: 'The man is like a wise fisherman who cast his net into the sea, he drew it up from the sea full of small fish; among them he found a large (and) good fish, that wise fisherman, he threw all the small fish down into the sea, he chose the large fish without regret.' " Crossan, ibid., p. 34. Jeremias had already connected this parable with The Treasure and The Pearl, *Parables*, p. 201.

200. Crossan, ibid.

201. Ibid., pp. 35–36.

202. Crossan gives the parallel references, including the references to the Gospel of Thomas. I give only the first reference in each instance.

203. These are the parables which interest Crossan most greatly. He discusses one in detail, The Good Samaritan, pp. 57–66, and offers short discussions of the others, pp. 66–75. He then discusses the theme of the group under the rubric "Eschaton and Paradox," pp. 75–78.

204. Ibid., pp. 96–120. Crossan here uses structuralist tools very significantly in his discussion, and he offered a further version of this discussion to the SBL Parables Seminar (now in *Semeia* 1, see note 192 above).

205. Dodd used them as the key to his "realized eschatology," *Parables*, p. 85; Jeremias has them as the key to his "realized discipleship," the most comprehensive of his rubrics in that it involves man's commitment, *Parables*, p. 198; I used them myself as the lead into the use of the parables in Perrin, *Rediscovering*, pp. 87–88. I say "unreflectively" because I know that my use was unreflective. It was not until I read Crossan that I realized that this is what I had done!

206. What follows is a summary, with occasional quotations of Crossan, *In Parables*, pp. 39–44, 50–52.

207. What follows is a summary, with occasional quotations, of Crossan, ibid., pp. 57–66.

208. What follows is a summary, with occasional quotations, of Crossan, ibid., pp. 111–115.

209. See above, pp. 151–152.

210. Among previous interpreters Dodd, Jeremias, and Linnemann had all read verse 15 as part of the parable, allowing this verse to influence their interpretation. Crossan, ibid., p. 112.

211. One example of this: Crossan determines that The Sower ends with the multiples 30, 60, 100—and not 30, 60, 120 as in the Gospel of Thomas—on the grounds that "the 30/60/120 of Thomas may be better mathematics than the 30/60/100 of Mark but it is not as good poetry." Ibid., p. 43.

212. I hope to point this out in an "Editors' Bookshelf" to be published in the *Journal of Religion* late in 1975.

213. Perrin, *Rediscovering*, p. 123: "The parable is itself an 'exemplary story' . . . ."

214. See above, p. 158.

215. See above, p. 158.

216. I had the honor to be an officer of the SBL at the time of the formation of the seminar, and I am a member of it. I speak, therefore, from

personal knowledge of the formation of the seminar, but I must hasten to add that I am offering a personal interpretation of its purpose.

217. See above, pp. 126, 133, 141, 156.

218. Crossan, "The Servant Parables of Jesus," and "Parable and Example in the Teaching of Jesus," *Semeia* 1 (1974), pp. 17–62 and 63–104.

219. Via, "Parable and Example Story: A Literary-Structuralist Approach," ibid., pp. 105–133.

220. Funk, "Critical Note," ibid., pp. 182–191; Crossan, "Structuralist Analysis and the Parables of Jesus," ibid., pp. 192–221; Via, "A Response," ibid., pp. 222–235.

221. Amos N. Wilder, "An Experimental Journal for Biblical Criticism: An Introduction," ibid., pp. 1–16.

222. See above, pp. 162–165.

223. Wilder, *Semeia* 1, p. 15.

224. What follows is a summary, with occasional quotations, of Via, *Semeia* 1, pp. 222–235, insofar as those pages concern The Good Samaritan.

225. See above, pp. 149–150.

226. He does this in terms of a claim that these eight realize the various possibilities of the "deep structure" of Jesus' parables in a way that others do not. See *Semeia* 1, pp. 108–110 and 127.

227. Those last quotations are from *Semeia* 1, p. 119.

228. What follows is a summary, with occasional quotations, of Crossan, "Structuralist Analysis and the Parables of Jesus," *Semeia* 1, pp. 192–221, insofar as those pages concern The Good Samaritan.

229. Funk, "Critical Note," *Semeia* 1, pp. 182–191, esp. 187–189.

230. See above, pp. 138–139.

231. Via, "A Response to Crossan, Funk, and Peterson," *Semeia* 1, pp. 222–235.

232. Patte, "An Analysis of Narrative Structure and the Good Samaritan," *Semeia* 2, pp. 1–26; Crespy, "The Parable of the Good Samaritan: An Essay in Structural Research," ibid., pp. 27–50; Funk, "The Good Samaritan as Metaphor," ibid., pp. 74–81; Crossan, "The Good Samaritan: Towards a Generic Definition of Parable," ibid., pp. 82–112.

233. It is also, in my view, an essay of such deplorable quality that it is difficult for the biblical scholar to take it seriously. I am not competent to judge it from the viewpoint of a structuralist critic.

234. *Semeia* 2, p. 98.

235. For the earlier discussion of this see above, pp. 131–138.

236. What follows is a summary, with occasional quotations, of Funk, "The Good Samaritan as Metaphor," *Semeia* 2, pp. 74–81.

237. See above, pp. 119–120.

238. Via, *Semeia* 1, p. 118.

239. Funk, *Semeia* 2, p. 80.

240. Unpublished comment on Funk's "The Good Samaritan as Metaphor." Tannehill had earlier found this same quality in some of the proverbial sayings, "The 'Focal Instance' as a Form of New Testament Speech," *JR* 50 (1970), pp. 372–385.

241. For the following reference to Patte, Crespy, and Crossan see note 232 above.

CHAPTER IV

The Kingdom of God and the
Parables of Jesus: Some Conclusions

We have now completed our review, both of Kingdom of God in the message of Jesus and of the interpretation of the parables of Jesus. It is time, therefore, to draw some conclusions from these reviews and this I will attempt to do, beginning at the level of the historical Jesus.

A. THE MESSAGE OF THE HISTORICAL JESUS

In the study of the Kingdom of God above I deliberately made no attempt to summarize the message of Jesus "in the form of propositional statements" because the characteristic linguistic forms of Jesus' proclamation "resist translation into other modes of discourse."[1] The study of the interpretation of the parables can only reinforce such a consideration because that discussion has shown how wholly inappropriate it is to subsume "the message of the parables" under a series of propositional rubrics. The parables must be allowed to speak for themselves. But, at the same time, we have seen that the most characteristic forms of Jesus' speech tend to revolve around two distinct poles, to have two distinct foci of concern. I would describe these poles or foci as "proclamation" and "parenesis."

The discussion of Kingdom of God and the parables has shown unmistakably how strong the element of proclamation is in the message of Jesus.[2] The *Kingdom sayings*[3] challenge Jesus' hearers to recognize the Kingdom of God as a reality in the exorcisms, to recognize that the ancient myth of the activity of God as king can now be realized in their experience in various ways, and to recognize that the fate of the Bap-

194

tist, and the potential fate of Jesus and his followers, are to be understood as a manifestation of the reality of God acting as king. The
Lord's Prayer[4] invites the disciple to pray for the "coming" of the
Kingdom, but uses "Kingdom" as a tensive symbol. The disciple is
taught to pray that he or she may know the activity of God within the
reality of their concrete historicality. The *proverbial sayings*[5] proclaim
the "coming" of the Kingdom as the hearer is jolted out of the effort to
make a continuous whole of human existence. The *parables*[6] proclaim
this coming in dramatic reversal, in the clash of worlds, in the sudden,
unexpected transection of the everyday by the incursion of the divine. I
would claim that the exegeses I have offered and the discussion I have
reviewed establish this beyond any possibility of doubt or cavil.

At the same time there is, however, a second pole, a second focus of
concern, one that I would call "parenesis," the element of *response* to
the reality being proclaimed. This is also to be seen in each of the
characteristic forms of Jesus' speech. In the *Kingdom sayings*[7] the
"breathtaking" claim that the fate of John the Baptist and the potential
fate of Jesus and his followers could be a manifestation of the Kingdom
of God necessarily involves the response of John the Baptist, Jesus,
himself, and his followers, to the claims of the Kingdom upon them.[8]
Without their response to the experience of God acting as king their
fate could not have become a manifestation of the Kingdom. In the
Lord's Prayer[9] the petitions are "explorations of fundamental possibilities for the experience of God as king in human life," and among them
is one, "Forgive us . . . as we herewith forgive . . . ," which clearly
intends "to link the experience of God to the response of man." In the
proverbial sayings we found a number of parenetical sayings, sayings
which we called "metaphors of response."[10] In the case of the *parables*
this aspect was not developed because the emphasis was upon the
problems of the interpretation of the parables in general, and upon the
way in which these problems are exemplified in the interpretation of
The Good Samaritan in particular. As it happens, The Good Samaritan
is a proclamatory parable, so we had no occasion to explore the possibility of the parables as parenesis. We turn to this possibility, briefly,
now.

A most important feature of the interpretation of the parables of
Jesus, at the historical level, is Dominic Crossan's use of the three
parables, The Hid Treasure, Costly Pearl and Great Fish as "key" or

"paradigmatic" parables.[11] He was justified in doing this, and he was justified, further, in claiming that the themes of advent, reversal, and action could be derived from these parables and therefore regarded as themes of the parables as a whole. In the course of the discussion in the SBL Parables Seminar[12] he further defined "parables of action" as parables "which invite and demand commitment to God in Kingdom." At the same time, Crossan argued, since the theme of reversal is so strong a theme in the parables as a whole, we must expect that there will be some parables which warn the hearer that the commitment "is to a God whose ways are not our ways."[13] In a very important diagrammatic presentation of his understanding of the parables of Jesus as a whole,[14] Crossan argues further that the parables of action are "images of . . . reactions to situations of challenge or crisis," and that they are of three types according to whether the reactions are (1) successful, (2) unsuccessful, or (3) both. Among the parables of *successful reaction* to the Kingdom as challenge or crisis are The Friend at Midnight (Luke 11:5–8), The Unjust Judge (Luke 18:2–5), and The Doorkeeper (Mark 13:34–36); among the parables of *unsuccessful reaction* are The Rich Fool (Luke 12:16–20; Thom. 92:3–10) and The Throne Claimant (Luke 19:12b, 14–15a, 27); and among the parables including *both reactions* are The Bridesmaids (Matt. 25:1–13) and The Talents (Matt. 25:14–30; Luke 19:12–27).

As I hope my review of the discussion has made clear, I am very impressed by Crossan's interpretation of the parables at the level of a historical understanding, and here he has made my point for me. The parables listed are concerned with the theme of action in response to the challenge of the crisis; they are, to use my term, "parenetical"; the parables reflect both poles or foci of concern as do the other linguistic forms characteristic of the message of Jesus.

The discussion has established the fact that in the proclamation of Jesus "Kingdom of God" was used[15] as a tensive symbol, and that it was used to evoke the myth of God acting as king. The challenge of the message of Jesus was to recognize the reality of the activity of God in the historicality of the hearer's existence in the world, and especially in the experience of a "clash of worlds"[16] as the hearer came to grips with the reality of everyday human existence.

B. THE INTERPRETATION OF KINGDOM OF GOD
IN THE MESSAGE OF JESUS

A major feature of the discussions above has been the deliberate attention given to literary factors. I was concerned to claim that Kingdom of God is a *symbol*, rather than a *conception* in the message of Jesus, and that indeed considering it as a conception had in fact caused difficulties in the discussion. Once it was seen as a symbol such unanswerable questions as whether it was present or future, or both, in the message of Jesus could be seen to be false questions, and one could begin to ask the true questions. The questions that should be asked, in my view, are questions as to what kind of symbol Kingdom of God is in the message of Jesus, and what does it evoke or represent.

In the exegesis I carried out, I argued the Kingdom of God was a *tensive* symbol in the message of Jesus, that it was, to use Wheelwright's terms again, a symbol of cultural range, a symbol having meaning for people in cultural continuity with ancient Israel and its myth of God acting as king, a cultural continuity in which Jesus certainly stood. On the lips of Jesus the symbol evoked the ancient myth, and the claim of his message was that the reality mediated by the myth was to be experienced dramatically by his hearers. Thus a literary concern was important to an understanding of the message of Jesus at the historical level.

As we move from a historical understanding of the message of Jesus to the possibilities for interpreting that message in a subsequent day and age, then a consideration of literary factors remains essential. The interpretation of the coming of the Kingdom of God in terms of the coming of the Son of Man in the New Testament involved an understanding of the symbol as a steno- rather than as a tensive symbol. The speculative theological use of the symbol by Augustine also involved literary features in that Augustine was reading the New Testament texts as allegories and Kingdom of God had become for him a speculative cipher to which he could give any meaning demanded by his overall theological system. With the rise of the historical sciences the interpretation of Kingdom of God in the message of Jesus became more self-conscious and Johannes Weiss carried through the first modern scientific (*wissenschaftlich*) interpretation. He thought of Kingdom of God as a conception and decided that as a conception it had nothing to say to modern man, thereby opening up what I have called the "hermeneutical gulf" between the message of Jesus and modern, technological man.

After Weiss we considered only two further interpreters and we considered these from the literary standpoint of their interpretation of Kingdom of God in the message of Jesus as a symbol evoking a myth. We considered Walter Rauschenbusch because he fully accepted the ancient myth and hence was able to return to a direct and natural use of the symbol. Using the symbol directly and naturally remains a hermeneutical option for those for whom the myth is still valid and meaningful. We considered Rudolf Bultmann because he is much the most important modern interpreter of Jesus' use of Kingdom of God, and because he represents the hermeneutical option diametrically opposed to that represented by Rauschenbusch. For Bultmann the myth is dead and the symbolic language, archaic; he, therefore, sought a means of translating the myth as an "expression of life," and found it in the hermeneutics of "demythologizing." Bultmann's interpretation remains an option for those for whom the myth is dead and the symbolic language archaic, but there are problems, both with Bultmann's understanding of myth—which he sees as prescientific cosmology—and with his understanding of the symbolic language—which he sees as symbolizing a conception and in which the symbols are steno-symbols. The question, therefore, arises as to whether Bultmann's demythologizing is the *only* hermeneutical option open to those who can no longer accept the myth and use the symbol as naturally and directly as did Rauschenbusch.

The answer to this question is, No it is not. Other possibilities arise if Kingdom of God is seen as a tensive symbol in the message of Jesus, and if the myth it evokes is seen as true myth, i.e., as a narrative means of demonstrating "the inner meaning of the universe and of human life," or as a means of verbalizing one's basic understanding of the historicity of human existence in the world in language meant to be taken seriously but not necessarily literally. In my SBL Presidential Address I expressed the hermeneutical option which challenges me personally as the responsibility to explore "the manifold ways in which the experience of God can become an existential reality to man" and to understand Kingdom of God not as "a single identifiable event which every man experiences at the same time," but as something "which every man experiences in his own time."[17] Since I would be fully prepared to argue that "activity of God" and an "event which every man experiences" is ultimately mythological language to be taken seriously but not necessarily literally, in the last resort my option may not produce a result significantly different from "a Bultmannian understanding of the eschatology of Jesus."[18] But I would claim that it had been arrived at by a more defensible hermeneutical method. Nor would I claim that the option which challenges me is the only possible option between those represented by Rauschenbusch and Bultmann. Others, more skilled than I in the understanding of symbol and myth, may arrive at other and more persuasive hermeneutical options. What I am concerned to claim is that a valid hermeneutics to be applied to Jesus' proclamation of the Kingdom of God must take seriously and deal most carefully with the elements of symbol and myth in that proclamation. The nature of the language of the proclamation demands this.

C. THE INTERPRETATION OF THE PARABLES OF JESUS

The interpretation of the parables of Jesus is perhaps the most fascinating of all the aspects of New Testament interpretation. The reason for this is twofold. On the one hand, the parables are perhaps the most characteristic form of the speech of Jesus himself. They challenge the hearer to explore the manifold possibilities of the experience of God as king, and they do so in ways which constantly remind the hearer that, on the one hand, God is to be experienced in the historicality of the world of everyday, while, on the other hand, they claim that God is to be experienced precisely in the shattering of that everyday world. Moreover, they do this in ways which constantly leave the hearer naked and alone before the possibility and challenge of the experience of God as king. The parables give no hint of a structured supportive community; they offer no help in the form of an expression of the possibility and challenge in the form of conventions which can ultimately be domesticated. Indeed the process of interpretation of the parables in the early Christian communities could well be described as the process of their domestication. Just as world-shattering aphorisms are mellowed down to the point at which they become radical challenges—challenges which, although radical, can be accepted and still leave the hearer's world fundamentally what it was before[19]—so also the parables are allegorized and moralized in the Christian traditions to a point at which one can live with them and draw helpful lessons from them. But when one approaches the parables as the recent American discussion has made it possible to approach them, then one finds them almost impossible to live with. They constantly shatter and probe, disturb and challenge, in ways which are for me personally analogous to the impact of great art. Even if I owned Picasso's *Guernica* I could not hang it on a wall in my house, and although I own a recording of the Solti Chicago Symphony performance of Stravinsky's *Rite of Spring*, I play it only rarely. One cannot live everyday on the boundary of human existence in the world, and yet it is to this boundary that one is constantly brought by the parables of Jesus.

The second reason for the fascination of the parables of Jesus at the level of New Testament interpretation is the sheer complexity of the hermeneutical problems they present. We have the problem of reconstructing the texts as Jesus told them from the allegorizing and moralizing of the early Christian communities, a problem we have traced from Jülicher's recognition of the allegorizing to Crossan's careful use of the Gospel of Thomas and Via's of the structural dynamics of story and discourse. Then we have the problem of understanding them at the historical level, the discussion of which we have traced from the failure of Jülicher's attempt to understand them in terms of Aristotelian rhetoric to the success of Funk and Crossan in reading them as stories told in a particular historical context. Then, further, we have the problem of understanding the parables at the literary level. We have reviewed this discussion from Jülicher's original distinction between parable and allegory, through the complexities of distinctions among similitude, parable, and exemplary story—and also those of *tertium comparationis, Bild*, and *Sache*—to the contemporary American discussion of metaphor and story, and to the introduction into the discussion of the structuralist analysis of narrative. Finally, we have the problem of interpreting these word pictures and stories from the past of Jesus and his contemporaries in ancient Palestine into the present of the interpreter and his audience in the modern world. We have seen Jülicher find in them general moral principles of universal application, and Jeremias the features of a fundamentally Christian piety. We have seen the practitioners of the "new hermeneutic" seek to understand their character as "language events" on the lips of Jesus and of contemporary Christian preachers, and we have seen Via apply a method of existentialist interpretation to draw from them a message addressed to any man. Most recently we have seen the American attempts to let the word pictures and stories speak for themselves, using the tools of historical criticism to recreate the circumstances of their first telling and of literary criticism to understand their natural function as language in the new setting of a modern interpretation.

The parables of Jesus are, therefore, very powerful texts, and they are also texts offering a complex challenge to the interpreter at every level of the hermeneutical process. As one reviews the history of their interpretation from Jülicher to the SBL Parables Seminar one gets the impression that it is the history of an attempt to allow the parables to speak for themselves. Their original force and power was lost as they were allegorized and moralized; Jülicher swept away the cobwebs of the allegorizing but left unstirred the dust of the moralizing. Jeremias saw the necessity for understanding them first in their original historical context but continued to draw lessons from them as he reconstructed their message. The "new hermeneutic" grasped something of their force and power in understanding them as language events but failed in the attempt to communicate this event character into the present. Via made great strides in understanding the fundamental, and permanent, meaning of the narrative parables as narratives, but then returned to drawing lessons from them. Not until we come to Funk and Crossan do we find the technical skills necessary to recreate circumstances under which the texts may speak combined with a willingness simply to allow the texts to speak.

In reviewing the history of the interpretation of the parables one is impressed by the skills which have to be developed, and by the effort which has to be expended, to reach a point at which the texts are able to speak for themselves. Textual criticism, historical criticism, literary criticism—this last certainly now to be understood as including structuralist criticism[20]—are all needed in the attempt to make it possible for the texts to speak for themselves. At the same time that review of the history of the interpretation of the parables shows how readily an interpreter can expend great skill and effort in order to make it possible for the text to speak, only then further to muffle it by a demand that it speak in a certain way. But the texts must be allowed to speak for themselves; all our efforts as interpreters must ultimately be geared to

that end. It is as important for the interpreter to know where his work
ends as it is for him to know anything else about the theory and
practice of hermeneutics.

D. SIMILE, METAPHOR, AND MYTH

The parables of Jesus are "parables of the Kingdom," their ultimate
referent is the Kingdom of God. But Kingdom of God is a symbol
which functions by evoking a myth, while a parable can be a simile or
metaphor. I must, therefore, discuss further the relationship among
simile, metaphor, and myth, as this relationship has become evident in
the course of the discussions I have reviewed. We have seen that a
parable can be a simile—"the Kingdom of God is *like* . . .—or it can be
a metaphor: "the Kingdom of God *is*. . . ."[21] The simile is essentially
illustrative and hence the parable as simile teases the mind into recognition of new aspects of the reality mediated by the myth of God active
as king. The metaphor, on the other hand, contrasts two fundamentally
different categories of reality and hence produces a shock to the imagination. It produces a shock which induces a new vision of world and
new possibilities, therefore, for the functioning of the myth, new possibilities for the experiencing of that existential reality which the myth
mediates.

Now if the parable is to function effectively as a parable *of the
Kingdom of God*, then clearly it can so function only if the myth of
God active as king is also functioning. Jesus addressed his parables to
people who fully accepted the myth and so his parables were effective
forms of proclamation of the Kingdom, or of instruction with regard to
response to the proclamation. In this connection the secularity, the
concrete everydayness of the parables is very important because this
element of the parables becomes an *interpretation* of the Kingdom: the
hearers are challenged to recognize the reality that is mediated by the
myth in terms of the concrete actuality of the everyday.

Now if the parable functions as metaphor, and if, further, it functions with reference to a myth, then we have a double problem of
interpretation. We have the problem as to whether the metaphor is
alive, dead, or dormant, and we have the problem as to whether the
myth is alive or dead, so far as new hearers or readers of the parables
are concerned. The interpreter must necessarily be aware of both of
these problems. The basic problem of all hermeneutics of the Kingdom

of God is the problem of the myth which that symbol evokes. Here the interpreter works in the context of the possibility represented at the one extreme by a Rauschenbusch or the possibility represented at the other extreme by a Bultmann, or that interpreter works in the context of some other possibility from the spectrum lying within the boundaries established by those two extremes. The further problem of the hermeneutics of the parables of Jesus is the problem of the similes and metaphors themselves, the problem of their effectiveness in a cultural situation very different from that of the Palestine of Jesus and his hearers. We may exemplify this problem by pointing out that for someone who must walk a dangerous street or road The Good Samaritan needs only be translated to come alive—which leaves the interpreter only (!) with the problem of interpreting the referent, the Kingdom of God. But for the man of the technological West, for whom agriculture is agribusiness carried on both scientifically and on an enormous scale, The Sower and The Lost Sheep would really seem to have died as metaphors. In such cases the kind of hermeneutical procedure represented by Via, who carried out a Bultmannian type of hermeneutics in connection with the parables,[22] would seem to be appropriate.

E. THE FINAL ELEMENT IN THE ACT OF INTERPRETATION

The purpose of interpretation is to allow a text to speak, to make possible an appreciative reading of the text.[23] In the course of these studies we have seen how very complex this hermeneutical enterprise can become in the case of the Kingdom of God and the parables of Jesus. Kingdom of God is a symbol evoking a myth; the hermeneutical possibilities vary enormously according to the viability of the myth and the functional possibilities of the symbol. The parables are similes or metaphors; in their case the possibilities depend upon the viability of the simile, and upon the status of the metaphor as alive, dead, or dormant. Indeed the hermeneutical enterprise is even more complex than our discussion has indicated because obviously myths become meaningless and metaphors die or become dormant in response to sociological and cultural factors. Moreover, some cultural situations limit the hermeneutical possibilities very severely. Augustine's interpretation of both Kingdom of God and the parables of Jesus was necessarily conditioned by the cultural dominance of allegory.

It is not my claim that any specific hermeneutical theory has been developed in these studies, except in the very general sense that any valid hermeneutics must clearly pay careful attention to textual, historical, and literary factors, and that the aim of any hermeneutics must be to make possible the moment in which the interpreter enters into dialogue with the text by reading it appreciatively. It is obvious by now that all of this is very much easier said than done, but the purpose of these studies has been to explore some of the possibilities in connection with Kingdom of God and the parables of Jesus.

NOTES

1. See above, p. 56.

2. In what follows I am deliberately building upon foundations I believe I have established in the studies above, and the quotations are from those studies.

3. See above, pp. 42–46.

4. See above, pp. 47–48.

5. See above, pp. 48–54.

6. See above, pp. 55–56 and Chapter III.

7. See above, pp. 42–46.

8. Fuchs makes a great deal of this possibility, as we saw above, pp. 107–113. In contrast to Fuchs I would want to restrict myself to what may be legitimately extrapolated from an exegesis of Matt. 11:12.

9. See above, pp. 47–48.

10. See above, pp. 53–54.

11. See above, pp. 159–160.

12. This aspect of the discussion in the seminar concerned the Servant parables. I did not review it because I deliberately limited myself to the seminar discussion of The Good Samaritan.

13. Crossan, *Semeia* 1, pp. 213–214, from an article "Structuralist Analysis and the Parables of Jesus." Among the parables warning that the commitment "is to a God whose ways are not our ways," Crossan includes The Unjust Steward (Luke 16:1–7) and The Vineyard Workers (Matt. 20:1–13).

14. Ibid., p. 214.

15. I am using the past tense to emphasize that this is a historical understanding of the message of Jesus.

16. Amos Wilder's phrase. See above, p. 170.

17. Perrin, "Eschatology and Hermeneutics," *JR* 93 (1974), p. 13.

18. As I admitted, ibid.

19. On this process in connection with the proverbial sayings of Jesus see above, pp. 50–52.

20. It is impossible to tell at the moment how important structuralist criticism may become in the interpretation of the parables of Jesus. The SBL Parables Seminar has been devoting a good deal of attention to the subject,

but with extremely limited results. The basic problem seems to be a disparity between the parables of Jesus as texts and structuralist criticism as a method. As I understand the matter, structuralism as a method is designed to concentrate on the fundamental generative structures of the human mind as these might be exhibited in various kinds of texts. If this is the case, then the method might be expected to be most helpful in connection with primal texts such as myths, classical Greek drama, or the great archaic biblical texts. But the parables of Jesus are highly personal and strictly occasional texts, as I have insisted throughout these studies, and hence will tend to resist such a method of approach. In this connection I find Dan Via's structuralist approach to the Gospel of Mark (in *Kerygma and Comedy in the New Testament*, published by Fortress Press, 1975) much more compelling than I do his similar approach to the parables of Jesus. Via compares the Gospel of Mark to Greek comedy and claims that it is close to "a deep, generative structure of the human mind" (Via, p. 92), and he may well be right in this. Certainly the things he is able to say on the basis of this insight are things that will have to be taken very seriously indeed by future interpreters of the Gospel of Mark, including Norman Perrin. But The Good Samaritan, for all its power, moves at a very different level from this. It is a text generated by an individual vision and geared to a particular set of circumstances, and for all that it features a clash of worlds, it moves at a level very different from the primal levels of the Gospel of Mark.

Another point to be made is that structuralist criticism also tends to work with categories which are drawn from an analysis of a whole body of literature, e.g., the Russian folk tale, categories in terms of which a given text within the genre may be further analyzed. Again, the very nature of the parables of Jesus as texts tends to make the application of such a method to them very difficult. They form a corpus of texts very limited in number and of a highly specialized type. It is not immediately apparent with what other texts we may link them so as to have a large enough number of related texts to form the basis for the kind of analysis that can be practiced in the case of the folk tale.

Events may well overtake any prediction that I might make, but as of the Spring of 1975, it does seem that structuralist criticism will have only a limited impact on parable interpretation.

21. See above, p. 135.

22. See above, pp. 144–145.

23. I am obviously close here to Ricoeur's "second, post-critical naiveté." The phrase "appreciative reading" was suggested to me in conversation by Daniel Davis, a graduate student in the field of religion and literature at the University of Chicago Divinity School.

Bibliography
and Indexes

Bibliography

The purpose of this bibliography is to give a brief, introductory bibliography for each of the areas of concern of the book.

1. KINGDOM OF GOD

Galling, Kurt and Conzelmann, Hans. "Reich Gottes. I. Im Judentum und NT." In *Religion in Geschichte und Gegenwart*. Third edition. Tübingen: J. C. B. Mohr (Paul Siebeck). Vol. III (1961), cols. 912–918.

An excellent survey, with a good bibliography.

Hiers, Richard H. *The Kingdom of God in the Synoptic Tradition*. Gainesville: University of Florida Press, 1970.

Hiers is a devotee of Johannes Weiss, whom he has translated, and he tends to give short shrift to other viewpoints. But this is valuable as one of the more recent discussions.

Klein, Günter. "Reich Gottes als biblisher Zentralsbegriff." In *Evangelische Theologie* 30 (1970), 642–670.

The most thorough recent discussion of the subject, with an excellent bibliography in the footnotes.

Ladd, George Eldon. *Jesus and the Kingdom*. New York: Harper & Row, 1964, London: SPCK, 1966.

A major discussion of the subject from the standpoint of a conservative biblical scholarship, which Ladd calls Biblical Realism.

Lundström, Gösta. *The Kingdom of God in the Teaching of Jesus.* Richmond: John Knox Press and London: SPCK, 1963.

Perrin, Norman. *The Kingdom of God in the Teaching of Jesus.* London: SCM Press and Philadelphia: Westminster Press, 1963.

These two books appeared at the same time and covered ostensibly the same ground. But they complement one another in that Lundström concentrates on continental European theological scholarship while Perrin limits himself to New Testament scholars and moves deliberately through the discussion from Schweitzer to the post-Bultmannians.

Schnackenburg, Rudolf. *God's Rule and Kingdom.* New York: Herder and Herder and London: Nelson, 1963.

A translation of the German *Gottes Herrschaft und Reich* (1958) and probably the best discussion of the subject, with a good bibliography. The fourth German edition (1965) reviews the discussion between 1958 and 1965 in an appendix, and it brings the bibliography up to date to 1965.

Weiss, Johannes. *Jesus' Proclamation of the Kingdom of God.* Edited and translated, with an Introduction, by Richard H. Hiers and D. Larrimore Holland. Philadelphia: Fortress Press and London: SCM Press, 1971.

This is a translation of the first edition of Weiss's epoch-making work. The Introduction offers a perceptive discussion of Weiss and a somewhat partisan review of the subsequent discussion.

Wolff, Ernst. "Reich Gottes. II. Theologiegeschichtlich." In *Religion in Geschichte und Gegenwart.* Third edition. Tübingen: J. C. B. Mohr (Paul Siebeck). Vol. III (1961), cols. 918–924.

A very informative survey, with a good bibliography.

2. PARABLES OF JESUS

Chapter III of this book discusses the modern interpretation of the parables of Jesus in great detail. The following works are discussed, in the order given here.

Jeremias, Joachim. *The Parables of Jesus.* Third revised edition, London: SCM Press and New York: Scribner's, 1972.

Jülicher, Adolf. *Die Gleichnisreden Jesu.* 2 vols. Tübingen: J. C. B. Mohr (Paul Siebeck). I (1888, 1899²), II (1899, 1910²).

Fiebig, Paul. *Altjüdische Gleichnisse und die Gleichnisse Jesu.* Tübingen: J. C. B. Mohr (Paul Siebeck), 1904.

Fiebig, Paul. *Die Gleichnisreden Jesus im Lichte der rabbinischen Gleichnisse des neutestamentlichen Zeitalters.* Tübingen: J. C. B. Mohr (Paul Siebeck), 1912.

Jones, Geraint Vaughan. *The Art and Truth of the Parables.* London: SPCK, 1964.

Dodd, C. H. *The Parables of the Kingdom.* Welwyn Garden City: Nisbet, 1935; New York: Scribner's 1961.³

Fuchs, Ernst. *Studies of the Historical Jesus.* SBT 42; London: SCM Press and Nashville: Alec R. Allenson, 1964.

Linnemann, Eta. *Jesus of the Parables.* New York: Harper & Row, 1966.

Jungel, Eberhard. *Paulus und Jesus.* Tübingen: J. C. B. Mohr (Paul Siebeck), 1962. (There is a second edition, 1964, but our quotes are from the first).

Robinson, James M. "Jesus' Parables as God Happening." In *Jesus and the Historian: Written in Honor of Ernest Cadman Colwell.* Edited by Thomas Trotter. Philadelphia: Westminster Press, 1968, pp. 134–150.

Wilder, Amos N. *Early Christian Rhetoric: The Language of the Gospel.* Revised edition, Cambridge, Mass.: Harvard University Press, 1971.

Funk, Robert W. *Language, Hermeneutic, and Word of God.* New York: Harper & Row, 1966.

Via, Dan O., Jr. *The Parables: Their Literary and Existential Dimension.* Philadelphia: Fortress Press, 1967.

Crossan, John Dominic. *In Parables: The Challenge of the Historical Jesus.* New York: Harper & Row, 1973.

Semeia 1 (1974). "A Structuralist Approach to the Parables." Edited by Robert W. Funk.

This has an extensive bibliography.

Semeia 2 (1974). "The Good Samaritan." Edited by John Dominic Crossan.

3. METAPHOR AND SYMBOL

Beardsley, Monroe C. *Aesthetics*. New York: Harcourt, Brace, and World, Inc., 1958.

One of the most important philosophical discussions of metaphor. Four theories of metaphor are presented and discussed with emphasis placed on the last theory, the logical absurdity theory.

Berggren, Douglas. "The Use and Abuse of Metaphor." *The Review of Metaphysics* XVI (1962–63), pp. 237–258 and 450–472.

An excellent critical description of the "theory of metaphorical tension," as developed in the work of Beardsley, Black, Wheelwright, et al., with a provocative discussion of myth, defined as a "believed absurdity," as the main abuse of metaphor.

Black, Max. *Models and Metaphors*. Ithaca: Cornell University Press, 1962.

A careful discussion of three views of metaphor: the substitution view, the comparison view, and the interaction view. The interaction view is presented as the most adequate in that it allows for the interaction of associated systems of meaning.

Frye, Northrop. *Anatomy of Criticism*. Princeton: Princeton University Press, 1957.

An excellent literary-critical discussion of the theory of symbols is provided in the second essay.

Richards, I. A. *The Philosophy of Rhetoric*. London and New York: Oxford University Press, 1936.

A classic work on rhetoric in which metaphor is discussed in terms of "tenor" and "vehicle." This work set the stage for much of the later critical discussion of metaphor.

Ricoeur, Paul. *The Symbolism of Evil*. Translated from the French by E. Buchanan. Boston: Beacon Press, 1967.

An important discussion of the relations between symbols and myths with an emphasis on the development from the primal symbols of evil to later narrative myths.

Shibles, Warren A. *Metaphor: An Annotated Bibliography and History*. Whitewater, Wis.: The Language Press, 1971.

An extensive bibliography of works on metaphor, emphasizing English language texts but including selected recent works in French, German, and Spanish. The annotations are usually good, often presenting the main arguments of the works listed, but the introduction is remarkably poor.

Wheelwright, Philip. *Metaphor and Reality*. Bloomington: Indiana University Press, 1962. *The Burning Fountain*. Bloomington: Indiana University Press, 1968.

An important critical discussion of metaphor and symbolism, taking examples from English literature, and attempting a classification of symbols according to types.

4. HERMENEUTICS

Betti, Emilio. *Die Hermeneutik als Allgemeine Methodik der Geisteswissenschaften*. Tübingen: J. C. B. Mohr (Paul Siebeck), 1967.

A 750-page translation and abridgment of a work originally in Italian, *Teoria generale della interpretazione* (2 vols. Milan: Guiffre, 1955). Betti is in the tradition of Schleiermacher and Dilthey in seeking a "general theory of hermeneutics applicable to the humanities, to fine arts, and to the social sciences.

Bultmann, Rudolf. "The Problem of Hermeneutics." In *Essays Philosophical and Theological*. London: SCM Press and New York: Macmillan 1955.

————. *History and Eschatology: The Presence of Eternity*. New York: Harper & Row, 1957.

————. *Jesus Christ and Mythology*. New York: Scribner's, 1958, London: SCM Press, 1960.

These are the main statements of Bultmann's hermeneutics.

Dilthey, Wilhelm. "Die Entstehung der Hermeneutik." In *Gesammelte Schriften*, vol. 5. Stuttgart: Teubner, 1964.

Dilthey has profoundly influenced the modern discussion of hermeneutics. Bultmann takes his fundamental insights directly from him.

Ebeling, Gerhard. "Hermeneutik." In *Religion in Geschichte und Gegenwart*. Third edition. Tübingen: J. C. B. Mohr (Paul Siebeck). Vol. II (1959), cols. 242–262.

Much the best survey of biblical and theological hermeneutics currently available, with extensive bibliographies.

Eliade, Mircea. *Images and Symbols*. New York: Sheed and Ward and London: Horvill, 1961.

A discussion of the interpretation of religious symbols in the modern world.

Hirsch, E. D., Jr. *Validity in Interpretation*. New Haven, Conn.: Yale University Press, 1967.

Perhaps the most important recent work on hermeneutics in literary scholarship, in which Hirsch argues strongly for authorial intent as the determining factor in interpretation.

Palmer, Richard E. *Hermeneutics: Interpretation Theory in Schleiermacher, Dilthey, Heidegger, and Gadamer*. Evanston, Ill.: Northwestern University Press, 1969.

A very good introduction to the hermeneutics of the scholars named in the title, with extensive bibliographies.

Ricoeur, Paul. *Conflict of Interpretations: Essays in Hermeneutics*. Evanston, Ill.: Northwestern University Press, 1974.

This is a translation of essays written by Ricoeur between 1960 and 1969. In many ways it is perhaps the best introduction to his hermeneutical thinking, since these essays offer concise statements of the views developed systematically in his major works. There is a very good introduction to the essays by Don Ihde, who edited the volume.

Robinson, James M. "Hermeneutics since Barth." In *The New*

Hermeneutic, edited by James M. Robinson and John B. Cobb, Jr. New York: Harper & Row, 1964.

The "new hermeneutic" itself has not proven to be a significant contribution to current hermeneutical theory, but this review of recent biblical and theological hermeneutics is magisterial.

Journal of Religion. Vol. 55, no. 3 (July, 1975).

This issue of the *JR* is devoted entirely to a discussion of hermeneutics, with an introduction by Anthony C. Yu, articles by E. D. Hirsch, Jr., Richard E. Palmer, Peter Homans and Norman Perrin, and with an annotated bibliography.

Indexes

INDEX OF BIBLICAL REFERENCES

217

INDEX OF PARABLES

(Parables mentioned only once are not indexed. References are given only to identify the parables. They imply nothing about the original extent of the parable.)

INDEX OF NAMES AND SUBJECTS

Mowinckel, S., 80
Myth:
  Bultmann's understanding of, 73–74, 78–79
  definition of, 22–23
  as evoked by symbol, 58–59, 71–72
  of God active in salvation history, 19–22
  of Kingship of God, 17–18
  of Salvation History, 18–19
  significance of historical experience for effectiveness of, 23–28, 73
  See also Allegorical myth

Nicholson, E. W., 80

Parables:
  as aesthetic objects, 141–155
  as comparison not allegory, 6–7
  as immediate and occasional texts, 8, 104–105, 140, 143–144
  discussion of:
    introductory, 55–56
    Jülicher, A., 92–97
    Fiebig, P., 95–96
    Dodd, C. H., 37–39, 97–100
    Jeremias, J., 101–107
    Linnemann, E., 113–117
    Jüngel, E., 117–120
    Wilder, A., 127–131
    Funk, R. W., 132–141
    Via, D. O., 141–155
    Crossan, J. D., 155–168
    SBL Parables Seminar, 169–181
    Summary, 199–202
  list of major, 41
  reinterpretation of in early Christian tradition, 101–102
  See also Allegory and parable
Parenesis in the message of Jesus, 48, 52–54, 56, 195–196
Patte, D., 175
Proclamation in the message of Jesus, 42–46, 48–53, 55–56, 194–195